Advance Praise for
Procurement Confidential

"If your definition of procurement done well is Savings R' Us, think again. **Procurement Confidential** *is an enlightened view that goes deep into what drives success in today's most impactful procurement organizations. Culture is a key component, so is strategy, execution, and cross-functional collaboration. Unlock the potential!"*

> — Willie Deese, president (retired), Merck Manufacturing Division, and chief procurement officer of Kaiser Permanente, SmithKline Beecham, GlaxoSmithKline, and Merck

---

"As I read this book, I was amazed at what seemingly large, sophisticated organizations were doing that they thought were best practices but were just the opposite. With the extensive experiences of Howard and Robert, there's plenty of 'what NOT to do' real-life stories that serve as important lessons learned that are instructive on what TO DO.

This book could be titled 'How Buying and Selling SHOULD Get Done.' Howard and Robert focus on the impact of organizational culture on how procurement and sales get done. Having a culture that focuses on VALUE — making a concerted effort to understand the needs and that of the seller (if buying) or buyer (if selling). In the end, it's all about making procurement and selling beneficial for ALL concerned. Looking for the '"win-win' will win all the time!

There is an expression that I used throughout my career— "The HOW is just as important as the WHAT" — and this book is a valuable resource to those professionals (procurement, sales, and supply chain) who wish to explore what it takes to add the HOW to the equation to get the best VALUE in all that they do. Sweet!"

> — Ross Born, CEO (retired), Just Born Quality Confections (makers of Peeps, Mike & Ike, and Hot Tamales brand products)

"**Procurement Confidential** is a time-tested roadmap for procurement leadership. Richman and Handfield provide excellent guidance on measuring functional success beyond the widely used price-only focus to fully align with the business strategy."

— Erik Stavrand, partner, SEAK LLC

"**Procurement Confidential** is a must-read for anyone involved in acquisition. And, if you read it, you will recognize that nearly everyone is involved at some level. The authors do an amazing job of providing candid, real-world examples that allow the reader to go beyond the abstraction of traditional management and procurement books and get into the application of 'how it's really done' based on a wealth of lessons learned. This book is for the manager that wants to go beyond self-help pontifications and more towards expert-level qualifications."

— Daniel J. Finkenstadt, PhD; co-author of *Supply Chain Immunity* and *BioInspired Strategic Design*; principal at Wolf Stake Consulting LLC

"More than ever, service providers and procurement organizations have to partner to ensure business objectives, investment objectives, and business risks are identified and mutually understood by both parties on behalf of the ultimate customer, typically an Operating Unit/P&L Center. This is especially true with more rapidly evolving business models and consumer expectations.

It is in everyone's interest to get the best insights, creative ideas, and value propositions which may or may not always be articulated in an RFP. Service providers and procurement must partner to define and understand RFP objectives so the ultimate business need is fulfilled."

— Ed Smith, VP, Business Development – Building and Construction, Engineering and Manufacturing, DHL Supply Chain — U.S. and Canada

Procurement Confidential

The Real Story of How Buying and Selling Actually Gets Done in the Corporate World

Howard Richman

Global Procurement Executive
Managing Member, Levelfield Enterprises, LLC

Robert Handfield, PhD

Bank of America University Distinguished Professor of Supply Chain Management
Executive Director, Supply Chain Resource Cooperative
Director, Ethical Apparel Index Initiative

W wessex

www.wessexlearning.com

Procurement Confidential: *The Real Story of How*
Buying and Selling Actually Gets Done in the Corporate World

Howard Richman, Robert Handfield

ISBN: 979-8-9901932-0-8 (hardcover)
       979-8-9901932-1-5 (softcover)
       979-8-9901932-2-2 (e-book)

Book / Cover Design: Anna Botelho

Copy Editor: Nicole Frail

Indexer: Laura Ogar

Wessex Press, Inc.
www.wessexlearning.com

Wessex Press is a New York State Certified Service-Disabled Veteran-Owned Business. Founded (2007) by Noel Capon, R.C. Kopf Professor of International Marketing, Columbia Business School, Wessex Press makes professional books, textbooks, simulations, and other learning materials more accessible and affordable for its core audience — college students, professors, professionals, and life-long learners globally. Wessex operates at the cutting edge of technology, providing traditional and e-learning tools. Focus topic areas are marketing, sales and account management, and other higher-education textbooks. We continue to expand our offerings into such areas as argumentation, economics, English as a second language, finance, general management, human resources, sociology.

Table of Contents

About the Authors

Howard Richman is a global procurement executive and now Managing Member of his consultancy, Levelfield Enterprises, LLC (www.levelfieldenterprises.com), which specializes in leading transformations of global procurement organizations, sourcing of indirect spend, risk management for hedging commodities, and an advocate for supplier diversity. He has spent 40+ years in finance and procurement roles for six major multinational corporations in the chemicals, defense, packaged goods, pharmaceutical, and software industries, as well as consulted for biopharma, manufacturing, healthcare, private equity, and hospitality firms on their strategic sourcing and procurement operations activities. Howard led his team at Citrix Systems, Inc. in winning the 2017 Procurement Leaders World Procurement Award for Cross-Functional Transformation. His degrees include an MBA in Finance from Columbia Business School, along with undergraduate and graduate degrees in Economic Geography from Clark University and Columbia University Graduate School of Arts & Sciences.

Robert Handfield is the Bank of America University Distinguished Professor of Supply Chain Management at North Carolina State University, and Executive Director of the Supply Chain Resource Cooperative (http://scm.ncsu.edu/). Handfield is considered a thought leader in the field of supply chain management, and is an industry expert in the field of strategic sourcing, supply market intelligence, and supplier development.

Acknowledgments

(*Howard*) This book would not be possible without the many years of encouragement and support of my loving wife Sharon, and the everyday joy I receive from my 3 kids, their spouses and my 5 grandkids. I also want to thank my mentor, Ron Ashkenas, for teaching me what "boundaryless behavior" can do to transform the culture of an organization; my collaborators in academia, Professor Noel Capon of Columbia Business School and my co-author, Professor Rob Handfield of North Carolina State Univ.; and my many leaders, teammates and proteges who have strived for excellence in everything that they do, including those of blessed memory.

(*Robert*) This book and my career are largely due to the loving support of my wife, Sandi, and my children, Simone and Luc. Thank you for continuous support of me over the years. I would like to also thank all of the executives who provided insights, ideas, thoughts, and candid discussions with me that helped shape the ideas of this book.

Preface

A word of advice — hold on to your hats. This is not your normal, everyday business book and certainly not a handbook, as we will focus on one thing and one thing only: ***telling the truth*** about how business really gets done in the corporate world. You will see a number of "Procurement Confidential" comments as we go along, where we will tell you what ***really goes on behind the scenes*** in the B2B large multinational corporate world of buying (*procurement*) and selling (*sales*), and of managing *supply chains* and *third-party logistics* (3PL). We also address why many attempts at *supplier relationship management* (SRM) often lead to nowhere (or worse yet, a string of broken promises), and propose some realistic solutions for approaching this differently. It does not have to be this way, and it is important to understand why things fail, and to admit our failures, in order to create opportunities for long-term success. We will get at the real truths behind supply management, exposing some of the misperceptions that novices may have about how purchasing really works; for example, spend planning doesn't really exist, and many Fortune 500 companies simply allocate general buckets of money without a solid procurement plan, especially around capital expense spending.

Corporate culture has been the subject of many books and studies, and it is often assumed that to get ahead, you need to adapt to and emulate your company's culture. Leaders (and to some extent, shareholders) are the only ones empowered to change the culture of a company. The problem is that companies are run by human beings — with goals, ambitions, and egos — who thrive and survive in cultures that lead to suboptimal decisions that are nevertheless rewarded.

People are, from the very beginning of mankind, tribal and clannish in nature. As such, we set up silos to protect our functions and create boundaries to protect our interests. Within our functions (like sales, procurement, and supply chain), our behaviors are driven by a desire for success: recognition, titles, decision-making authority, span of control, reporting relationships and compensation structures, all of which feed into our conceptualization of self-worth. Nobody wants the descriptor of *tactical* or *site* in their job title if they can have *strategic*, *regional*, *global*, or *worldwide*. Most of us want the power to hold the "D" (*decision*) as well as the respect and acknowledgment from others that comes with that responsibility. Most of all, when we get involved in the transactions of the company, either on the buy side or the sell side, we want to WIN! That's what we get paid for, right? For making the numbers, however measured, which then fulfill the strategic goals of the company. If only that were true.

There are exigent forces, natural cycles, which disrupt our environment and play havoc with our plans. "To Everything There Is a Season" was a folk song written by Pete Seeger in 1959, and later adapted by The Byrds in 1965 as "Turn, Turn, Turn." You've heard the song many times, which borrows from the first eight verses of the third chapter of the book of Ecclesiastes to emphasize that there is a time for everything that happens in life (and as Howard likes to say, "Timing isn't everything; it's the ONLY thing!"). Whether you buy or sell or transact in between, understanding the importance of these cycles (and timing) in all things that we do in corporate life will act as a competitive advantage. Yes, a butterfly flaps its wings in China, and it sets off a string of connected events that many do not anticipate but some have the foresight to interpret and act upon. Some of these cycles are part of the wonders of our physical world, others more socioeconomic, including the:

- 11-year solar cycle that influences the magnetic activity of sunspots;

- 5- to 6-year El Niño to La Niña climate cycle of the warming and cooling of ocean waters, which both cause and accentuate periods of drought and rainfall in many places of the world as well as drive huge changes in agricultural and aquatic environments (which then drive changes in human and economic behaviors as we adapt to these);

- 60-year boom to bust cycle of growth to economic depressions, interspersed with shorter term economic up and down cycles;

- cycle of corporate restructuring from centralization to decentralization that happens in a company about every 10 years, then the move back to centralization;

- sales cycle of focus on regions, then moving to focus instead on customer verticals, and then back to regions again; and

- cycles of technology leaps, then consolidation to current technology, then back to another technology leap.

In many companies, these factors make a joke out of long-term planning, and with that, the failure of many attempts to establish something other than tactical buyer-supplier relationships and contracting. This is compounded by unfavorable reporting relationships for many of the heads of the procurement and supply chain functions, and the view of these functions in a number of companies as commercial proving grounds for "up and coming" executives, as opposed to respected professions that are integral to delivering the strategy of the company. As a result, a carousel of procurement leaders comes in, stays for three years, and then gets off, resulting in a lack of a consistent supply management strategy over time. Companies are all seeking to gain a competitive advantage, increase their market share, and make forays into newly developing markets, but the incentives for managers and executives promote many of the wrong behaviors as corporate cultures put quarterly results over long-term value generation.

But you know this already, right? In your heart of hearts, and in your water cooler gatherings, it's discussed all the time in whispers and innuendos. You talk about how to play the game, how to sandbag the numbers so that you under-promise and over-deliver, and how to look good despite the absurdities that engulf you. There are "best practices" galore available to you, but your company's (and manager's) priorities (and funding) can be at odds with applying them. What people say they want or need in their functional responsibilities may be more about building out their function for greater importance or control but not be what the company actually wants and needs to be successful.

But now it's time to shine the spotlight on all of this because our very competitiveness and survival in this fast-changing world of commerce and technology depends on it. Recognizing the potential pitfalls in procurement, sales, and supply chain interactions, including SRM, can help you "up your game" by optimizing what you do and how you do it. There are ways to realistically change your culture for the better and to implement changes in metrics and measures to reward the right behaviors that will make the company more resilient to the exigent cycles at play and help you align your function better with the strategy of the company.

Each of these chapters in the book will cover a distinct but important lesson on how this can be done. Whether you are a sales, procurement, or supply chain professional, or work in a function that interacts with or relies on these functions for support (including finance, HR, marketing, information technology and security, engineering, R&D, or the shared services functions), you can explore the topics that most interest you in this ever-changing corporate world and use them to your advantage. After all, why else would you bother reading this book?!

In Chapter 1, ***It's the Economy, Stupid!,*** we set the groundwork for why all of this matters, and the impact of the sales, procurement, and supply chain functions on our economic well-being. We also look at a case study of what can go wrong when short-term thinking and poor metrics are applied to solving a supply chain third-party logistics (3PL) business problem or challenge and that we can adjust and learn from our mistakes.

In Chapter 2, ***How "Purchasing" Gets Done in Many Corporations ("Old School") (and what salespeople really need to know to be effective)***, we focus on how Sales needs to view its interactions with Procurement, and why Procurement has such a hard time getting out of its "Savings R Us" / "Contracts R Us" / "Negotiations R Us" reputation, image, and mentality.

In Chapter 3, ***What Procurement Needs to Know about Sales (Transforming the Purchasing-Sales Relationship)***, we look at the sales function and how Sales can improve its success rate in *requests for proposal* (RFPs) and profitability with a value-driven approach when dealing with *procurement*. The impact of technology, such as ChatGPT, on nullifying the value of the RFP question interchange is also rendering this a more challenging environment. We examine the traditional sales and procurement models, and we evaluate how these two approaches are truly at odds with one another and how to repair the damaged relationships that may have occurred as a result in the past.

In Chapter 4, ***What Sales Needs to Know about Procurement (Transforming the Purchasing-Sales Relationship)***, we cover the complex nature of the Sales and Procurement relationship. We provide some guidelines for salespeople, in particular, to understand how decisions are made with respect to third-party spending in organizations. Understanding the "tangled web" of how procurement decisions are made can lead to an improved understanding of how to add value to relationships by understanding the multipronged needs of organizations and the requirements for developing, sustaining, and nurturing interorganizational value chain relationships.

In Chapter 5, ***The "Ask" of the Procurement/Procure-to-Pay (P2P) and Supply Chain (SC) Organizations (and why they are not usually aligned to the strategy of the company)***, we examine why these functions are often not aligned with the strategy of the company. We look at

Finance's role in determining how companies are funded and structured, and how the *financial planning and analysis* (FP&A) process operates in a vacuum relative to Procurement's category strategy planning, and how to bring these two processes to alignment. We will also explore how Procurement's category strategies and goals (especially savings) are often completely out of sync with the financial planning process and company objectives.

In Chapter 6, **Organizing and Understanding the Procurement Organization**, we explore the many ways that Sales can work to better understand the Procurement organization and process; evaluate Procurement's effectiveness in the organization; and find ways to make Procurement a champion of Sales as opposed to "the enemy" when value-added approaches are proposed (including two case studies).

In Chapter 7, **Putting the Procurement Team in Place (or "People are not your greatest asset… people are your ONLY asset!")**, we talk about recruiting and organizing a diverse Procurement team that can effectively deal with the array of issues stacked against them and secrets for turning them into a high-performing team.

In Chapter 8, **Culture Eats Strategy for Lunch**, we give examples of how a change in culture and performance metrics can have an oversized impact on the performance of the Procurement function and how it can align it to the strategy of the company as it seeks to become a *trusted advisor to the business*.

In Chapter 9, **Understanding and Segmenting Your Supply Base**, we examine *supplier relationship management* (SRM) best practices and more realistic ways to approach SRM, based on NC State University Supply Chain Resource Council (SCRC) research.

In Chapter 10, **Organizing the Procurement Function for the New Global Reality**, we look at the importance of the *chief procurement officer* (CPO) reporting relationships and how to position the *procurement operations, strategic sourcing*, and *category management* roles for success in the B2B corporate world.

Finally, in Chapter 11, we look at *The Ongoing Transformation of Global Procurement and How We Work (The digitization of the function)*. Here, we explore the potential to redefine what we do and how we do it in an age of "plug & play" apps that are enabling us to break away from the yoke of multisuite systems and provide lighter, faster access to data and solutions to everything that we do.

In summary, this book is really about corporate culture and change management. But in order for change to happen, we first have to recognize that there is a reason that change must happen, and then own it. Most people on the burning platform in the corporate world look at change efforts and think "This too shall pass," and don't realize that they have two choices — to either jump 100 feet into the ocean below, or burn to death. Procurement in particular has to change, and people in the function need to see that the days of seeking control and hierarchical decision-making along with false metrics of success, like "savings," need to change with it. We have to see ourselves and our roles differently, or we will never be aligned with the strategy of the business, and we will never achieve the status of "trusted advisor to the business" that we desperately seek. But as you will see, it is within our grasp if we are willing to look at the Sales–Procurement–Supply Chain relationships differently, and if we adapt to the new reality of a fast-changing digital world.

Chapter 1:
"It's the Economy, Stupid!"

Yes, back in 1992 during the presidential campaign between Bill Clinton and President George H.W. Bush, James Carville (a strategist for Clinton) coined this phrase. Little did he know at the time how this relates to **the importance of best practices in Sales, Procurement, and Supply Chain and the consequences of poor business decisions when "price" becomes the only decision criteria in the process**.

There's a big difference between "price" and "cost," yet the two are used interchangeably as though they are the same thing when they clearly are not. *Price* is a transactional quantity or payment or compensation expected, required, or given by one party to another in return for goods or services (thanks, Wiki). *Cost*, on the other hand, can be measured in many different ways. Some examples are more accounting oriented, and others more financial and marketing oriented.

Cost of goods sold (COGS) is an accounting term that can consist of adding volume times material price paid per unit but also can include other cost elements included into the price, such as labor, equipment, tooling, research and development (R&D), quality, marketing and advertising expenses, licensing expenses, administrative overhead, warehousing and storage, distribution, shipping and handling charges, and taxes. Many of these costs are buried in the *sales, general, and administrative* (SG&A) line item of a *profit and loss* (P&L) statement or part of an overhead calculation, and accountants often try to differentiate between those that are fixed costs versus variable costs. Earnings Before Interest, Depreciation, Taxes, and Amortization (EBIDTA) is a well-established financial performance metric used to look at the financial impact of operating decisions by eliminating the impact of non-operating management decisions such as tax rates, interest expenses, and significant intangible assets.

But what about other financial and marketing cost criteria that help decide whether you produce the good or service in the first place, or which goods or services you produce, use, or buy (and from whom)? Sometimes you vertically integrate to make or produce the goods or services internally, and other times you source these goods or services from third-party suppliers. The decision criteria for what you do may include price but also looks at financial investment, cash flow, and marketing criteria such as the *weighted average cost of capital* (WACC), the learning curve for reducing the cost of production over time, economies of scale that reduce cost of production or cost to procure per unit of output, market presence/brand positioning or shelf space, *total cost of ownership* (TCO) over the lifecycle of the product, *return on investment* (ROI), *internal rate of return* (IRR), *free cash flow* (FCF), and/or the expected *annual recurring revenue* (ARR) from selling your goods or services.

So let's start by laying the groundwork — why all of this matters! Decisions are complicated, and the performance of the Sales, Procurement, and Supply Chain functions are at the heart of that decision-making! These functions get a lot more visibility now in the business press due to the "black swan" events that have led to massive disruptions that we've encountered during and after COVID and the Russian invasion of Ukraine. We saw what happened when global supply chains were halted in their tracks during COVID. The volume of media mentions on supply chain, the efforts to nearshore or bring home production of products to protect against losses of intellectual property and security, and the impacts of global inflationary pressures has escalated in the last three years. Supply Chain continues to be a lead story on the front pages of the *Wall Street Journal*, in headlines on CNBC, and in popular business journals like the *Harvard Business Review*.

Why all the fuss? People are tuning in to the fact that Sales, Procurement, and Supply Chain professionals are responsible for decisions that have a massive impact on competitive performance of organizations and on the economy as well. And the differences matter. In effect, Sales, Procurement, and Supply Chain activities are the essence of the global economy — the execution of financial and marketing decisions made at the highest level.

Consider the following graphs that demonstrate critical U.S. statistics that are followed by the business press and what they mean. These releases influence the Federal Reserve policies, cause stock prices to rise and fall, and influence C-Suite executives on decisions of whether to invest, hire, and expand or to pull back, conserve, lay off workers, and write off expenses. All of these are driven by the performance of Sales, Procurement, and Supply Chain employees. The numbers shown in these charts tell the story in a dramatic fashion.

To begin with, consider how U.S. manufacturing supply chains have been severely impacted before and after COVID. Professor Miller from Michigan State University developed a new supply chain pressures index based on a post from the Cleveland Fed,[1] going back to Q1 2004. Miller used the index that compiles the reasons manufacturing plants in the U.S. gave for operating below full capacity on the Quarterly Survey of Plant Capacity Utilization from the Census Bureau. The Census uses a large stratified random sample of approximately 7,500 plants each quarter. The index consists of a checklist of reasons for not operating at full capacity (see *Appendix* for more details). As shown in Figure 1, the three primary reasons for supply chain disruptions during COVID and through 2021 and 2022 include "insufficient supply of labor," "logistics/transportation constraints," and "insufficient supply of materials." The level of pressure on manufacturing supply chains to deliver continued to escalate during 2021, and only in late 2022 eased up. However, the capacity levels are well above pre-pandemic levels, and lead times for many manufacturing sectors have continued to escalate.

---

1 Federal Reserve Bank of Cleveland, *https://www.clevelandfed.org/en/newsroom-and-events/publications/economic-commentary/2021-economic-commentaries/ec-202117-semiconductor-shortages-vehicle-production-prices.aspx.*

Figure 1: Supply Chain Constraints Affecting Manufacturing Capacity Utilization

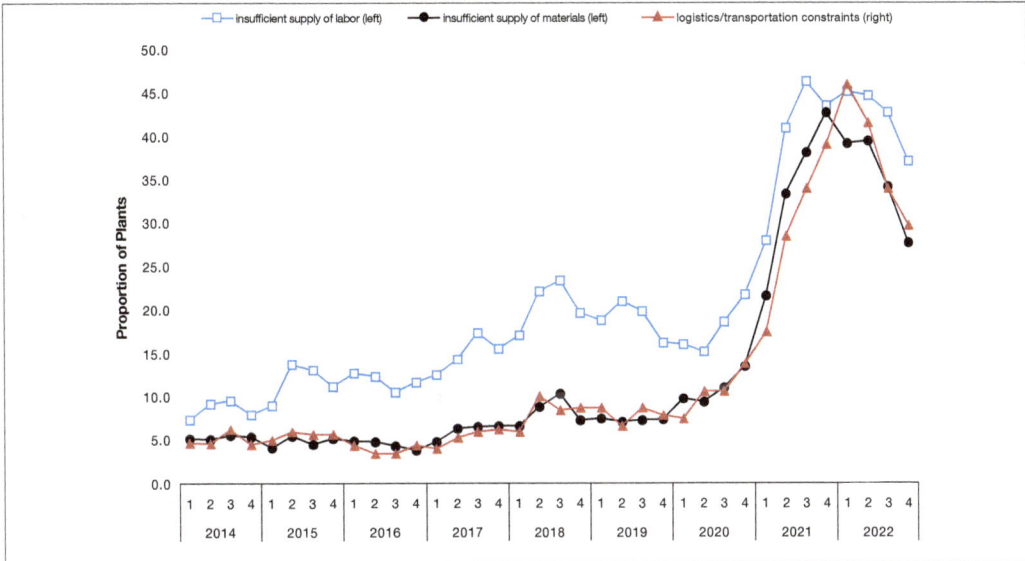

Source: Census Bureau

The chart in Figure 2 shows the Producer Price Index (PPI). One can observe how the cost of almost all goods escalated following the COVID period (shown in gray) — and is only now starting to come down. The PPI is created when the Bureau of Labor Statistics polls *procurement professionals* and asks them if the price they are paying for their goods and services are going up or down. Procurement is the primary driver of this index that Wall Street and the Fed relies on for an indicator of inflation.

Figure 2: PPI for Final Demand, 12-month percent change, not seasonally adjusted

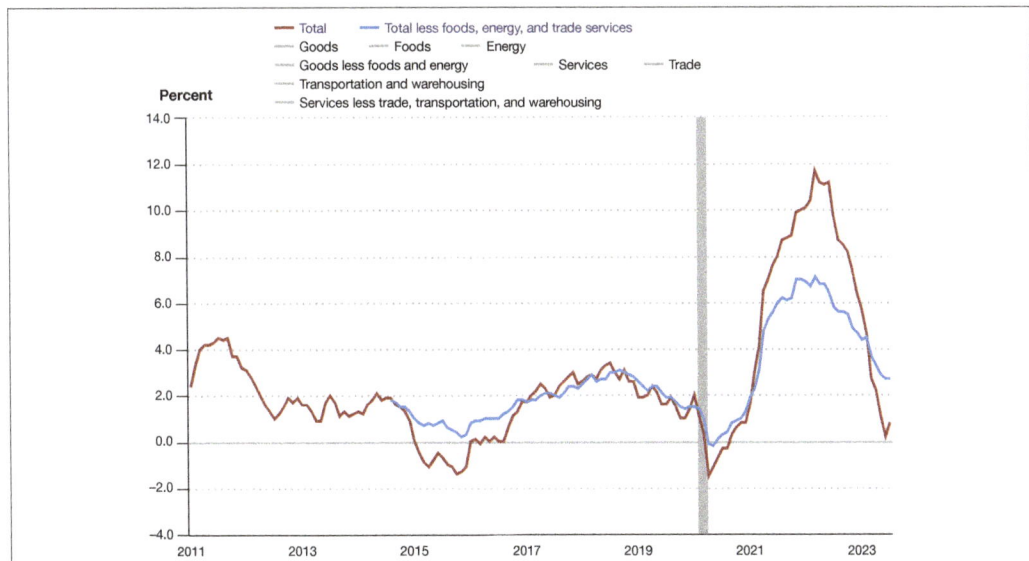

Source: U.S. Bureau of Labor Statistics. All data are subject to revision four months after originally published.

The last chart we will look at is the Purchasing Managers Index (PMI) for Manufacturing, which assesses the overall level of growth in the economy based on the level of industrial purchases for manufacturing.

Purchasing Managers Index (PMI) for Manufacturing

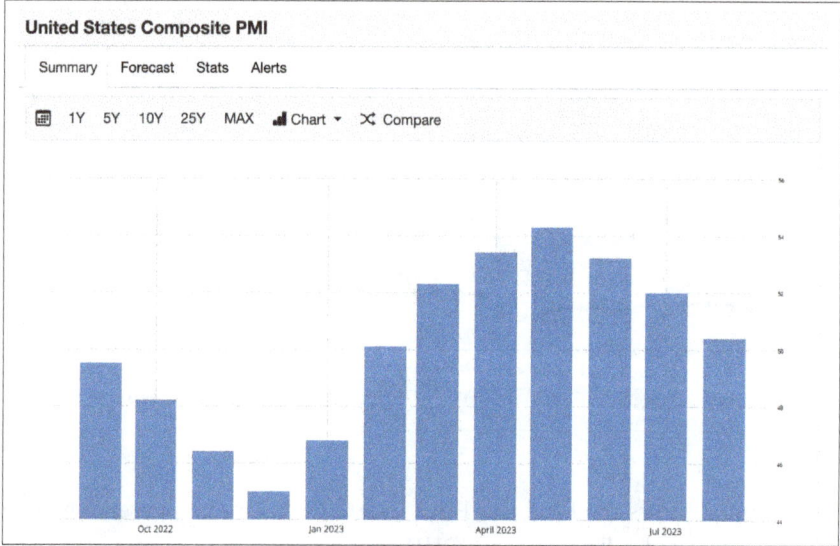

As one can see, the index had been dropping steadily in 2022 — and was at its lowest point ever. Any level of the PMI below 50 indicates the economy is shrinking — and this index is also followed closely by economists and Wall Street. It is purely driven by purchasing activity.

Consider, for instance, the top companies evaluated for the highest level of supply chain maturity in 2022 by the Supply Chain Resource Cooperative, using their Supply Chain Maturity Index:

	Top Supply Chain Innovation Companies	Top Social Responsibility Supply Chain Companies
1	Microsoft	Apple
2	Alphabet	Microsoft
3	3M	AT&T
4	HP Enterprises	Intel
5	Dell Technologies	3M
6	NXP Semicondutor	HP Enterprises
7	Apple	Alphabet
8	Procter & Gamble	Facebook
9	Nike	Colgate-Palmolive
Tied	Colgate-Palmolive, Ford, Cognizant, Norfolk Southern, ON Semiconductor	Abbott Labs, Ford, Target, General Mills, Kellogg's, Target

Not a bad list! These organizations are not only investing in supply chain innovation — but they are also the top performers when it comes to Environmental-Social-Governance (ESG) performance. Because guess what — supply chain functions have the biggest impact on ESG performance than all other business functions combined — impacting almost 90% of Scope 3 emissions, which includes carbon emissions from all of the supply chain.

While there may be political and cultural disputes ongoing around the topic of ESG, as well as Diversity, Equity, and Inclusion (DEI), it has become a reality of life as companies' boards of directors have responded to investor shareholder concerns (especially institutional investors such as pension funds and activist investor funds including SPACs (*special purpose acquisition companies*) in publicly held as well as privately owned companies. ESG performance helps to increase the credibility of those who make these functions their professions. The credentials of individuals doing this work keeps increasing, and for good reason — procurement and sales-people drive the economy, globally. Sales and marketing get a lot of credit already and have emerged as a popular career for many people. But procurement … not so much.

Despite the importance of procurement activities, the people performing them are looked at as SG&A expenses on a P&L statement, and not as key drivers of financial performance and success for the companies they work for. They see reporting lines to managers and executives that do not have the subject matter expertise to make the necessary strategic sourcing and supply chain decisions in a timely manner. But more often than not, it is procurement that draws the ire and reputational disfunction on itself (sometimes deservedly so, sometimes not), and it all revolves around this issue of "price" versus "cost" and the worst of all Procurement measures, called "savings," which drives their reward system and decision-making toward price and not cost. People do what they are incentivized to do — and if they do it well, watch out! If we've learned anything in our 70-plus combined years of working financial, supply chain, and procurement issues, it's that when you take a bad process and make "improvements" to only one part of the bad process, it only makes things worse for the company that relies on that end-to-end (E2E) process.

The reason procurement gets such a bad rap is that their reputation precedes them! The following are two descriptions of procurement, one from a large 3PL business development team in a workshop, the other from comments solicited at a meeting of the Strategic Account Management Association (SAMA), a sales executive group:

"Single word" description of procurement by a 3PL Development Team	"Two-word" description of procurement by SAMA Sales Executives
"Value-Prevention-Team"	"Sales Prevention"
"Confrontational"	"Price Takers"
"Price-Focused"	"Hardball Negotiators"
"Transactional"	"Short-sighted"
"Non-strategic"	"Aggressive" (not 2 words!)
"Biased"	@#$%&* (not 2 words!)
"Mistrustful"	*&^%$# (not 2 words!)
"Aggressive"	?&%!@# (not 2 words!)
"Power-hungry"	*%@?!! (not 2 words!)

As you can see, some of these are not fit to print. You can't make this up!

Before we delve into what procurement does "right," let's dive into what happens when procurement's behavior verges on the terrible. The following case study provides insights into a company that came close to self-destruction because of a procurement policy that was hell-bent on pursuing cost reductions over everything else — including the customer! Read on …

CASE STUDY

Procurement's Bad Rap — why the disrespect?!

The 3PL Case Study from Hell, or "How I Destroyed Shareholder Value by Saving $25 million"
(a 2015–2019 retrospective)

Kraft-Heinz Company's Impact on Procurement of 3PL Services

One of the worst things that can happen which drives destruction of solid procurement functions is a takeover by a private hedge fund. I (Robert) collected significant evidence to support the fact that individuals at The Kraft-Heinz Company (KHC) were under duress from a big hedge fund, 3G Capital, to come up with immediate cost savings improvements that effectively destroyed the company's value. I first heard KHC mentioned during an interview I had with a senior vice president of business development at a large 3PL that provides the bulk of their 3PL services:

> *One of the most challenging issues we face with our customers is when they have a change in leadership, and they come in with a new vision of where they want to take the company. They are not as committed to us like the old relationship contact, and want to make their mark. So they will always, first thing, put the business out for bid, and issue a Request for Proposal. The new leadership will always put everything we are doing out to bid — and the Kraft merger with Heinz did just that. And we lost the Kraft and Heinz business for some of those bids, as we were not the lowest cost.[2]*

During this same time period, another executive highlighted the need for discussion around the KHC account during our executive workshop program, citing the following:

> *KHC is our number two customer in this vertical (fast-moving consumer goods [FMCG]), and since the 3G acquisition, has changed their contract manufacturing management approach from*

---

2 Interview with DHL executive, November 2016.

an operational base to a heavy reliance on procurement outsourcing. Most of our relationships were with the operational people in the business, who understood what we could do for them. Unfortunately, we found that their procurement team were a bunch of millennials who were largely unaware of the business needs, and we had to try to build relationships with them and help them understand the business. As a result, the relationship has become very transactional.[3]

Additional comments from the 3PL working with this company described the situation as follows.

We were dealing with the people we had worked with before on this deal. We previously had a great relationship with them, and worked hard to drive productivity improvements at their distribution center, continuous cost savings through improved efficiency activities, as well as transportation savings through improved network optimization and full truck load savings. But their procurement people came to us and out of the blue announced that they needed a 10% cost savings on the unit price rates we were quoting them. We tried to emphasize that we had already generated a bunch of savings for them, but they kept coming back and saying "No, we really need you to come down by 10%!" I got the impression that they were really under the gun from their leadership team, and they even seemed embarrassed to keep coming back to the 10% number. We even told them our margins weren't 10%, but they said they had to meet this objective. I got the feeling that this was being imposed on them because of the 3G merger, and they hinted as much.[4]

In a subsequent interview I conducted with a senior executive at the 3PL, they confirmed that they have lost some of the KHC business but not all of it. I did not learn if the executive mentioned above was able to close the deal. However, he did confirm much of what I have learned since then about KHC.

Kraft has gone through a substantial accounting repositioning, and things have gotten much worse for them lately. They are in a bunker mentality. We have actually won some contracts, and lost some. They have gone completely towards bottom-line price, and RFP'ed (request for proposal) every part of their supply chain. When we bid on these, they would come back and tell us that "I don't believe your cost" — and they took some businesses away from us. This has hurt them and they have paid the price, as they don't understand the concept of "total cost," not just bottom-line price. For instance, they took a big operation away from us and gave the business to a competitor (not mentioned) — who then, once they got into the business, promptly came back to Kraft and asked for a 40% rate increase! I don't mean to say that we were right! It doesn't make us right — but it doesn't make us wrong either.... Perhaps it is somewhere in between.

If you think Kraft was bad — Heinz was worse! We never did ANY business with Heinz before they merged with Kraft, because we knew they were always looking for the lowest price, and we stayed away from all of their RFPs. I am always upfront with our customers, and will tell them the same thing: "If you put us out for an RFP, and you are looking solely for the lowest price, we will not win and are not interested. We focus solely on total cost of ownership, which includes

---

3 Interview with DHL executive, February 2017.

4 Interview with DHL executive, April 2017.

inventory, delivery, efficiency, and the entire system cost. In fact, I will tell you, that if you are looking solely at price — and we are the lowest cost provider — then have we done something wrong! I get the shivers thinking about this, because that is not who we are; we are always selling total cost."

We saw a lot of new faces at Kraft and they looked like rats on the sinking ship. The environment had gotten so bad, it became an intolerable place to work. I don't know what the market cap is now, but it has gone down a lot. I recognize that anytime you change a provider, you will see some loss of productivity and there is always a struggle with the start-up. But when we lost their business, they picked other providers that I would call NOT experts in Fast Moving Consumer Goods (FMCG). It just wasn't an industry that was in their flight zone. We stood back when we lost the business and said to ourselves that this is going to be ugly! And it was. We have seen this same scenario play out with other companies who went down this road, including Continental, SC Johnson, and others who put out an RFP, told us we were too expensive, and we responded that they weren't looking at all the relevant costs involved. Sure enough, we are now hearing back from Kraft's procurement people, and they are telling us they want us back, after dealing with the people they awarded the business to. And we are hesitant in responding, and saying, "Well, it depends on what you are asking for now!"

They are in a bunker mentality, and everyone is hiding for cover.[5]

This executive's comments suggest that the morale at KHC was significantly impacted by 3G Capital's takeover and their application of their infamous Zero-Based Budgeting. Another executive I spoke with at a 3PL also noted that the company was desperate to drive cost savings, even asking suppliers to produce cash, and that the entire procurement team was fundamentally inexperienced and did not have the relevant experience that the prior team did.

Procurement, in general, likes to cause disruption. The Kraft procurement team completely changed overnight after 3G Capital came in. They had one mission, to drive down cost, and we are still feeling the pain of those decisions from the procurement team and their mode of cleaning house. It was really painful dealing with them, and the skill set required to negotiate these types of complex deals was completely absent. They brought in a lot of young new faces, with MBAs, and put them in a position where they were told to change things quickly and burn it down. We are all 25-year professionals on the other side of the table, and trying to educate these guys, and they weren't buying it.

We were amazed when they told us they wanted us to cut them a check to support their cost savings! They originally came to us with a request to cut them a check for $2M, and then came down and said the minimum they needed from us was a check for $1M. They were shaking us down to keep the account! We tried to show them where we were adding value, and added up all of the productivity improvements and operational cost savings that we generated for them, that added up to well over $1M. But that savings didn't affect their personal budget, as it didn't affect Procurement's cost savings bucket.

---

5 Interview with 3PL executive, February 2017.

Fortunately, we didn't lose any business, but what they did agree to is we looked at growth incentives, and came up with a deal that if they were to bring in new projects we would help them find ways to accrue for the cost savings on these projects. This forced us to get creative, and we were able to position ourselves to a point where they brought a lot of new projects to us, and our volume with them is up over 50% in the last year alone (2018–2019). Fortunately, we held our ground and didn't write them a check, but we heard that a lot of their suppliers did at that time. Eventually KHC got their hands slapped.

After the SEC audit, 3G brought in a completely new procurement team, and hired a whole new set of leaders, and they seem to be more well-rounded, and have more insight into the operating principles for the company, are aligned with their operations team, and come across as being more strategic. They are much more sophisticated, and understand the value of long-term partnerships with 3PLs, and how we can help their business grow, as opposed to short-term contractual bidding. They are looking for strategic partners who can help them with their strategy of increasing external contract manufacturing. They have taken a 180-degree approach from last time, back in 2017 we were pulling our hair out.

I think they learned the hard lesson that you can always find a lower bid — but in this industry, is it sustainable? And what happens is a lot of companies like KH will go to the lower bid and find the transition alone outweighs the cost savings. The challenge and disruption of start-up and manufacturing can outweigh the potential price savings, and unfortunately that did happen to KH procurement in this case. We didn't experience it personally, but I know they moved business around. Today in our manufacturing site, we have over 66% of Kraft's business, as we proved to them what we could do as a partner. It is difficult for them to make a change given that level of volume.[6]

Was Procurement Responsible Entirely for the Problems?

This case suggests how critical leadership mindset is not only to procurement but to the entire organization.

KHC Cuts in R&D

Interviews confirm significant cuts occurred not only in Procurement, but also in KHC's R&D function, and that their product lines were suffering. However, there is also evidence that they have turned the corner on this. And that is because much of their innovation comes from suppliers! One executive noted:

In 2018 Kraft started to focus on what was happening to their revenue, and started to transition their leadership, and by Q1 2019 went through a complete overhaul. One area that has been significantly changed is R&D. They have become more steady in terms of new product development, and their current focus is on the resurgence of their legacy brands. Their leadership is focusing on reviving their legacy brands and are driving marketing budgets around these brands. Unfortunately, the whole outer perimeter of grocery stores is where the major growth is, in the organic

---

6 Handfield Interview with 3PL senior executive, February 2017.

and fresh categories, which is what they seem to be missing. Perhaps we need a good recession to pump up sales in the center aisle again! But during the 3G period, they had massive cuts in R&D and are now bringing in new teams of R&D and marketing folks. The prior team was failing to drive any organic growth for Kraft, and that also explains why they were missing revenue targets.

What we have seen more recently is that we are starting to have more strategic conversations, and Kraft is looking for companies that have a bigger wallet to invest for them. But they really need to rejuvenate their innovation arm internally, and to start creating new products and options for growth. That is a big change after all the cuts they made, and they recognize this and are adding capabilities and capacity, which include a number of new capital investment projects and programs that have a longer-term ROI. For instance, they want us to move to facilities that are 24/7, adding capacity, and looking for opportunities where external manufacturers will purchase their equipment and run their factories for them. They seem to be shedding assets and reducing overhead like crazy.[7]

I also interviewed another provider of market intelligence to KHC procurement function, who worked with their Chief Procurement Officer at Kraft since he was hired in 2014, and their contract expired in 2017. Here is what he believes occurred at Kraft:

Kraft's problems were also outside of procurement. A lot of the 3G Capital cuts were in R&D and Sales and Marketing. Kraft-Heinz believes in hiring a lot of young MBAs and throwing them in the mix, and often put them in charge of working with markets and key distribution channels. This didn't work very well. Supermarkets expect a certain amount of respect from the brands — and while a lot of negotiations occur online, in the retail sector a lot of decisions also occur in the aisles. Kraft experienced a lot of revenue issues that were related to no investment in R&D. More importantly, their personnel cuts took out a layer of sales and marketing people that they considered to be expensive dead wood — but their senior management didn't realize the value they were bringing, and the importance of personal relationships with store category managers.

Procurement is hard-nosed — and they definitely burned some bridges by being too aggressive. It's likely though that they put everything out to bid, because they believe in obtaining cost savings and improving operating margin by any means, including bidding every category out when they came in. They likely cut into their muscle, and this impacted them.[8]

3G Capital's Zero-Based Budgeting (ZBB) Approach

Many of the problems associated with KHC can be attributed to the 3G infamous zero-based budgeting (ZBB) approach. This technique was developed in the 1960s by a Texas Instruments accountant named Pete Pyhrr and was originally focused on how to build better budgets:

In zero-based budgeting, managers plan each year's budget as if starting their department from scratch—a contrast with the prevailing method of adjusting the previous year's spending. The system calls for managers to break programs or activities into individual "decision packages," including all associated costs, to help identify how funds are used. The technique forces them to

---

7 Handfield interview with retailer, March 2017.

8 Handfield interview with market intelligence executive, February 2017.

justify the costs and evaluate benefits every 12 months, and to scrutinize whether dollars should be shifted from less-profitable to more-profitable projects.[9]

This is noted in a good article published by Reuters about the time of KHC's announcement:

3G Capital [uses a] notorious embrace of a tool called zero-based budgeting (ZBB), used to keep costs low and profit margins high. "At some point, having best-in-class margins doesn't matter if the sales growth doesn't eventually come," said Guggenheim analyst Laurent Grandet. … Zero-based budgeting is an approach requiring corporate managers to justify each item of spending every year, or even build their budgets from scratch, rather than the more common process of using the prior year's budget as a starting point. It came back into fashion among corporations over the last decade, after 3G Capital used it to great margin effect at brewing giant Anheuser-Busch InBev, whose creation it orchestrated, and then at Kraft-Heinz.[10]

There are a number of advocates of the approach:

"The cuts can be impressive, and that's a big win," said consultants Boston Consulting Group in a report from 2017. They noted, however, that faster growth was not a guaranteed result. "When it's applied clumsily, ZBB can have a demoralizing impact that distracts the organization from growth and value creation." Unilever, Mondelez International, Diageo and Kellogg are among companies that have used ZBB, though none has seen as bad results as Kraft's. "I think it's a black eye for Kraft-Heinz management for not implementing it in as a sophisticated way as might be necessary, or maybe they just implemented it too hard, too fast," Investec analyst Eddy Hargreaves said. "I don't think ZBB per se is the problem."[11]

However, the article goes on to point out that ZBB can't fix the problems of lack of product innovation, which may be another factor at play at KHC.

The head of investment at a European consulting firm said ZBB was not the answer for problems ailing Kraft and its packaged food peers, which are suffering as consumers eschew traditional staples like macaroni-and-cheese and bologna for fresher, less-processed or healthier options. "To catch up with the shift of consumer demand for better-for-you and sustainable food, you have to innovate. And to innovate you simply can't use ZBB," he said.[12]

An article by AT Kearney (now Kearney) points out the advantages and disadvantages of ZBB[13]:

Advantages:

- Allocates resources based on needs and benefits, rather than history.
- Encourages managers to run operations more cost effectively.
- Identifies areas of waste.

9 *The Wall Street Journal.* https://www.wsj.com/articles/meet-the-father-of-zero-based-budgeting-1427415074,

10 Reuters.com, *https://www.reuters.com/article/us-consumer-kraft-heinz/kraft-heinz-problems-shine-light-on-controversial-budget-tool-idUSKCN1QB2CF.*

11 Ibid.

12 Ibid.

13 *https://www.kearney.com/industry/aerospace-defense/article/-/insights/zbb-the-basics-of-zbb-article.*

Disadvantages:

- Costs that are eliminated can creep back in if left unchecked.
- People in organizations dread ZBB and can be paralyzed by it.
- Management energy is used completely on what's perceived as "mission impossible."

To conduct ZBB properly, Kearney recommends using ZBBplus, which suggests that targets need to be set not only from the top down using external benchmarks but also from the bottom up, producing targets that are based on stronger information. In addition, they advocate looking beyond traditional back-office spending as well as providing a framework for how work is done, resources are used, and how decisions are made.

The ZBB approach, however, has also been criticized in the supply chain management (SCM) press:

> *… previous 3G-led purchases of Anheuser-Busch, Burger King, Tim Horton's and Heinz itself have quickly resulted in large-scale job losses, shuttered factories, slimmed-down headquarters and the imposition of "zero-based budgeting". The latter, which forces managers to justify their proposed expenditure from scratch every year, rather than simply adjusting last year's budget figure, has been used by 3G to slash everything from corporate jets to colour photocopying, as part of its broader strategy to improve margins at the growth-challenged food companies it's bought. …. Although media coverage of the Kraft-Heinz merger has largely concentrated on internal cost-cutting, the odds are that a decent slice of the annual $1.5 billion that 3G has pledged to take out when it combines the two companies will come from suppliers. 3G partner and Heinz chairman Alex Behring was quoted in the* Financial Times *recently saying: "Scale will yield procurement savings." … the real test of whether 3G Capital's move is good news or bad for procurement is whether it encourages collaboration with key suppliers to remove unnecessary cost and waste from their supply chains — as Kraft has been doing of late — or simply takes the axe to supplier pricing. The legacy of professional procurement at both companies would suggest that it ought to be more the former than the latter."*[14]

While ZBB may have some merits in terms of a management turnaround strategy, the fundamental question is whether it was deployed in the proper fashion at KHC. I conducted a number of other interviews with executives who were formerly at KHC and who provided insights into what occurred during the period when 3G Capital attempted to deploy ZBB within the organization.

It is my belief that 3G Capital applied ZBB in a brute-force fashion at every company they acquired. For instance, while working at Anheuser-Busch Inbev, I spoke to a procurement executive who made the following comment:

> *"After this merger, my plan is simply to beat the crap [sic] out of our suppliers some more for 5% cost savings. This is the playbook."*[15]

---

14 Kearney.com, https://www.kearney.com/industry/aerospace-defense/article/-/insights/zbb-the-basics-of-zbb-article
15 Interview with Anheuser-Busch Inbev procurement executive.

The original intent of the ZBB model involves exploring the underlying assumptions for budgets in certain categories. The approach was originally developed to prioritize which of scores of new product-development projects should be pursued and how much capital they should get each year. Corporate travel is another good example. Aggregating airline and hotel usage across the company and then negotiating preferred rates with a handful of providers is one way to save money. But once those benefits are achieved, further cost-cutting will necessitate flying economy/coach or using web conferences instead. Pete Pyhrr uses the travel example as a way to ask the question: "It's really saying: why are we going to all these places and how many of us are going?"[16]

Impact of 3G's Cuts in Marketing on Top-Line Revenue

Multiple individuals I spoke with confirmed that there were significant cuts made to KHC's procurement, sales, and logistics organization, which had resulting impacts on their "top line," as well as growth in revenue. These cuts came about because of 3G's approach to ZBB but had significant impacts on firm performance.

> *I have heard of 3G Capital, but have had nothing to do with them. However, I heard a lot of things about what they did at Kraft Heinz. Specifically, I knew someone (a Danish gentleman) who was in transition and who left Kraft Heinz to join my FMCG company in Dubai. After he left to join our company, he was in touch with his ex-colleagues, and shared with me a number of stories about what they were facing. He told me about the type of approach to restructuring they took along with Berkshire. He described it as "completely ruthless restructuring as part of a very focused turnaround approach." This approach was impacting the very basic foundations of the company, and a number of people who were really critical to its operation were severely affected. It didn't just hurt those who lost their jobs, but for those who were left, what they did to the company was really bad.[17]*

Another executive I interviewed was the former chief procurement officer at Kraft who recalls why he left the company shortly before 3G Capital acquired them. It is important to note that he had already applied many cost-savings approaches at Kraft during his tenure there (July 2014 to August 2015). This suggests that there may not have been much in the way of "savings" to achieve in the procurement area.

> *While I was at Kraft Foods, I was able to achieve a 150% increase in our savings rate. I developed a big data analytics platform and was able to achieve it in 7 months. It took me 5 months to convince the CEO to give me the investment for the platform, and then for the remaining 7 months, I drove the RFP process using the tool and generated 150% in our savings rate. When 3G came in with their playbook, I realized that they don't ever pivot from it, and wouldn't listen to me. I told them that I had already leveraged my spend over the supply base, but they just told me in so many words that "I don't care what the leverage component is for any specific supplier, I will just simply beat them up."*

---

16 *https://www.scmworld.com/is-3gs-growing-influence-good-or-bad-news-for-procurement/*
17 Interview with senior VP of a large FMCG company in Dubai, October 25, 2019.

After I left, I heard a lot of stories about what happened. They got their asses handed to them by their transportation providers after they beat them up on their prices, and a lot of their trucks weren't showing up to move their product to customers. Their providers told them: "You put us over a barrel, but you have now become a loss leader customer. We prefer to cycle our trucks to customers where we can make a buck!" When transportation stopped coming to pick up product, Kraft ended up choking on inventory in their plants, and they couldn't move the stuff after they made it! **So their response was to fire all of their own transportation people, which made it worse!**

There were a lot of other issues that also occurred. Kraft is such a big player in the commodities market, especially in areas like cheese, milk, dairy, and nuts. As such, they are a big market changer, and can impact prices and demand in the food commodities market. In these cases, there are specific prohibitions on trade that come into effect if you are a market maker, and Kraft started violating some of these. In fact, the Kraft-Heinz 3G guy was busted, indicted, and incarcerated for market manipulation! This really impacted their supply chain. Thankfully, I didn't stay in that job!

Another big problem was that the guy they put into that job had no knowledge of the food business, and had never managed a COGS spend that was as big as Kraft. He had previously worked in a company with $6B of spend, and Kraft has over $18B. In addition, he has never had experience with the level of commodity and materials exposure that Kraft had. He tried to use brute force (the 3G Way) in the supply market for commodities, but someone found out and was betting on the other side of that trade. He got caught in the cross hairs, and it hurt them.[18]

Another executive at Walmart, who had previously been at Target working in grocery during the period of the cuts at KHC noted the importance of the rep/merchandiser/marketing relationship and how this was disrupted when KHC brought in all new reps for their brands after the cuts:

A lot of the planning goes on when the merchandiser and the brand rep come to me, sitting on the inside [in marketing at Target or Walmart], and they will present to me the decisions on what we will carry at this retailer, and how to promote the brand. This allows us to then integrate the brand into our marketing for the retailer. If a brand has a group of experienced reps working their products, and then had significant turnover, and send in a bunch of new reps, it becomes a challenge working with these new people! You want to be objective and want to work in the interest of the enterprise; but if there is high turnover, and the new person struggles because they are so new to representing their brand and don't understand how to sell it, it is harder to get work done. I do recall that it was difficult for merchandisers to work with a new rep, particularly if they are new to the role.[19]

I also interviewed a senior supply chain analyst, who had worked with KHC as a consultant, and understood the environment being faced by their organization and by KHC under the

---

18 Interview with Walter Charles, former CPO, Kraft Foods, March 2017.
19 Handfield interview with retail executive, February 2017.

3G model. He echoed the notion that transportation and sales are critical elements that drive revenue, and that this is the primary reason why KHC took such a bit hit to their revenue.

The whole 3G effect looks good on paper — but it isn't good. I got to know Heinz as a consultant, and have also worked with other companies who have been "3G'ed" (his term!). The firings of the key marketing and supply chain staff is the biggest issue I have with it, and the reordering of the bodies and replacement with new folks who don't understand the business at all. Their business model is simply that you are harvesting brands (Mac and Cheese, Heinz ketchup, Oscar Meyer) and taking out cost, with no value added whatsoever. They wouldn't invest in marketing, no formulation updates, or anything that produced innovative ideas to further promote and improve the brands. But the biggest problem was the impact on the relationships in the supply chain. In the grocery sector, it is a very transportation-intensive sector. You rely on transportation providers for cold-chain and ambient-temperature capabilities, involving moving products which require a temperature range to comply with FDA standards. It is also fast-moving, especially with fresh produce, to make sure you pick up and drop off to hit aggressive targets. It is also about last mile, in which you are delivering to specific retail locations, and have a window to hit in terms of schedule, which is often last minute. To achieve these outcomes requires a lot of collaboration and having capable people who can work together closely on the brand side and the transportation side and the retailer side to make it all happen and fall into place. So when you bring in a bunch of new faces with no experience on the brand side, you can't expect them to know how to operate. And then you can't start a new RFP process with a new bunch of carriers with whom you have no relationship. The same goes for the sale side, where you are working closely with merchandisers to promote your product with the Safeways, the Walmarts, and the Krogers of the world. So I believe that you are absolutely right when you say this was the reason behind their top-line misses![20]

These insights are confirmed by a report on CNBC, which stated:

3G has been lauded for its ability to quickly integrate deals and slash costs. In two years, it extracted roughly $1.7 billion in savings from Kraft-Heinz. To help achieve those goals, it laid off thousands of employees, including those with years of experience in the consumer goods industry. None of the business unit heads in place when Kraft and Heinz merged are in the same role, and many have left.[21]

Cuts in Transportation

I interviewed an executive who shared with me his experience. After working at the company's Chicago headquarters for 30 years, he was in the first wave of individuals fired from Kraft Heinz.

I was in the first wave of people to be let go, and I have to say they were fair in giving me a fair package during the transition. When 3G came in, I knew they were all about ZBB and I knew that playbook very well. It was well-publicized and I saw it first hand at Heinz, and had been

---

20 Interview with senior analyst formerly with Gartner, November 18, 2019.

21 CNBC, *https://www.cnbc.com/2019/05/07/misconduct-at-kraft-heinz-puts-spotlight-on-pressure-to-meet-targets.html.*

following it since that time. I still have a few friends there, and they told me that they basically burned the furniture when they arrived.

I was working in supply chain and transportation for most of my career. The last role I was in was supply chain customer development. In this role I was an intermediary between our supply chains operations, sales team, and customer teams, which involved a lot of program management, continuous improvement, and customer issue resolution activity.

But I knew the cuts were coming, and knew there was a high potential that I could be on the list, regardless of my stellar performance record over 30 years. Part of me was curious that maybe I could learn something about the ZBB approach, as I was never under the impression that we had "all the answers" at Kraft. But as it turns out, I never got that chance, as I was let go. After I left and I heard about the things they were doing, and started talking to my former customers, I'm glad I was let go when I was, as it was a disaster. They brought in a bunch of young MBAs who knew nothing about customer relationships, and you just can't do that in retail without pissing off customers.

As a result of the arrogant attitude of these new customer relationship managers, Kraft lost a bunch of shelf space. Although ZBB is an interesting approach to business, they are seeing now the effects of cutting off business relationships. You can't keep doing that stuff. 3G was able to cover a lot of sins by having one acquisition after another, and every new acquisition provided something new you could cut that could cover the problems you were hiding in the business you had just acquired. After Kraft, they went after Unilever, who said "no thank you," so now they had no fresh supply of cuts to fuel their operating margins, and the stock took a huge hit.

3G was never any good at the top line. They didn't do anything for any company ever that improved the top line (revenue). Their whole game was to improve margin through massive cuts. Their last quarter this year was better, as they have someone who is more marketing and finance focused.

After they took over when I left, they went after their transportation providers for cost savings. This was during a period when the transportation market was already very tough, with not a lot of excess capacity. (It is a bit softer now, by the way). Just as I left, I told one of my people that she had better get her résumé out, because it was going to get really bad in terms of transportation performance. You can't cut your providers in a tight market. If you beat up transportation providers, they just won't send over their trucks to pick up your product! Which is exactly what happened to Kraft, and they missed a lot of store deliveries, which further hurt their already damaged relationships, and they lost a ton of shelf space to other companies.

I didn't live through the damage, but I can tell you that they cut almost everybody that had any experience at the company. Today, if you have two years' experience at Kraft, you are considered a veteran![22]

---

22 Harry Hagen, Loyola University.

I also spoke with a former senior supply chain executive who spoke confidentially on what happened at Kraft, where he was formerly with Nabisco and then part of Kraft's logistics leadership team.

> *When I joined Kraft with the Nabisco acquisition, there were a lot of great people there who had deep knowledge of how the supply chain ran. Kraft was a $50B company after they added Nabisco, and driving change there was a bit like turning a battleship in a bathtub! But I enjoyed that big infrastructure. Then the leadership decided to split out Mondelez, taking with them some of the best snack brands in the market, including Cadbury and Nabisco. This left Kraft with all the low-margin, low-growth grocery items. And then 3G came in after the Heinz merger (Heinz was owned by Buffett) and I heard from some of my former colleagues about what happened next. For instance, people told me that the 3G model was to bring in two people, who both had 15 years' experience, and give them each 15 minutes to "tell us why you get the job over your colleague next to you in the room." It was all about cost cutting. But what 3G didn't realize is that, in the grocery industry, which is all low margin, the most important thing is that it is all about the customer! All of the big brands, P&G, Unilever, and all of them, know that SCM is all about making sure the consumer/customer comes first. For instance, P&G has what they call their two moments of truth, the first being what the customer sees on the shelf, the second being what they experience after you have bought the product and bring it home. And when companies go in and suck out marketing budgets, this impacts service, which impacts what customers see on the shelves, which hits revenues.*
>
> *Kraft had a huge transportation spend, about $1.3B annually. And so 3G believed that they could take out dollars, but didn't realize that buying transportation isn't like buying corrugate. 3G elected to allow procurement to run transportation sourcing, claiming that they were "good at it," but not realizing that the key to transportation is ensuring good customer service. There are also many complicated issues that veterans know, including understanding how and when to use intermodal, rail, truck load, and less-than-truck load services. Ensuring good service means knowing your carriers and having great relationships with them, to ensure that they will have the trucking capacity in times of need and for emergencies, as well as planning for a lot of seasonality and cyclicality that is common in the grocery industry. Procurement at Kraft were confident that they could handle all of that, and proceeded to learn that relationships are important when you don't have them, and beating up on transport providers will significantly damage customer service, which impacts top-line revenue.*
>
> *No one at 3G understood that transportation wasn't an infinite resource. When they ripped out costs, they saw significant deterioration in customer satisfaction levels, as they impacted their service and logistics activities negatively. Even in a great economy, trying to cut costs in logistics is a mistake. But it happens all the time — some new chief supply chain officer comes in, wants to implement new productivity tools, and is responding to a new CEO who wants to cut costs to boost earnings — and they know they are only there for a short while. After they leave, the real effects start to hit the enterprise.[23]*

---

23 Interview with Rick Blasgen, CEO, CSCMP, November 14, 2019.

Insights from Interviews and Research

These interviews point to some preliminary insights regarding what unfolded at KHC during the period after 3G took over in March 2015.

- Extreme pressure was put on procurement managers to drive cost savings with suppliers.

- Extreme cost cutting targets were established, with little regard for what transpired prior to 3G's arrival. It seems like they automatically assumed that there was a lot of "fat" in their supply contracts, despite having a series of professional procurement executives who had already gone in and leveraged suppliers for cost savings.

- Kraft engaged in commodity market trades that manipulated commodity markets.[24]

- It seems as if KHC sought to capture savings in advance of when prices were actually renegotiated in contracts.

- Kraft tried to reduce costs in transportation, which severely damaged their relationships in a tight market, and many providers failed to show up to pick up their products for delivery to retailers. This further hit top-line revenue, as Kraft lost credibility with major retailers (including Walmart, Kroger, and others) and lost massive shelf-space in retail aisles. This was further damaged by poor retailer relationships as all their customer service representatives with deep relationships had been fired, replaced by young aggressive MBAs who didn't have the experience to manage retailer relationships.

- KHC reduced headcount in their sales staff, firing experienced relationship managers that were familiar with the nuts and bolts of how to represent the brand in retail stores. The loss of these individuals significantly damaged the relationship with key merchandisers, that resulted in significant hits to top-line revenue. The new personnel simply didn't have the knowledge and expertise and familiarity with the brands, and sales declined significantly during this period.

- KHC suffered significant operational improvements that may have led to market share loss. Missed deliveries in grocery retail stores are often penalized by loss of shelf-space, which would in turn help explain why revenue targets were missed when transportation providers failed to deliver their products to stores.

In summary, we now see why all of this matters, and the difference that good Sales, Procurement, and Supply Chain practices can bring. They help drive the economy, have the potential to improve business practices from the standpoint of Total Cost of Ownership and the Net Present Value of Future Cash Flows, bring efficiency to the processes, and increase shareholder value to both buyer and seller when executed in a competitive but constructive manner. Understanding how these business functions operate together is the essence of what makes corporations successful. Sales and Marketing are the eyes that are informing everyone of what the customer wants — but if they are not exposed to the right things, they won't get it right. Procurement needs to listen to internal customers as well as salespeople and communicate what the best

---

24 *https://www.cfo.com/fraud/2019/08/kraft-settles-futures-market-manipulation-case/*

decision should be to improve value. But often that's not how it works. When Procurement people are incentivized and rewarded for achieving "savings" (however defined) as opposed to implementing solutions that optimize the business (of which savings can legitimately be a part of that solution), the business usually suffers in the long term.

The net effect of all of this was a loss in equity value for KHC of $30 to $40 billion during the worst of these times, and this was when the stock market as a whole was significantly increasing in value. As shown in the share price stock listings below,[25] KHC's share price plummeted from a high of $93.08 on February 24, 2017, to an all-time low of $25.41 in August 2019, a drop of 73% in share price. The massive cuts in headcount, product innovation, and a procurement strategy focused on price reduction eventually caught up with it. However, there is a happy ending to this story.

HOME > KHC · NASDAQ

Kraft Heinz Co

$37.34   ↓18.79%   -8.64 MAX

Jan 25, 10:04:40 AM UTC-5 · USD · NASDAQ · Disclaimer

| 1D | 5D | 1M | 6M | YTD | 1Y | 5Y | MAX | | Key events |

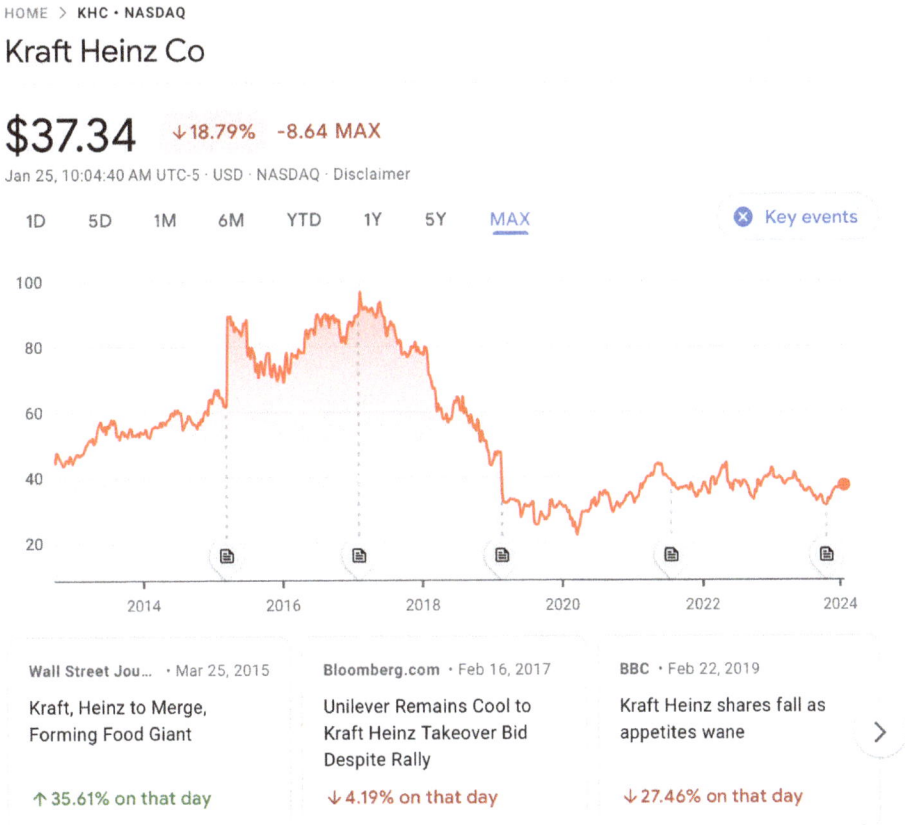

Wall Street Jou… · Mar 25, 2015	Bloomberg.com · Feb 16, 2017	BBC · Feb 22, 2019
Kraft, Heinz to Merge, Forming Food Giant	Unilever Remains Cool to Kraft Heinz Takeover Bid Despite Rally	Kraft Heinz shares fall as appetites wane
↑ 35.61% on that day	↓ 4.19% on that day	↓ 27.46% on that day

---

25 Google Finance, *https://www.google.com/finance/quote/KHC:NASDAQ?sa=X&ved=2ahUKEwiG-vevodWAAxXoTDABHUMxAHoQ3ecFeg QILBAh&window=MAX.*

Learning, Change, and Redemption is Possible — Fast Forward to May 2023

In May 2023 on LinkedIn, Marcos Eloi Lima, chief procurement officer (CPO) at KHC, posted the following:

> "Incredibly proud to announce that The Kraft Heinz Company has won the Procurement Leaders Award for Supplier Collaboration & Innovation. This recognition reflects our commitment to excellence and is a demonstration of the power of collaboration and the incredible potential that emerges when we work and innovate hand in hand with our partners. A huge thank-you to our incredible suppliers and cross functional teams for their unwavering support and collaboration. Join us in celebrating this milestone!"

The CPO's statement was also reposted on Linkedin by Janelle Orozco, the newly appointed CPO, North American Zone at KHC, with the following: "Incredibly proud of the team at The Kraft Heinz Company behind this award! Amazing work collaborating with our most important suppliers to find new spaces for value creation and innovation." She also posted, "Thrilled to be able to attend the Procurement Leaders World Awards, showcasing amazing work by fantastic companies. Incredibly proud of the Kraft Heinz team for taking home the award for supplier collaboration and innovation. We cannot be successful without our supplier partners — so pleased to see this shift through a consistent program and looking forward to seeing even more as we build it for the future. Let's Make Life Delicious together!!"

According to Janelle, in an earlier post on LinkedIn, Procurement Leaders shortlisted KHC for four awards for different initiatives in Supplier Collaboration and Innovation, Risk & Resilience, and Transformation, the result of the "passion, collaboration, and resilience the procurement team has shown over the past few years. #HereAtKraftHeinz we are building a great story and we are looking forward to share all about it soon. Good luck to our amazing team!"

KHC also posted the following on LinkedIn after winning the award: "Congratulations to our Kraft Heinz Procurement Team for winning the Procurement Leaders Award for Supplier Collaboration & Innovation. This team is our gateway to innovation and efficiency, bringing the latest and greatest in technology, new ingredients and packaging to our business. We are proud of their commitment to driving value for our entire organization, and thankful to our Suppliers for their partnership as we pursue growth together. Join us in celebrating this incredible team."

KHC's stock has remained relatively flat since 2020. As shown in the chart below, however, during the same period of these events, when we compare KHC share prices to other major indices, it shows that while the price of KHC is down 50% since the inception of the company as a merged entity, the S&P 500 is up 150% and the Consumer Cyclicals index is up almost 100%. This is still an extraordinary loss in shareholder value, attributable to a failed procurement and supply chain strategy.

An important development was the Kraft Heinz Securities Group class action litigation settlement which was announced May 9, 2023, for $450 million, a massive settlement that makes the list of all-time largest settlements.[26] The action alleged that while KHC claimed following the merger that the company was reporting increased profits and profit margins due to cost cutting "synergies" between the combined companies, in fact 3G was imposing comprehensive cost cuts that "gutted" the company's investments in R&D, quality control, and its supply chain. The plaintiffs allege that these undisclosed cost cuts caused a deterioration in the brand value of the company's food brands and harmed key customer relationships, which drove the goodwill impairment. In response to the impairment and related news, analysts criticized the company for having concealed "bad news." The Settlement Amount "will be allocated amongst the Kraft Heinz Defendants, 3G Capital, and Defendants' insurers, pursuant to a confidential agreement entered into by the Defendants."

Source: TD Ameritrade, Thinkorswim platform, closing prices on August 23, 2023.

Is the Procurement Leaders awards a happy ending for The Kraft-Heinz Company, or a work in progress? Only time will tell. Regardless, we admire the turnaround and what it took to get there. For many companies, though, and their Procurement and Supply Chain functions, you are only as good as your last quarter's results. But as you will see in the coming chapters, it doesn't have to be this way.

Chapter 2:
How "Purchasing" Gets Done in Many Corporations ("Old School")

(and what salespeople really need to know to be effective)

As much as chief procurement officers (CPOs) like to throw around clichés about the best practices of their procurement organizations — describing elements as being "Best in Class" by incorporating "strategic sourcing," "category management," "source planning," "supply chain optimization," "digitization of procurement," "ESG (Environmental, Social, & Governance) compliant supply chains," and "risk mitigation" — we find that much of what really goes on is not actually reflective of the interactions between Sales and Procurement. This chapter will focus on how Sales needs to view its interactions with Procurement, and why Procurement has such a hard time getting out of its "Savings R Us" reputation, image, and mentality.

Introduction: The Blue Sheet

I (Howard) have never attended a Strategic Account Management Association (SAMA) meeting or conference during my procurement career, and I will state right now that it was probably a mistake not to do so. After all, why would an up-and-coming procurement executive attend a conference for salespeople? (And besides, where would I find money in the procurement budget to justify my attending these meetings? Not that SAMA would let me attend anyway.) Let's face it, it's hard enough to get funds just for your Procurement people to go to procurement conferences. So instead, we did some research on SAMA and their publications to learn more about how salespeople view the world of procurement.

But before we go into that, what does it mean to be a *strategic account manager* (SAM) or, better yet, a *global account manager* (GAM) in a Sales role? Having worked with corporate sales employees who have attended executive development training to become certified as SAMs/GAMs, I know their responsibilities are very much like the other side of the coin when compared to procurement *global category managers* (GCMs). SAMs/GAMs are responsible for defining and delivering the short-term and long-term revenue commitments from their accounts, expanding use of current product lines and introducing new product lines, and a host of other responsibilities that now go by the designation of "customer success." That's the "what," but what about the "how"?

The Blue Sheet

It was during a consulting assignment that I was introduced to the concept of the Miller Heiman Blue Sheet. The Blue Sheet is an "old school" sales tool that was used before Salesforce.com came into being, and it is still used or incorporated into the SAM toolbox, although it's typically digitized now. One of the SAMs working on the revenue side of the business befriended the procurement function and offered up a day of training for Procurement on the life of a SAM. Lo and behold, he brought out the famous Blue Sheet and taught us how SAMs used it to understand who (and how) to deal with in an organization to best sell their products and services, and how to feed that information into their sales funnel. It focused on short-term and longer-term revenue generation and timing from the customer, identified who the customer decision-makers were, what (and who) the potential "red flags" were, and the priorities for the account. Accordingly, the account management assignments were then set for the account.

I'm not sure why I was surprised by this, because this was a composite of the same type of tools that we were using in procurement category management, except we were using different tools called *source plans, stakeholder mapping, communications plans*, and RACIs (*responsible/accountable/consulted/informed*). Procurement GCMs were expected to update their category source plans and stakeholder maps every 6 to 12 months to make sure that the category strategy being employed by the GCMs leading the sourcing teams were aligned with market best practices and the internal stakeholders (usually major budget holders) were being properly consulted and informed. This was a little tricky because we could share the source plans, communication plans, and RACIs with our stakeholders, but they had no idea that we were doing stakeholder mapping behind the scenes, and we were labeling them in terms of who had decision-making power and their degree of influence, and who were considered to be supporters or blockers of our activities, and how we should involve them or skirt around them. We were blue sheeting our stakeholders in our own company!

Sample Stakeholder Map: Category: Marketing – Creative Agencies

Name	Position	Level of influence (L/M/H)	Supporter/ Neutral/ Blocker (S/N/B)	RACI or decision-maker (R/A/C/I/D)	Comms (weekly, monthly)	Sourcing team role
H. Brown	CMO	H	N	D	monthly	sponsor
V. Ebert	VP Brands	H	B	C, I	weekly	core
L. Meeks	Dir. Creative	M	S	A	weekly	core
J. Smart	Dir. Marketing	M	N	R	weekly	core
M. Butts	Dir. Mktg. Fin.	H	S	C, I	monthly	support
Y. Hernandez	Legal	L	S	I	monthly	support
F. Taylor	GCM	H	S	A, R	weekly	team leader

I came to realize that in major accounts — especially in enterprise software firms like Oracle, SAP, IBM, and Microsoft — their SAMs and GAMs knew so much more about our internal operations and had successfully blue sheeted us to a much greater degree than procurement GCMs had been able to do to them. They were experts at this. They knew everything about their counterparts in Procurement. They practiced their pitches, reviewed and "role played" the interactions, and the activity was staffed, funded, and ingrained in their culture and work responsibilities. They had quota and bonus systems for revenue realization, but also made sure to award people who were in roles that supported the sales activity.

It was also the culture in these enterprises to use *closers* (also known as *elephant hunters*) as the SAMs and GAMs, and once they landed the whale (or the elephant, or any other description you can give to a large enterprise account), within 1 to 4 weeks, we would see an announcement that the SAM/GAM with whom we had invested all this time to negotiate a major deal was pulled off of our account. That was always their plan, and they were then assigned to the next potential whale. In their place, they gave us a more junior salesperson to maintain and grow the existing business and to feed off of the carcass. So much for building honesty and trust in the relationship. But let's face it, trust is not something that develops between companies — it's something that develops between contacts, human beings, who then carry out *supplier relationship management* (SRM). This was the only way for Procurement to salvage all of the verbal promises that were made between executives but never reduced to written guarantees in the contracts.

So we started to read the SAMA literature about what they were preaching to the SAMs and GAMs and discussing at their conferences, and it was no surprise to find that the main theme was how to get around Procurement. They applied their Blue Sheets, and if they could find decision-makers and budget holders in the organization that were willing to write their products and services into the specifications (instead of creating functional specifications that were supplier agnostic), they would do so. It was the SAM's job to do so, and they spent a lot of their time and company money positioning themselves in the organization to help the client solve problems using their goods and services. Also, if they could go to senior executives through their "old boy" connections, and then get C-Suite leaders to agree to sponsor their offerings in meetings that would flow down as purchase requisitions/orders to Procurement, they would do so. SAMA published interviews with sales executives, asking them to describe Procurement in two words, and as noted in Chapter 1, the typical responses included "sales prevention," "price takers," "hardball negotiators," "short-sighted," "aggressive" (not two words!), and a host of other names, some of which are not fit to print.

While very few statements by the sales executives were complimentary, and in their roles, they had worked around purchasing for many years, they also had observed some level of shift in the strategic recognition of what Procurement and Supply Chain do. However, they still saw many remnants of the "old school" and felt that these old-school elements were still prevalent.

In one of my discussions with a former VP Sales for a global electrical lighting control company, he confirmed his experiences at SAMA meetings and their emphasis to always go around Procurement. But he also knew that Procurement, if they inserted themselves into the game at any point, would be looking to either block the deal or delay it until they had a victory to claim, usually in the neighborhood of 5 to 10 percent cost savings. This was especially true in the medium-sized business accounts that represented the largest market for their sales pipeline, where Procurement was usually brought in at the tail end of the process. But they anticipated that and gave their salespeople room to make the concession to close the deal. Talk about win-win scenarios! Sales gets the net price they were expecting to get anyway, and Procurement gets to trumpet about how they were great negotiators and claim that they had achieved "below-market pricing." (We've got a story about "below-market pricing." See Chapter 8, "Culture Eats Strategy for Lunch.")

The discussions with Procurement didn't all start out in a contentious manner; there were always the typical friendly statements in the early phases, such as "We are your friends, let's collaborate and build a trusted relationship and partnership," "Success of the project is the highest priority," "Everybody has to make a profit," etc. But then, right before the contract was signed, the mood changed. There were the pressures from the top to make sure it's a good deal; that the contract terms were unfavorable and they wouldn't work off of the supplier's boilerplate T&Cs; that Legal would never approve the indemnification clause, and they don't have enough insurance; that there are insufficient penalties for late milestones or substandard performance, and the schedule doesn't meet the desired timeline; and that guidelines around how change orders will be priced looked like a huge unbudgeted hole that would kill the project funding. Before you know it, each side had reverted to its old self, which was hands-off, aggressive, and antagonistic.

Are Sales and Procurement Best Friends Forever?

Consider a presentation by SAMA and ISM (Institute for Supply Management) made at a World Commerce and Contracting (formerly IACCM) conference a number of years ago. Both sides were preaching the importance of collaboration and strategic partnership. Then it was pointed out that SAMA had regular training programs on "How to Avoid Procurement in Your Sales Efforts" and ISM was promoting "How to Negotiate Better Prices with Sales Sharks." So much for collaboration and strategic partnering! There's a desire by both parties to somehow reach a new level of commercial relationship, but the old-school tactics keep rearing their ugly heads. Why is this happening? Is it possible to change, and are there instances where it has? The answer is yes, but like all other things in these Sales-Procurement relationships, exigent forces are at bay that stir the pot and have people reverting to their natural state.

During a World Commerce and Contracting (formerly IACCM) conference, I once presented on the subject of software procurement and the many pitfalls that can befall the buyer if they are not careful. To say the least, I showed my true colors for those who were blue sheeting me and (in my humble opinion) were trying to screw my company in software contracts. (There's a special place in my heart for software, both having to buy it for many years but also having worked at the end of my career for what I felt was a very ethical software company.) The response was intriguing, to say the least. One of the attendees at the presentation was a Sales EVP from a software services company from the Boston area that sold products that enabled companies to translate their documents into many languages for both legal and marketing use. The EVP began to question whether his own sales executives understood how poorly they were being perceived by the buying community, and he invited me to come to his company to address his sales team on the subject. I felt like this was a breakthrough of sorts, an example of Habit 5 of Stephen R. Covey's *The 7 Habits of Highly Effective People* ("Seek First to Understand, Then to Be Understood"*). I made that presentation to his team, and some 20 years later, I am still connected to two of the executives from that firm (though they have moved on in their careers as well).

But these pitfalls are no longer confined to enterprise software companies. With the Internet of Things (IoT), there is now software and service that can be sold with every piece of hardware, even dimmers. Sales VP David Odess confirmed for me that this has been a gamechanger for Sales, making their products more dynamic with update features that could be designed into it, and new streams of revenue for Sales to take advantage of. This also creates challenges to how the procurement function is organized to cover multicategory products that cross traditional lines of buying authority (see Chapter 5). But this also has implications for how salespeople need to sell and with whom they need to interact in Procurement. At one major account, David ended up selling a lighting control system solution to a global retailer who assigned the negotiations to the Procurement person responsible for the cabinets category. The company had classified it that way in their spend profile, because 52 percent of the lighting was built into the cabinets! This is real life, folks.

Regardless, I have also been in the position of defending my firm on multiple occasions from multimillion-dollar claims of unauthorized use of software licenses, and on three occasions, the firms I worked for ended up writing seven-figure checks to those software companies. How could they know this and make these claims without ever auditing our usage (though they had the right to conduct audits as part of the licensing terms)? The answer was simple — they had blue sheeted our company and trained their salespeople to talk with our people throughout the company who were not knowledgeable about the licensing terms or Procurement's and IT's role in managing the tracking and distribution of licenses. Like they say in the Navy, "Loose lips sink ships." From these seemingly innocuous, supporting queries that they made of people in the company, they learned of instances where licenses were being shared or distributed outside of the allowed licensing rules, and the software salespeople let them propagate and build to a point where they could send in the Business Software Alliance to conduct an audit. Their blue sheet endgame was simple — force your customer into eventually buying an enterprise license that was a much more costly "all you can eat" arrangement because tracking of license use in many multinational companies is quite complex (especially with turnover of employees). The recent growth of subscription cloud-based Software as a Service (SaaS) licensing has not eased that burden.

Both sides are at fault here, due to a lack of trust, and that lack of trust is earned ... too many people on both sides are "talking the talk" but not "walking the walk." The exigent forces at bay promote the behaviors, and maybe one should just accept the fact that, like in a court of law, there are only two strategies: conciliate or annihilate (told to me by one of my lawyer friends). The world of commerce is designed to be competitive, and while win-lose scenarios rarely result in value creation in buyer-supplier relationships (since most ongoing commercial relationships do not involve one-off leveraged buys but continuous buys over time), everyone wants to report back that they achieved a Win-win result, with each stressing the upper case "W" on their side. The WIIFM ("What's in it for me?") is real, as the results of every deal are influenced by personal goals for recognition, influence, decision-making authority, budget control, and enhancing one's potential for earning bonus compensation and promotions. If anybody tells you "It's not about the money," you can be sure of one thing: It's about the money! Everyone wants to get paid, me included.

Yet there are many people on both sides of the buyer-seller relationship that are highly ethical, collaborative by nature, enjoy the success and feelings of fulfillment from creating Win-win, and would never cross certain ethical boundaries of behavior to get there. In our opinion, they actually make up the majority of people we have dealt with over our careers. So if that's the case, what are these exigent forces that seem to muddy the waters and create the mess of the many buyer-supplier relationships?

The Problems that Arise Between Sales and Procurement

I think that looking at it from the Sales side, it's quite simple — it's always about the money and building a pipeline of recurring revenue for your company that can become a reliable annuity in the sales funnel. But Procurement doesn't spend enough time trying to figure out how salespeople get compensated, whether by commissions, or unit sales, or bookings, or some other incentives, and it can differ between different roles that each person on the Sales side plays, be it enterprise software, hard products, or technical field services support. Knowing this matters, and it impacts how the various people in the company approach and support their customers.

That being said, there are many salespeople, while facing the pressures of meeting ever higher quotas every quarter or year, who are also focused on longer-term customer success that comes from reliable performance and helping your customer become a successful competitor in their business. They love to help customers solve business problems using their products, and ethically will not push the sale of the products they have in their line sheet that will be detrimental to that cause. These sales professionals push back on the drive for revenue based on their own company's hockey-stick marketing projections, and they think in terms of the sales cycle and sales motion required to not only meet quotas, but also encourage the right behaviors of their salesforce. I never, ever knowingly and purposely wasted a salesperson's time just to fulfill a "3 bids and a buy" mandate. I felt it to be unethical, and I let them know up front what it would take to be successful or if their products or services were a good fit for purpose. Time is money, people's livelihoods are at stake, and I never took that lightly. They appreciated that level of honesty, and we would discuss what would need to change in the future to rebalance the odds of success.

I was not alone in my approach to Procurement, but I can also tell you that a number of Procurement people did not have the training, toolkit, or skill set to work in that manner. As one of my Procurement teammates once told me, "If the only tool in your toolbox is a hammer, every problem starts to look like a nail." And hammer away they did, because that's all they were taught to do, and they didn't have the drive or desire to take a different path, one of solving business problems, not procurement problems. But then again, their culture and reward system reinforced this behavior.

Who Is in Control?

Fortunately for me, I became enlightened early in my procurement career after suffering through four years of defense contracting that rewarded and allowed only the use of a sledgehammer, never mind a hammer (we won't get into the specs on that sledgehammer). Those who strayed from this philosophy were quickly demoted or dispatched in other ways. I walked away from that experience much wiser, but spiritually and physically numb, unbelieving of the fact that I was willing to do what I did for as long as I did and rationalize my behavior as having been acceptable. It was win-lose all the time, engaging in confrontation and purposeful breach of supplier contracts as accepted negotiation ploys. I learned that people will do whatever it takes to survive in their surroundings and adopt the behaviors that are rewarded. I also learned that while suppliers did get mad, they more importantly never forgot what was done to them, and there was always a time when they would get even. When they did, it was always at the worst time, and we deserved it. I promised myself that I would never let this happen again in my career, and I kept that promise.

But why does this happen, and why does it persist in these enlightened times? I thought about this for many years, and I have come to the simple conclusion that "Culture eats strategy for lunch" (the title of Chapter 8, and the attribute for this saying is not settled, but former Merck CEO Richard Clark used it often). For many years, as Procurement struggled for its seat at the table, tired of the end runs of the SAMA-educated salesforce, the culture became one of control — how do you control the spend of the company? How do you force the company into letting you make the decisions on which company to use and how much you should pay for their goods and services?

First, you need systems that tell you how much was being spent on what and with whom, by whom, in your company. Then you have to set up processes and mandates to use these processes to force competitive bidding on everything that you bought. Then you have to insist that only Procurement be authorized to negotiate and control the contracts with the supply base. Then to justify all of this investment in Procurement people, processes, and technology, you had to have measures that showed the benefits of the activity, i.e., "savings."

All of it seemed to work for a while, especially with direct spend — for example, spend on goods that were inputs to the manufacturing process that had specific SKUs associated with them, and they could be included in budgetary planning with tracking of *purchase price variances* (PPV) and price and volume variances to forecast. It could also be extended to capital projects — for example, *property, plant, and equipment* (PP&E), which had a defined capital budget and was tracked in Finance on a project-by-project basis. But what about indirect spend?

In most companies, Procurement couldn't or wouldn't touch indirect spend, which includes IT spend (hardware, software, outsourced services, and telecom), legal services, HR benefits, contingent labor, executive search and recruitment, management consulting, marketing creative agencies, real estate and facilities, or even travel, meetings and events spend (and choosing the corporate credit card for T&E). These buying responsibilities were the property of the functions that managed them, and to get Procurement involvement and/or control took a hands-on battle in the C-suites. This took a new set of people, processes, and technology to attack it, which brought about the birth of the multistage *sourcing management process* (SMP), a 5-, 6- or 7-stage process designed to analyze business requirements and the supply base, launch the formation of executive-sponsored cross-functional teams, and development of project charters for leading them to executing a sourcing strategy that would be reinforced through SRM. Often times, these indirect categories of spend amounted to as much as 70 percent of a company's total spend with third-party suppliers!

Procurement and Supply Chain became so much more advanced but not as respected a profession as we would like it to be. Nobody knows this better than the SAMs and GAMs. The days of bribery and payoffs are mostly a thing of the past, and many of the leaders and CPOs of today have both undergraduate and graduate degrees in relevant fields of study. Yet at every procurement conference I have attended, there is the same Rodney Dangerfield griping session of "I don't get no respect." Everyone in Procurement complains that they are not achieving what they want, which is to have a seat at the table of their internal stakeholders and budget holders and be considered a "trusted advisor to the business" functions that they support. I have been part of six multinational global procurement transformations that have trained everyone in the procurement function on category management and a multistage sourcing management process, along with the installation and use of new digitized processes and systems to help make the activity more efficient. Yet here we are, still complaining that "I don't get no respect." **Despite all of this progress, the respect will never come until the procurement culture changes from control and savings to strategic alignment and value generation that helps give their business a competitive advantage in the marketplace.** But how do you measure that, and how does one account for the human nature part that is simply ego — that people love being in the position of power and having others rely on them for decision-making?

Procurement CPOs have done a lot of work to give "savings" a lot more credibility with their stakeholders. First, they didn't count "cost avoidance," only actual purchase price reductions, and limited the benefits to 12 months to align with corporate budgeting. If it was a first-time buy for a new product or service, they applied alternate measures of savings based on comparisons to budget or market, or reductions in price proposals by suppliers through negotiations (sometimes against the average cost of the best three bids, sometimes against just the lowest bid). It is all well-meaning to do this, especially if Finance actually reduces the stakeholder budgets by some amount commensurate with the savings achieved. This way, the impact was real and allowed Finance to reallocate the money toward needed R&D, revenue generating, or capital investments to improve infrastructure or productivity.

And this is where I proclaim that *savings are the worst procurement metric, with the exception of all other procurement metrics*. It's a cultural misalignment to value added activity, and it promotes procurement behaviors that are contrary to becoming a "trusted advisor to the business."

It starts with Finance incorporating savings targets into the budgeting process. This is a good thing, because it joins the budget holders and Procurement at the hip, making the SMP activity a high priority and collaboration a must in order to meet the agreed budget. But it also sets up Procurement as the "bad cop" who has collaborated with Finance to cut their budget, leaving no room during the fiscal year to deal with unplanned events that may result in added expense for the budget holder. It also adds risk to the plan if the savings targets are not met for any reason, including forces outside of their control. But there is a more important issue at hand here — it's called the market.

It's an even worse situation in government agencies. Departments are given annual budgets —
and are expected to spend all of their budgets and are even encouraged to blow through them!
That means that as the end of the fiscal year approaches, the pressure is on to spend as much
as possible if there is still money in the budget, and even spend it on things that aren't urgent.
Why is that? Because if the budget is exceeded, that means it will be increased the following year.
That means there is absolutely no incentive for cost savings in government acquisition at all!
This could have something to do with why there exists a massive deficit in most governments
worldwide.

The Market, and Why "Savings" are a Bad Metric for Procurement!

If you have ever been a buyer or trader of stocks, bonds, energy, chemicals, real estate, interest
rates, or other commodities, you know that market forces can cause volatility in pricing. People
who are good at analyzing markets, including fundamentals of supply and demand for specialty
services, understand that when the momentum swings toward a buyer's or seller's market, you
need to act fast based on logic, facts, and data. Nobody is expected to pick market highs and
lows, but knowing trends and momentum in an up or down market is the key to shrewd management of price and cost risk to the business. Procurement savings metrics tied to budgets
accentuate all the wrong behaviors in volatile markets.

How Do Procurement Savings Metrics Cause Bad Decision-Making?

Here are a couple of real-world examples. The company goes through the budget setting cycle in the third
quarter of the year, and it finalizes the budget for the following fiscal year by early fourth quarter. Your
Procurement contracts are negotiated annually, usually pricing your goods and services through the end
of the year. You start your bidding and negotiation cycle, and there is a sudden and significant move in
the market to the upside. What do you do? You've committed to a certain baseline that you anticipated
would exist at the start of the year, but you are already higher in price. If you lock in for a year at that
price, you have already created a negative budget variance. So what do you do? You panic and do the worst
thing possible: Commit to the higher price for the first quarter with the hope that the market will reverse
itself and get you back to budget later on. But the market forces smell blood, and the price shoots even
higher, and you repeat the same mistake as before in the second quarter. You are what's known as "short
& wrong," and you're chasing an escalating market that is also exacerbated by supply chain shortages. The
cycle continues until you throw up your hands in despair and commit to the higher prices for the rest of
the year, locking in the negative savings and budget variance. Then of course, the market reverses and you
are sitting there with above-market purchase commitments (in the commodities business, that's known as
being "long & wrong").

The opposite scenario of course is you take the price at the beginning of the year and commit, then the
market softens and you are locked in at the "long and wrong" prices, so you lose your company's competitive advantage — but at least you've made budget and can declare your savings, despite the poor decision.
The lesson in all of this is as follows: The market doesn't care about your budget!

In effect, *the budgeting process and the fiscal plan is mandating a buying strategy as opposed
to market forces of supply and demand.* Your best decision for the business might be to lock

in for three months, or three years, but your savings metrics punish you for doing so. You go through hours of research and planning for the SMP and SRM processes to understand your commodity and supplier dynamics, but your buying decisions are totally devoid of the most important element — the market. If you see the potential for an escalating market and you lock in on a three-year deal, paying a little more in interest and carrying charges to do so and ensuring availability of supply, you get hounded for negative savings and budget variances (and take a hit to your bonus compared to other GCMs) when it could be a life-saving strategy for the business. During the energy shocks of 2005, 2008, and the supply chain shortages of 2022, we saw many buyers panic and do the wrong thing because it was contrary to their savings metrics.

What other exigent factors contribute to this? There are several, but mainly it's the culture of Procurement, a culture built around spend control and a "Savings R Us," "Negotiations R Us," and "Contracts R Us" mentality. This mentality still sees their supplier's salespeople as the enemy, and we rely too heavily on bidding and negotiation tactics to meet objectives. This leaves internal stakeholders viewing Procurement as a tactical, "beat them over the head" organization (because it acts as one), and SMP gets thrown out the window when pressed to deliver quick results (though not sustainable). When push comes to shove, it becomes a self-fulfilling prophecy as Procurement reverts to getting out the hammer (or sledgehammer) to do its thing, because it's in its nature to do so.

Not all procurement leadership or organizations act this way — I should know, as I have been part of six global procurement transformations in my career to convert those organizations. The goal was to move them from being tactical, "beat them over the head"/grab unsustainable short-term gains organizations to one that approaches categories of spend strategically, applying a bevy of tools to decide what to buy globally, internationally, regionally, or locally; and how to best set up the buying strategy based on whether they are in the tactical, leverage, critical, or strategic quadrant. These advanced methodologies train their people how to run cross-functional teams to define the business requirements, and to agree on a strategy for fulfilling those requirements and turn them into a recurring, sustainable, competitive advantage for the business.

There are many multinational companies that do this. But there is one recurring problem: It rarely lasts more than a few years before the cycle reverts to a decentralized approach, which happens about once a decade. New management comes along, sees how much the procurement function costs from a G&A standpoint, doesn't believe the savings metrics being reported, and starts pressuring the organization to skinny down. Stakeholders start complaining that too much power is being concentrated in procurement's control and want it devolved and reassigned to their own functions where they can set up shadow procurement organizations and direct the spend (and control it) in a way they deem fit for the function. The pendulum swings from a centralized to a decentralized approach. It will swing back again to centralization over time, but these business cycles are as reliable as the business cycles that move economies from expansion to recession to expansion again. Nothing in the world is static, and there is nothing more constant than change.

But why does this happen in procurement? Best practices are best practices, right? Yes, and no. Some best practices are timeless, but the march of technology under Moore's Law continues to change the way procurement can and should be done, and this threatens the status quo. Procurement functions, like all other functions, are in a constant battle for funds with the other functions facing the same pressures, and since Procurement uses savings as their metric to justify their performance and existence, over time, doubt creeps in. The organization claims to be saving 4 to 5 percent of total spend every year, yet every year the spend budget for the company is increasing by 3 percent instead of going down. Can that be solely attributable to growth in the company, or is there something amiss in the savings calculations?

In every survey of procurement executives taken annually on what their goals and priorities are for the organization, "savings" always comes out as either #1 or #2. There are so many other priorities to be considered, whether its risk mitigation, supply chain optimization and security, meeting ESG metrics and criteria, meeting *diversity, equity, and inclusion* (DEI) goals, helping drive revenue growth through the supply base, helping improve cycle times of new product launches to market, reducing budgetary impact, finding areas where spend can be eliminated, substituted, or volumes reduced, etc. A list of all of the different objectives that Procurement should shoot for is shown in the figure below. Note that these objectives should be tied to the business strategy of the organization, which may have nothing to do with purchase price savings! But in the end, it's almost always just about savings, and savings calculations are often a game, but a necessary one to justify the procurement budget.

Category Value Objectives that Link to Internal Partners			
Reduce total cost		**Increase revenue**	**Support partner goals**
• Reduce purchase cost	• Remove effort for noncore activities	• Add new features or services for market	• Drive product and service flexibility
• Lower risk of supply disruption	• Reduce working capital	• Reduce time-to-market on NPD	• Variabilize asset structure
• Improve process flow and internal costs	• Provide process and design cost ideas	• Support marketing in developing markets	• Support sustainable supply chains
• Reduce fixed costs	• Reduce cycle time	• Create "game-changing" business capabilities	• Strengthen the brand
• Improve visibility to market trends	• Local source of human intelligence		• Drive second tier supplier integration
• Subject matter expertise	• Support network integration	• Support marketing negotiations	
		• Drive budgeting and pricing strategic plans	

Savings Targets Drive Human Behavior

Human behavior for procurement GCMs and others in the function are greatly influenced by savings criteria. There is a constant battle to have ownership of the categories that generate the most savings potential, because in the end, when people are "totem poled" for performance at the end of the year to decide who gets the most bonus money and salary increases from the pool that has been allocated to Procurement, savings matter. It is always the #1 factor in the weighted scorecard for procurement professionals. In many ways, it's no different than sales quotas on the selling side. Often times, meeting or exceeding savings goals barely gets you anything — the top rewards go to those who exceed their savings goals by 25 percent or more. In fact, in many organizations, that becomes the baseline! This is part of the reality of how Procurement people get recognized and rewarded, and it drives their behaviors accordingly. Sandbagging savings projections so that you can under-promise and over-deliver becomes a culturally accepted staple for survival in this jungle. Why would any procurement GCM agree to a three-year fixed price contract in an escalating market, which is probably the best strategy, if it screws them in years 2 and 3's savings potential? Unless they are moving on to another category (another category whale, just like in Sales), they have to live with the longer-term ramifications of their decisions.

Though some CPOs come up through the procurement organization throughout their career, many do not. According to the Institute for Supply Management (ISM) Center for Advanced Purchasing Studies (CAPS) statistics, the typical CPO tenure is 3.4 years; that is because they move on to another role after exhausting their typical playbook — which is to do a spend analysis and put every contract up for bid. These individuals take credit for short-term cost savings — and then move on, leaving those left behind to deal with poor service, poor quality, terrible delivery, and massive disruptions and shortages that impact revenue and customer satisfaction. The reality is that in many companies, Procurement is viewed as a commercial training ground for up-and-coming executives that helps round out their experience. But in order for them to move up, they have to make a short-term impact. At companies that do this, and there are many, it becomes a cycle of wash, rinse, repeat.

Like all functions, new blood and leadership are the key to affecting a transition from "old" to "new." You know that a procurement transformation is serious if the new CPO is brought in from the outside, if it has C-Suite sponsorship, and if it is granted extra budget that is not normally available when internal candidates rotate into the position. These are all clues as to whether it will be "flavor of the month" or a real change, with expected results that are realistic and tied to the board's guidance to Wall Street.

So in the end, both internal stakeholders and suppliers are collaborating to go around Procurement, cut their own deal, and then are often subjected to a resentful, reactive function looking to make its mark through extracting its pound of flesh. The most shocking part of procurement transformations was not the reaction of the supply base, whom we often challenged for 20 percent price decreases over three years, but the reaction of internal stakeholders who said, "You can't treat my supplier that way." From these transformations, I developed "the one-third/one-third/one-third rule" in two instances (both highly accurate and predictable during these transformations), described below:

The one-third/one-third/one-third rule

First, internally within your own procurement function, you can expect that one-third of the buyers in the function will be fully on board with a transformation and will see it as a way to up their game and grow professionally; one-third will be wary of the changes to their job and their new responsibilities but will be willing to go along with it and give it a try; and one-third will simply say, "I never signed up for this."

Second, the top 100 firms in the supply base will react predictably when challenged with coming up with 20 percent reductions over three years (especially if the challenge is also accompanied by a promise that you will listen to their ideas on how to add efficiency to the process and they will have access to other lines of business in exchange) — one-third will say they intended to fully cooperate and write white papers on how to best improve their commercial relationship to cut cost and expense and expand opportunity; one-third will say they can't do 20 percent, but maybe could do 10 to 15 percent and want to fully cooperate; and one-third will tell you to shove it where the sun don't shine. It really depends on whether they are in the leverage or critical quadrant, and whether they want to migrate to a strategic quadrant with your firm.

Sales executives, SAMs, and GAMs need to know this, and need to know what type of procurement organization they are dealing with before blue sheeting their customer. Are they dealing with a tactical, short-term defensive organization brought in for last minute negotiations and price cutting, or one in the midst of a procurement transformation learning how to approach categories of spend strategically, or one on the tail end being decentralized into the functions? This is so important to know and to design the selling approach into the company accordingly.

Design the Selling Approach

To emphasize how important this is, a colleague of mine (Michael Fitzgerald, of blessed memory) and I designed a training program for the field quota salespeople in my company on how to deal with difficult customers where Procurement was getting involved in their deals. We taught them how to analyze the procurement function they were dealing with and which selling strategies were most effective under the circumstances. Ironically, this came back to haunt us when a year later, due to the influence of an activist investor, we ended up spinning off that part of the business and then having to negotiate for the purchase of those licensed services from the people we had just trained to negotiate! Talk about having to eat your own dog food! Regardless, it was so successful that another colleague of mine, Max Ribbler, then designed a training course for our inside Sales team to help them work with customer procurement functions to renew existing agreements. Savings as a metric…ridiculous.

Much earlier on in my career, after helping design and run a global procurement transformation, I was reading an article written by a Sales professor at Columbia Business School, Professor Noel Capon, that GAMs were more and more running into GCMs at multinational firms, and this was challenging their selling strategies and approaches to these companies. I contacted Professor Capon and gave him my thoughts about the article. We then decided to write a case study about such a situation to be taught to his Sales students. This case study is still taught annually by us to his class there, and it gives me an opportunity to air these thoughts about the buyer-supplier relationship and how it's evolving and constantly changing over time. The cycles continue, so the ending is constantly in flux based on where we are in the cycles. Like I said, there is nothing more constant than change.

Is it Possible to Resurrect an Improved Relationship Between Sales and Procurement?

The relationship between Sales and Procurement has always been a contentious one. The issue at the core of this tension is the concept of value recognition. Sales account managers accuse Procurement of being purely price focused and not recognizing the components of value. Procurement executives, however, complain that Sales account managers are always trying to "work around them" and to make the commercial sale to engineering, operations, clinicians, or other business stakeholders. "Salespeople are always trying to raise prices and *design themselves in* to our organization, without being competitively tendered." But salespeople complain that Procurement "does not recognize the value we bring to the business, in terms of quality, service, and reducing the total cost of ownership!"

But there is hope on the horizon. According to my friend, David Odess (former VP Sales), good salespeople are always thinking, "What is the goal of the person across the table? 1) Can I get there?; 2) Do I want to get there?; 3) Is it worth getting there?" Is there any repeat business opportunity to pursue, and do I even want it? Who am I competing with, and what are their strengths and weaknesses, and what will it cost me to beat them? Who am I negotiating with, and are they the real decision-makers (and what is really important to them)? They also think constantly about where they can add value in exchange for the 10% ask that they know is coming, be it through logistics, documentation or new technology. Most importantly, though, they need to be willing to say no if these criteria cannot be satisfied. No is an acceptable answer (which may or may not be at odds with how others teach "Sales").

In my opinion, good Procurement people need to anticipate all of this plus fully understand how the Sales people you are dealing with are compensated and who has the power to grant extra concessions as you climb up the sales ladder to higher levels of authority. And like a game of chess, if you are not thinking about your move three turns ahead on the board, you will suck at it.

So who is right? We recognize from the outset that these conditions will vary by firm, by industry, and indeed by individual characteristics. This situation does not always occur — as there are cases where harmonious partnerships exist between Sales and Procurement. But this is the exception, not the rule. In an effort to better understand this issue, the NC State Supply Chain Resource Cooperative held a one-day executive summit to discuss these issues in an open forum. We invited eight procurement executives from oil and gas, electronics, business services, industrial manufacturing, chemicals, and healthcare industries, and brought them in to meet with five sales executives from a large third-party logistics provider. In this forum, we covered several major questions, and held open debates on these issues. In addition, both groups shared their internal tools and mindsets around customer/supplier segmentation, key issues that define strategic relationships, the effective use of performance measurement, and the types of disagreements that occur around contract negotiations. The outcomes provide a compelling picture of the great misunderstandings and myths that often exist in both sales executives and procurement executives as they approach one another. We will be working on information to document these findings, and on offering solutions for helping improve the nature of the Sales-Procurement relationship over time.

Conclusion

Reaching an understanding of how Procurement and Sales really operate in the real world — their processes, motivations, reward systems — is a topic that is too often ignored when each side is putting its strategies in place for buying and selling goods and services. People matter, and the impacts of decisions made on how you go about your work will shape the outcome. Understanding the WIIFM — "What's in it for me?" — can never be overlooked if you want to be successful over the long term. But watch out — short-term results may be the reality of how people are rewarded in their system, and if that's the case, trying to apply long-term strategic *pie in the sky* approaches will probably come up short. Assess the environment first, and remember to "Seek First to Understand, Then to Be Understood."

Chapter 3:
What Procurement Needs to Know about Sales

As we stated in Chapter 2, at a World Commerce and Contracting (formerly IACCM) meeting, I (Robert) observed an ISM (Institute for Supply Management) representative and a representative from SAMA (Strategic Account Management Association) discussing how collaborative they were. And yet — I stood up and pointed out that they were really bluffing. Because, I noted, that SAMA had an announcement on their website for a learning event titled "Procurement are the Guys You Want to Go Around." While on the ISM website, they had a learning event titled "How to Fight Your Supplier on Price Increases." These two business functions were not collaborating but seemed to be saying one thing and doing exactly the opposite.

Supplier Cost Metrics

In most Western organizations, the primary goal of Procurement is to achieve cost savings. Typical cost savings performance measures in Western enterprises are built into request for quotations (RFQs), with a typical goal of 3%–3%–3% savings year-over-year for direct material spend. By default, these types of contracts are built into the supplier's price, one way or the other. More recently, Detroit's Big Three have moved to 5–5–5 or 5–5–3, which produces the same result in the end. It becomes tougher to achieve the savings after three years, based on standard costs. This approach is built on the objective of closing the gap between the cost standard and the supplier's quotation.

However, if costs are identified correctly at the beginning and aggressive but realizable target costs are established up front, they are typically 8 to 15% less based on Honda's experience. There is no expected cost improvement built in, unless the realities of the product or process or market are explicitly identified. In fact, Honda has been known to notify suppliers of price increases over an initial contracted cost if the supplier can prove that the market has changed, which could jeopardize their agreed-on margins. They have a vested interest in ensuring the supplier makes a profit — so they can continue to be productive, on-time, quality-focused, and a reliable component of their extended supply chain.

Larry Bossidy, CEO at Allied Signal, established long-term agreements with suppliers that required 6 percent cost reduction year-over-year, but insisted that this was a collaborative effort — the suppliers needed to provide ideas on how to achieve this. When GSK and Merck CPO Willie Deese put out challenges to reduce cost by 20 percent over three years, they always invited suppliers to provide a "white paper" on how to get this done. How do we cost you money? And what practices are in our *statements of work* (SOWs) and *standard operating procedures* (SOPs) that create rework and confusion? Internal stakeholders objected to this line of thinking at first. Their point was, "Are you are telling me I'm doing a bad job with my suppliers?" In effect, internal stakeholders had designed processes that made their job essential to the SOP, with built-in checks and balances that were probably more than necessary (some would call it overkill). The suppliers then built a "pharmaceutical premium" into their pricing to cover these extra costs, as well as take advantage of the fact that pharmaceutical firms were selling high-margin products and the Procurement people they were dealing with were under less pressure from budget holders to drive for lower prices. By forcing conversations with suppliers through white papers, their suggestions for reducing waste helped identify these redundancies and unnecessary check steps in the SOPs, which reduced their costs to service the account (and subsequently allowed them to reduce the price being charged).

> If you think about it logically, a **great procurement person**, working closely with their business stakeholders, should *value engineer* an SOW and SOP before it gets issued. If you properly condition the supply base ahead of any *request for proposal/quotation* (RFP/RFQ) being issued, the responses should come in at the lowest possible bid that makes sense for the suppliers. The goal should be receipt of highly competitive proposals that require little to no price negotiation. In addition to value engineering, they do this through target costing, supplier development, and supply chain management — the discipline of acquiring and moving material. For understanding how to do this well, reference the book *The Purchasing Machine* by R. David Nelson, Patricia E. Moody, and Jon Stegner.
>
> Unfortunately, most of the performance metrics (specifically "savings") get squashed by this approach, and it works against the procurement person leading the category because there is only small, incremental negotiated gains that can be achieved, despite the tremendous value generated.
>
> In fact, there is actually an incentive to do a poor job up front in the RFP/RFQ process because it increases the potential negotiated "savings" that come after the responses are received. No good deed goes unpunished.

Stupid Money. The following case example illustrates the importance of what has become known as post-award contract management. A few years ago, I (Robert) had the opportunity to host a good colleague of mine in my supply chain relationships class. We worked together years earlier to help define a baseline framework for strategic sourcing and category management that was deployed within a large oil and gas company's lubricants group, and which later became deployed across the entire procurement organization. Much of our work together focused on the importance of market intelligence, cost models, using the appropriate price index, negotiating the right contract archetypes, and establishing the right internal stakeholder needs. This work was instrumental in shaping my thinking about how to structure category management at a global level. In my class, my colleague spoke further about how procurement is markedly different in an era of $40 oil.

This conversation was further clarified in my mind when I spoke with a journalist from the Mexican journal *Manufactura* about the importance of procurement in Mexico. As the industry is becoming privatized with more private companies coming in to explore, the need for procurement will continue to escalate. This is due to the fact that local suppliers, particularly in contracting services, will need to be developed to identify the right skills and talent that can enable safe, efficient, and profitable operations when revenue is dropping.

As my colleague emphasized, CFOs and COOs are much more interested in what procurement can offer them in an era of $40 oil versus when oil was $100 a barrel. All of a sudden, it is critical to find cost savings and identify opportunities to drive out costs. But this requires that oil companies don't pursue the traditional approach of demanding price cuts from suppliers. Rather, it requires true collaboration with trusted supplier partners. The day after my class, he was scheduled to fly out to one of their major rigs in the Gulf of Mexico.

He noted the following: "They walked into a room of about 30 people, representing 5 suppliers as well as Shell people. For these meetings we would bring in benchmark data, comparing the different operating cost categories for Shell, and another chart that shows the cost models for all other rigs operating in the Gulf of Mexico. This allowed us to compare this rig's cost versus others, and the cost of our fleet operating relative to other fleets on 10 different performance metrics." He also noted: "What is interesting is that people in the room hardly look at the data. We have a rule, that we only want operators in the room, no salespeople! Many of these guys are from the Bayou, have been working on rigs for 10 or 20 years, and they know the rig inside and out. They also know how their company makes money, and they know the things that they are getting paid to do that isn't a core part of how they make money. So I ask a very simple question: 'We all know we have to save money given the environment. So I need your help. What is it that bugs you about the way we operate today? What is the *stupid money* we are throwing away today in the way we operate that doesn't make sense?' Now consider that it costs about $1.2 million per day to operate a rig, which includes the lease, the people, the surrounding infrastructure, etc. And the people involved in operating that rig are drillers, pipefitters, seismic people, mudders, and others. In every case, people will open up and tell me: 'Look — here is something that you are asking us to do that is probably costing you $100K a day!' We will then look at the chart — and sure enough, we will see the differential in the cost category that they are talking about. Now in a period of $100 oil, no one is going to look at $100K per day — because it is all about 'first oil' – getting the oil out as quickly as possible. Don't talk to me about skimping to save a few dollars. But suddenly, $100K a day is a big deal. Safety is number one, so we also have to consider if that savings improves or doesn't compromise safety."

My friend also emphasized to students that to be able to engage and talk to people and be successful in procurement and supply chain, you need to also think about your "brand image." He said, "You need to develop a brand image, which will help you throughout your entire life. You want to develop a brand around your strengths, and what you do well. If you are good at analytics, that is okay; but you can't just be in the room and not be able to also talk about what you did, and the meaning of the data that you analyzed. Other possible strengths might be your ability to network within the organization, your ability to influence people towards a solution, your ability to lead a team, or even just being known as someone who is on time and will do what they promise!" For me in my role, I need to get clarity from the business on what they want — or I will not be able to cut a good contract. For upstream, it is all about getting the well out of the ground in an efficient and safe manner. So I know that my personal brand is about being clear and always following up on my commitments to individuals.

> In developing a "brand image" for your work, as much as you want to be responsive to your stakeholders, you must never become someone who when told to "Jump," answers "How high?" This is not customer service, it's just being a servant. You need to be willing to ask the 5 WHYs and find ways to add value to the solution for whatever business problem is being addressed from an end-to-end perspective.
>
> Adding value = customer service; jumping high = being a servant.

The Sales Perspective

Sales is under pressure to meet its growth targets and establish robust sales pipelines of opportunity, balancing three types of revenue generation: continuous annuity, periodic, and episodic. *Continuous annuity* can best be described as a highly reliable renewal of services, licenses, or maintenance on fixed infrastructure or software that is embedded in the customer's operations, or increases of volumes that will naturally be required with the customer's growth. *Periodic* sales are those that come up with expansion of the account into the same or other business units and may involve other product lines. The relationship will also determine whether they are associated with formal RFP/RFQ processes. Both continuous annuities and periodic revenue can be helped along if Sales is successful in getting the customer to write their products or solutions into the specifications or SOW. *Episodic* revenue is usually large, funded capital projects for new goods or services for which Sales will have to compete, and the probability of success in winning the job can vary greatly, as may the timing of when it hits in the sales funnel. A sales pipeline tracks all of the different sales opportunities that exist — ones that are already in full stride, those that are on the verge of signing, those that are in development, and those that are in the early stages of business relationship development. This is an essential part of the sales activity. Wouldn't it be great if procurement also had a pipeline that viewed suppliers they were currently contracting with, those that had high potential and were in discussions, and those that would be worth contacting and exploring capabilities with in the future? This parallel has always struck me as something that is really missing from the procurement toolbox.

Sales is always aware of hitting their "target," which will generally become part of their bonus or commission. It is thus important to understand the balance of value generated with a sales encounter: how much goes to the firm, and how much to the person? Generally speaking, Sales relies on Marketing to get the right leads — but knowledge of the markets sits with the global/regional account managers while the sales account managers possess the intellectual capital of what is really happening with their customers.

The essence of the value-driven sales approach is not just about selling to customers but sustaining the relationship. There is often a shifting set of values that underlie the decision-making process on the Procurement side and often diverse perspectives on the buying criteria. It is important to simplify the business delivery process, to qualify and formally quantify the customer criteria, and ensure internal alignment of the sales organization's internal capabilities to deliver to the customer. There are three major reviews that occur in this process to qualify the customer, which includes criteria such as geographic scale, ability to integrate with customer systems, and understanding of business processes. Each assessment point is more granular in nature over time. The sales team's ability to design the solution is highly dependent on reasonably accurate data, so a data quality assessment is needed to get a full view of what we are stepping into.

If a current business relationship suddenly is put out for bid through an RFP, it is important to develop insights into what is driving this. This includes understanding the true reason a potential switch in suppliers is occurring and the rationale behind the RFP. It is worthwhile dedicating significant resources and assigning them to explore the required investment in the customer, including real estate, IT, and labor. When there is a positive response from the customer in the negotiation and contracting phase, there are requirements to understand that both parties are aligned, as well as details on how the materials will flow, how information will flow, and how the order-to-cash process will occur. There is a contracting phase to ensure contract terms versus business risk. This then moves into implementation, involving a smooth transition and handoff from the contracting party (often Procurement) to the business-unit stakeholder. The last part involves the post-award contract management phase: whereby the ongoing relationship is managed and improved over time and includes an assessment of how the business can be improved over time.

When applied rigorously, the value-added sales process can have a major impact on the success rate of Sales "wins." An account executive using this approach notes that:

> "Initially over half our targets were not coming through, not because of budgeting issues, but because of flawed implementation. Since rolling out this process two years ago, 'win rates' have improved by 27 percent. The customer interacts with this process throughout the process, and we are able to get a much more in-depth understanding of the sources of customer value. We have a much better understanding of the system requirements, the complexity, the risk and the 'win-ability' of the account, as well as the kind of relationship we have today, what the relationship should look like, and the portfolio of services we can bring into the relationship."[1]

Opportunity Cost of Lost Sales Pursuits

Procurement often believes that Sales goes after every opportunity and every RFP — but this is not the case. Sales may not pursue an opportunity if there is not a good business case. This was news to many purchasing executives.

The reason for this is simple: Preparing responses to a potential customer opportunity is a matter of return on investment. Typical pursuits for sales companies can take 6 to 12 months, and there

---

1 Handfield interview with senior business development executive, February 2017.

is an opportunity cost associated with not winning these bid events. Many sales organizations have a "hit rate" of less than 50 percent.

One sales executive noted that:

> *We spent 6 months working on an RFQ, with 10 people working on it for 10 months. The opportunity cost was over $500K of paid employee time. But the entire time, we weren't aware of the procurement strategy, and missed the value proposition entirely!*

This situation is not atypical in sales organizations. This occurs often because Procurement is focused on driving cost savings, and the easiest way to achieve this is to put supplier contracts out to bid. After three years or so, when the CPO has run out of cost savings opportunities and is ready to move on to their next opportunity after having achieved their "5 percent annual cost-reduction target," some very good suppliers get hurt along the way, and business value may be lost.

Another sales executive told us that they have an 80/20 rule that says that 80 percent of their sales revenue comes from 20 percent of their customers (which pretty much mimics the spend profile of major companies where 80 to 90 percent of their spend is with 10 to 20 percent of their supply base)! Also, when dealing with general contractors in construction contracts who are in charge of subbing out work and writing specifications for their customers, they are only successful in 30 percent of their efforts to have specs rewritten to include their products. Knowing when to pursue these opportunities and how much resource to assign to them is the critical decision they have to make. For this reason, there needs to be a much more focused business strategy for sales organizations — one that explicitly considers the challenges and strategies underway in the procurement organization.

Because salespeople are often picky, and only pursue RFPs that they have a legitimate chance of winning, many companies will turn away at least 40 percent of all RFPs they receive. This insight was very surprising to procurement executives with whom we met ... few could believe that Sales would actually not try to pursue every opportunity that came their way! There are four primary reasons why customer pursuits are halted in their tracks:

1. *Limited access to the decision-maker.* If Sales does not have an opportunity to present to the decision-maker, then they won't proceed. If Sales has the opportunity to make a presentation to the decision-maker (whether it is at the corporate or local level), they are almost always going to succeed. An important issue here, however, is the need to understand WHO the decision-maker is. The internal Procurement–stakeholder relationship is therefore critical to understand by Sales at this stage and will thus strongly influence the outcome of the opportunity. Sales notes that if there are three coaches (influencers on the decision-maker) that you can speak to, then you have a good chance of success fully influencing the process.

2. *Lack of existing relationship.* This is often known as a "cold" RFQ. If there is no pre-existing relationship with a customer, and no prior engagement, the odds of success are also very low. This means that an entire education process has to occur. Also, it is important to

recognize the cost of change that the customer will need to go through, and evaluating whether the benefits provided by a potential change in sourcing strategy will outweigh the costs of doing so. Procurement may not even understand the value proposition, and they are using the supplier as a "check in the box" to get a third quote to their RFP in the hopes of putting more cost pressure on the incumbent supplier!

3. *If the potential customer has never outsourced before, they are unlikely to understand the value proposition of a third-party logistics provider.* If the decision-maker does not recognize the value statement, and doesn't understand the value provided, there is a low chance of success.

4. *Competitor environment, strong incumbent.* If a business development leads goes into a situation where there are multiple other suppliers in the running, then you are clearly viewed as a "commodity" supplier by the customer, and there is a low likelihood of success.

Procurement knows that the internal customer generally doesn't want to change suppliers unless there is a compelling reason to do so, such as poor quality and service, usually seen as a lack of attention given to the account by the supplier or the assignment of subpar resources. Other reasons might be the missing of service level agreements (SLAs) such as uptime guarantees that impact operations or revenue generation opportunities. Absent of these pressures, new suppliers cannot match the current offer — they have to overcome a "hurdle" of a certain percentage, often 5 percent lower in price or more, in order to be even considered for a switch, and more than likely, Procurement will just take that and use it as leverage to reduce price with the incumbent and capture savings that can be claimed against their objectives. Suppliers are not stupid — they know this and it impacts their decision on whether to play the RFP game.

In all four of these cases, however, there is an education process that must occur, and an opportunity for Sales to help Procurement understand the nature of the business decision they have to make. The Sales team needs to offer a process and business model that presents an opportunity that will cover the cost of change. Is there enough value on the cost of change on their side? If not, then the sales opportunity is simply not present. On the other hand, Procurement is selling ideas as well — up the chain. And selling procurement on the tool kit to help them sell the sales organization, and coaching them through the benefits and business case, will be important here.

A sales executive notes that:

"The sales value-added process is critical to bring the team along and sell internally. On a 'cold' RFP, it is possible if you have someone who wants you to win. If you don't get the right information from coaches or the customer relationship, then you won't have a good outcome and hope is not a strategy. That's why we still lose 65 percent of our responses to bids."[2]

---

2 Comment by executive at Supply Chain Resource Cooperative workshop, January 2017. *https://scm.ncsu.edu/scm-articles/article/getting-sales-and-procurement-onto-the-same-team.*

Who is the Customer?

One of the challenges upfront involves who the actual customer is that you are selling to. This is an issue that confronts both the sales organization, but is also one that Procurement must contend with: Who is calling the shots?

There are at least three tiers of stakeholders determining the outcome of a new business proposal going out to suppliers: the corporate head office, the budget holder, and the local business. Each level has a different set of interests, and these are not always aligned. The corporate procurement function is typically focused on value as a function of cost savings across the global footprint of the company, and it is interested in deriving a global category strategy that can cross multiple business units. This may result in suboptimal pricing for a specific functional budget holder or at a given location, but the benefits at a global level outweigh functional or the local benefits. The functional and/or local operations stakeholder may be interested more in performance, often focused on delivery, service, and quality performance. As such, Sales must contend with different sets of issues, and it becomes important for both Procurement and Sales to be transparent about the criteria being considered for both parties. In some cases, Sales may "ride the local interest" and win, but risks alienating Procurement and the global category lead, or GCM. There is a need to explicitly consider this disparity.

An important element to consider here is how Sales goes about understanding the decision-maker in the Procurement relationship. A senior procurement executive from the electronics industry notes that:

> *In some cases, Procurement does a purposeful job of clouding who the decision-maker is and how that decision is made. Procurement may emphasize that Sales is forbidden from contacting anyone else in the organization during the bid process. It is not uncommon for the RFP language to include this stipulation, with a specific list of contact people. This language exists not to prevent Sales from speaking to decision-makers, but to ensure that Procurement provides a fair and balanced view of the proposal to all bidders and everyone in the organization. World-class procurement seeks to create transparency of a sales value proposition, and wants to promote the supplier's position to everyone in a balanced manner.*

Another executive, a healthcare procurement professional, also emphasized the importance of internal stakeholder engagement.

> *Sales may not be able to create the right relationship with the decision-maker to the deal. No procurement team worth its salt believes that a supplier needs to lose money to get their business. In fact, Procurement is more of a facilitator, and can actually help you to sell your offering inside the business to multiple stakeholders. And I can do it faster than you can without my help. In healthcare, physicians often have decision rights on the clinical decision, so Sales used to go to them directly and forced Procurement to buy it. Today we are implementing clinical category teams led by physicians that will sell across multiple hospitals, so you aren't selling it to one physician at a time. Now we can pull it through, rather than going behind our backs and upsetting a lot of people.*

Understanding the decision-maker in the process is clearly an area that requires an in-depth assessment, as this can heavily influence the nature of whether to pursue the customer. In the past, Sales would rely on internal relationships with the CEO or COO, who was the presumed decision-maker. As procurement organizations have matured and come into their own, Sales' reliance on C-suite relationships can occur at their own risk. In one healthcare provider, a supplier went to the CEO when turned down by Procurement due to performance issues and was promptly told that they needed to go back to Procurement, who held the decision rights! Many sales deals in logistics services are more than $50 million, and these decisions are made carefully and with a great deal of due diligence. There is often a "tactical" element to the procurement process, especially with the advent of RFQ tools such as those in Ariba. These processes often result in impersonal interactions, and value-based relationships may be damaged in the process.

But how about when you are the incumbent? Sales cannot get lazy and take their status for granted. Example: I (Howard) was new at a software company, and the janitorial contract was going to expire in a week. The Facilities team came to me and asked me to sign the new contract. It had a 2 percent increase, as minimum wage was going up 2 percent, and I said "No, I won't sign it!" I told them I didn't know what is in the *scope of work* and how it was developed! So I assigned a lower-level Procurement associate to work with it and she went through the scope of work and found all these hours being double counted by doing cleaning on certain restrooms and common areas — and we ended up with a 23 percent decrease! We went out on bid, and someone gave it to us for 30 percent less, but Facilities begged us not to change suppliers, as they didn't have the manpower to execute a supplier change.

I've been facing these battles my entire career, and all it took was for me to say no. It would have been so easy to say yes — a reasonable thing to do. This is the kind of challenge we always face in procurement, not only with salespeople for our suppliers but within our own functional relationships. You have to know you are getting a fair price and you have to question basic assumptions. In the end, I know that no one will sign a contract if they are not making money on it, or at a bare minimum covering all variable costs with some degree of overhead and profit thrown in (unless they plan to buy their way in and make it up on change orders).

Procurement people need to ask the salespeople, "What is real value here — did you invest in new technology solutions and optimize your processes to eliminate waste, create productivity, and give customers like me the price they deserve?" If the answer is no, then go find a company that is doing so. The notion that you can choose only two out of three — fast, cheap, high quality — is completely old-school thinking. Those companies willing to invest in technology and eliminate waste from its processes can do it all, and at lower cost and higher margins for themselves. They can respond to and meet your *key performance indicators* (KPIs) and *service level agreements* (SLAs) and manage and measure performance that provides feedback and continuous improvement. But Procurement must take a *total cost of ownership* (TCO) mindset that looks at the complete lifecycle of the product and services being bought, cradle to grave, and not just a purchase price.

So what should Sales do about this? What should they learn and do differently?

- *Quarterly business reviews.* Insist on having them with existing customers and not waiting for the renewal — and starting to discuss it in Year 1. Get Procurement to understand the value being created, and question why would they want to go out and bid this — and what is the value of that to them?

  - If Procurement is just savings oriented and not pursuing the real value, which is working capital and creating competitive advantage, think about how you can help them incentivize people to do the right things, and be paid and promoted for doing so. Address their WIIFM, this part of human nature.

- *Propose Incentives.* Toyota has an arrangement where they provide cost targets to their suppliers — if you beat >5 percent, you get to keep it and then it goes to next years' target.

- *Be like Shell and ask "Where is the stupid money?"*

- *Strategic Account Management.* Show them that you have identified them as a high-value relationship, and you will assign resources for customer success and continuous improvement programs.

- *Talk with them about cost structure and what their finance organization needs to see to meet their goals.* The nature of revenue generation is changing in a cloud-based Big Data subscription service world as the selling model shifts from buy to lease, and from on-premise licenses to in-the-cloud, on-demand subscription services. This is a huge financial structure change, as projects that were once fully capitalized and amortized over the life of the asset are now having to be expensed and immediately hitting the P&L. Look for ways to work with them to identify how best to address this so that their P&L stays intact.

By focusing on these tactics and discussions, you will learn a lot more about the supplier — and discover opportunities that you never knew existed. But it requires more than an RFP and a cloud of dust. I believe that the real savings that exist in the future lies with improving buyer–supplier relationships. Let's explore that now in more depth.

While we have covered what Procurement needs to understand about Sales in this chapter, the reverse also applies. In the next chapter, we discuss how Sales can better understand what procurement executives are all about.

Chapter 4:
What Sales Needs
to Know about Procurement

Tim Cummins, CEO of World Commerce and Contracting (WC&C, formerly IACCM), is intent on driving change. He is traveling around the globe, speaking with foreign ministries in Dubai, the Australian navy, the Canadian Department of Defense, and the General Services Administration in DC. I was fortunate enough to host this expert on collaborative contracting in the midst of his global itinerary, so he could speak to our group of supply chain executives at the Supply Chain Resource Cooperative. The following is an abridged version of Tim's speech to the group.

"Today I am asking you to make sure that you shift your mindset. First, stop thinking procurement — and start thinking about trading relationships! Second, stop thinking that relationships are personal — they are not. They are about virtual interdependencies. The programs and projects you are undertaking involve an array of stakeholders who you will never meet and who will never meet each other. This is critical in the context of what we mean by relational contracting. Third, stop thinking of your organization as an enterprise working independently. An enterprise, including a virtual enterprise, is formed from an amalgam of parties working to achieve a common outcome. Let me ask you a question: Are you hiring an integrated enterprise when you hire a supplier? Yes! In effect, you are hiring an entire ecosystem, not just a supplier. And fourth, stop thinking about contracts, and think about contracting. We need to think about contracts as they relate to categories of goods and services, and within those categories, there are a variety of relationship types that emerge, ranging from a purchase order to a joint venture. If you don't understand how you define the category, you won't have good results."

At a recent IACCM meeting, we had a protracted debate: Is procurement a subelement of contracting? The decision was YES, after much discussion. When you are engaged in contracting, the primary task involves how you define requirements and who is assigned to oversee performance. How is that done? The opportunity is for a responsible person to take on the task of ensuring the quality and integrity of contracting. *Service level agreements* (SLAs) and *statements of work* (SOWs) require time and effort to develop, and sometimes the business doesn't welcome having Procurement "waste" time on these activities (this is too much work — just get the contract done!). And we have seen that trend increasing; more and more procurement functions are stepping away from spending the required time necessary to develop good SOWs — because the volume of contracting is increasing. Between 1994 and 2015, the volume of contracted services as a percentage of revenue, as well as the value of business transactions, went up by 300 percent. Outsourcing went from 19 percent of spend to 56 percent of spend. Today it is over 60 percent of spend.

What is the key risk in outsourcing contracts? The number one risk is the quality of communication; all other risks are subcomponents of poor communication. As we get into relational contracting, how many people out there could confidently say this appears in their risk register? We don't consider it, but it is in fact a huge risk! It should be one of those uncertainties that matter. Because we don't have defined protocols for effective communication during contract management, we are likely to have negative financial impacts.

Too often we view the major issues in contracting as having to do with litigation. However, it is also true that in many cases, organizations hesitate to sue because they recognize that they are partially to blame for the issues that arise. Too often, we don't spend time working on the details of the work, and the thinking is "Here is the template — just get it signed." Mindlessness will be rewarded.

Why be interested in contracts? If you impose forms on suppliers, what is the quality of the data flow and communication between the parties? We have spent huge dollars constructing technologies that facilitate global trade, but we haven't improved the relationships between organizations. And in some cases, we have summarized contracts into 14 pages with 19 URLs, many of which do not work! As organizations become more disaggregated, we have extended the problem, because in effect we are hiring the supplier ecosystem. If we aren't communicating with suppliers and they aren't communicating with their subcontractors, then it is no wonder that we are seeing higher costs.

Some of the key insights Tim gained over his lifetime are the following:

- Contracts based on classical legal theory do not work!
- Contracts cause delay and have limited value when people cannot readily understand them.
- Perceived unfairness in contract terms undermines loyalty and performance.
- Risk is about much more than compliance.
- Global business drives major increases in the cost of commercial operations.
- Current enterprise systems are incapable of handling the complexity of global business relationships and virtual contracts.

What is the next big thing? Tim advocates that we are moving into the *relationship resource planning* era — and that we need to start doing things with external relationships that drive efficiency and virtual enterprises. Contracts need to become the scaffolding for high-performing relationships.

The WC&C view is that the future will consist of the following:

- Ongoing development of networked technologies will drive continued enterprise disaggregation and importance of contracting.

- Digital solutions will steadily address the challenge of managing across organizational boundaries and force standardization.

- Roles will shift from transactional oversight to new forms of global outsight and business enablement related to quality and cost of commercial operations, on-demand knowledge, and proactive problem resolution, design for users, and standards and norms — not templates — and market intelligence and differentiation.

Assessing Procurement's Maturity and Decision-Making

The previous discussion involves characteristics of a "mature" procurement organization. The degree of procurement maturity has a direct and strong relationship with the higher order level of team-based decision-making between the sales organization, the business, and procurement.

Typical Supply Base Segmentation

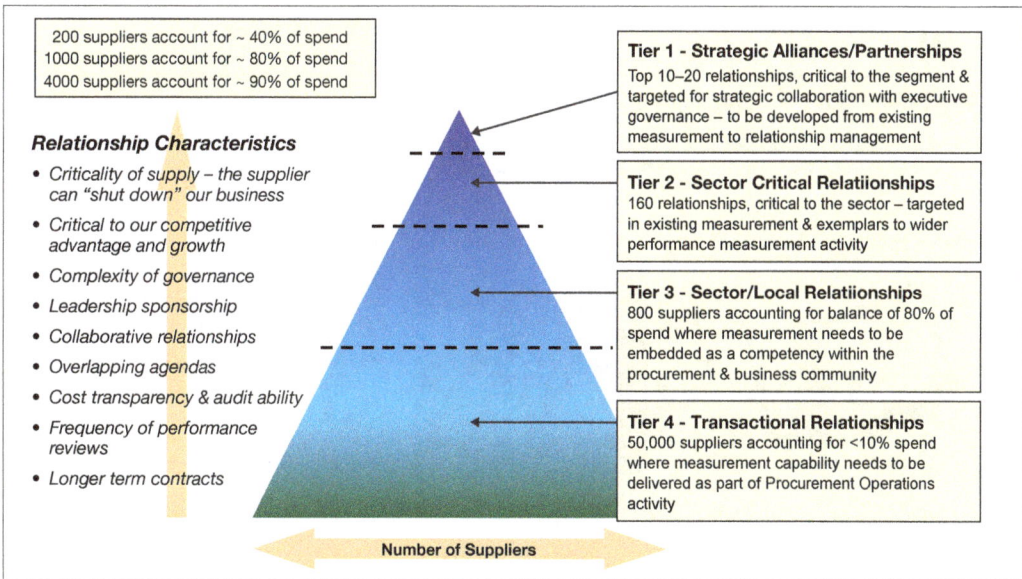

200 suppliers account for ~ 40% of spend
1000 suppliers account for ~ 80% of spend
4000 suppliers account for ~ 90% of spend

Relationship Characteristics

- *Criticality of supply – the supplier can "shut down" our business*
- *Critical to our competitive advantage and growth*
- *Complexity of governance*
- *Leadership sponsorship*
- *Collaborative relationships*
- *Overlapping agendas*
- *Cost transparency & audit ability*
- *Frequency of performance reviews*
- *Longer term contracts*

Tier 1 - Strategic Alliances/Partnerships
Top 10–20 relationships, critical to the segment & targeted for strategic collaboration with executive governance – to be developed from existing measurement to relationship management

Tier 2 - Sector Critical Relatiionships
160 relationships, critical to the sector – targeted in existing measurement & exemplars to wider performance measurement activity

Tier 3 - Sector/Local Relatiionships
800 suppliers accounting for balance of 80% of spend where measurement needs to be embedded as a competency within the procurement & business community

Tier 4 - Transactional Relationships
50,000 suppliers accounting for <10% spend where measurement capability needs to be delivered as part of Procurement Operations activity

Number of Suppliers

In mature procurement organizations, there is a common and aligned view of the supply base that is consistently communicated and emphasized in all business transactions. An example of a typical "segmentation" view of the supply base is shown in the figure above. In this case, there is a tiered structure, whereby Tier 1 suppliers are viewed as strategic partners. The sales organization in most companies has a similar segmentation that portrays how customers are viewed by the sales organization. If you are in a tier 1, you are viewed as a strategic resource who acts as a trusted advisor to deliver business value and promote organizational objectives. There are typically only a handful of suppliers who are in this role in most organizations. Tier 2 suppliers are strategic, but do not have access to the same regular performance reviews and in-depth senior executive engagements. Tier 3 suppliers are primarily working with local business relationships, while Tier 4 are purely transactional. In terms of logistics providers, a Tier 4 is viewed as someone who provides labor and no other value.

Putting People into a Box: Segmentation Approaches

One of the first topics identified in the workshop is that both Procurement and Sales put one another into a "box" through their segmentation analysis. Procurement uses a set of strategic segmentation tools that commonly look at several criteria. As shown below, Procurement will focus on creating category, or "market sector" strategy teams that seek to create an overall strategy for a given classification of spending (e.g., castings, professional services, logistics services, insurance, etc.). The first "cut" is to examine the business impact of the overall category and the value to be derived, in terms of importance to stakeholders and potential for savings. Next, a "supplier preference" classification attempts to target suppliers that deem the customer a "core" or "developmental" high-potential target. The next segmentation looks at the level of power in the relationship, and buyers prefer to be in a position of high power to drive a relationship. Finally, the degree to which results can be achieved are highlighted, with difficult, complex, low-value opportunities receiving less priority. This "filtering" process results in less than 1 percent of the supplier population within a market sector being a true target for closer relationships meriting performance management reviews and strategic aligned planning.

Segmentation Using Multiple Filters Target Suppliers for Strategic Partnerships

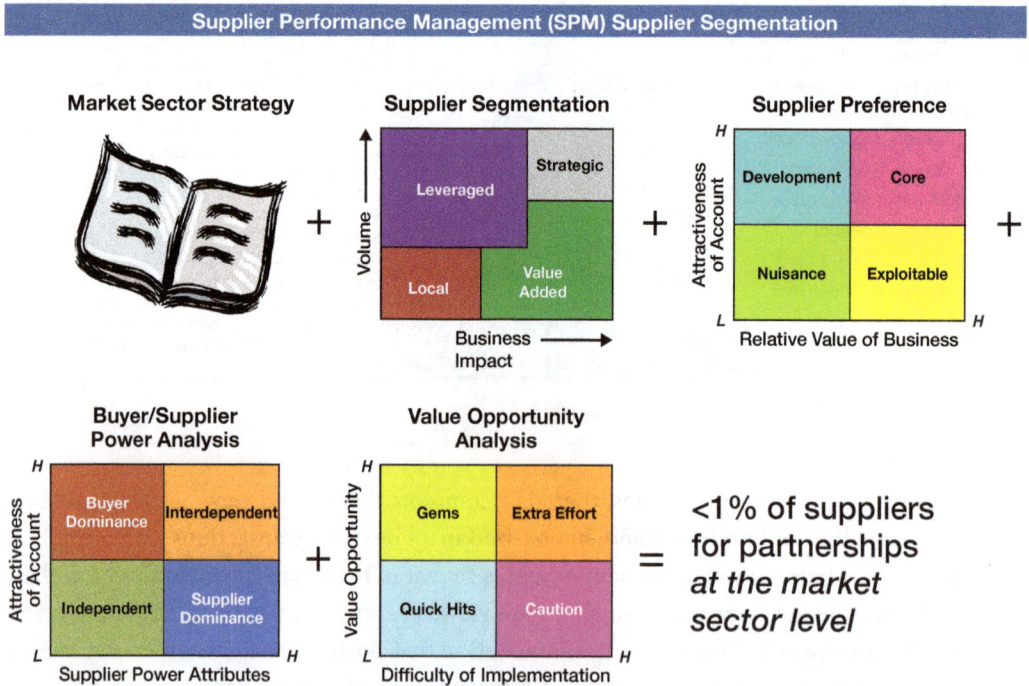

Supplier Performance Management (SPM) Supplier Segmentation

In our discussions, sales executives were astonished at this framework. Many noted: "We had no idea we were being viewed in this manner!" They also noted that the portfolio approach could vary depending on application across the enterprise versus at the local business level. For instance, someone mentioned that "at the business unit level, they don't broadly know about which quadrant we are in. But at the enterprise level, they are much more aware of this."

The businessperson will state "I want this player to serve me" and won't think in terms of the portfolio view.

On the other hand, Sales also establishes sales targets using the criteria of "value" and "winnability." A process known as an *opportunity risk assessment* seeks to answer a series of questions about the following issues:

- Are we seen as strategic to this customer?
- Is it something we are good at?
- Can we differentiate ourselves in a discrete opportunity?
- How actionable is the data?

These questions can help influence the sales organization's view of competitiveness, and it determines if different commercial strategies are needed for this customer.

It is important for the sales organization to understand how they are viewed by Procurement in this context, as a number of assumptions on how Procurement will work with you as a sales organization will follow from this perception. However, it is also important for the sales organization to recognize how Procurement views them as well!

A five-stage model for procurement maturity is based on four primary evaluation criteria, including spend management, supply base segmentation, category management, and relationship management processes. Understanding the movement toward a mature supply management organization along these dimensions can be an important component of understanding how to engage a potential sales target. Ideally, it is important to understand whether the supply management organization views the "supplier" as a strategic partner and hopes to drive a high level of communication and information sharing. Some of the questions that can be used to assess the maturity and state of the relationship include the following:

- What is the level of our relationship? At the corporate or local level?
- What is the most senior level of executive we are in communication with?
- Are we viewed as a value-adding partner in terms of cost, innovation, and continuous improvement ideas?
- Do we have relationships with both procurement and operational stakeholders?
- If not, are they well-aligned in terms of their approach to the relationship?
- Has there been a recent change in the leadership team, which would indicate a shift in the business or procurement strategy?
- How are the different business functions rewarded in terms of the outcomes that we are seeking to drive for their business?
- How many opportunities are we bringing to this business that are being considered and adopted?
- Does the contract reflect the priorities of the relationship at the highest levels in the organization?

In the sections that follow, we address these questions in more detail, reflecting the discussions of the executives that participated in this roundtable research event.

What about other types of services such as creative agencies, or professional services such as legal services, management consulting, or HR benefits suppliers? The procurement "touch" in these categories is often very light, as they have historically been like touching the "third rail" in the subway (and you don't want to do that unless you know what you are doing or don't mind 50,000 volts of electricity shooting through your body). When Procurement does get involved, as it should, you need to get educated first and do your homework before engaging your internal stakeholders in the process. Not surprisingly, many of the contracts with these service providers are severely lacking in performance measures that are monitored, tracked, and used to guide the desired outcomes. In legal services, good luck in even finding a contract with law firms — they often operate on "engagement letters" because nobody wants to get into a battle of the forms on the T&Cs. The performance criteria, therefore, are based on the subjective judgment of the user or budget holder on whether they did a good job. Why? Because it keeps the power of the relationship in the hands of the budget holder, where one could argue it should be in the first place. The only way Procurement can share in that ownership is to be educated in the category, present performance criteria that make sense to the business and the supplier for determining success or failure, and through doing so, earn a seat at the table with shared ownership interest in the supplier relationship.

Question 1: What are the specific performance criteria most valued by Procurement for outsource providers, third-party logistics (3PLs), and other types of suppliers?

In addressing this question, it is important for the sales team to be able to quantify the elements of value and, in this case, educate the customer. In some cases, the procurement organization may not have a full level of understanding regarding the different forms of performance and value that a third-party outsourced provider is delivering to their business. In every case, safety is the preeminent concern, and is the foundation for all elements of 3PL provider performance. But five other elements come into play that should be explored and defined specifically with the customer in the context of the current and targeted business.

1. *Cost.* What are the elements of not just the price of the service, but the total cost associated with operating the logistics channel?

2. *Serviceability.* What are the elements of delivery, warehouse operations, responsiveness to special requests, and transportation performance? This will impact factors such as the degree of expediting, the size of the warehouse, the number of carriers, etc.

3. *Quality/Safety.* How is quality defined? What are the key safety performance issues that are unique to this situation?

4. *Innovation.* What are the proposed ideas to drive improved outcomes across all of these other factors?

5. *Contract Compliance.* What is the track record in terms of invoicing, payment, and all contractual terms and conditions defined in the contract?

6. *Sustainability.* Don't forget about this! This criteria is becoming much more important in evaluating supplier capabilities, particularly if you are offering innovative new technologies that reduce carbon emissions. Companies are increasingly focused on their Scope 3

emissions, and if you get the business, you become part of that! Any reductions in emissions will be a bonus in addition to the elements noted above.

These elements may need to be reviewed and defined in specific terms at the beginning of the request for quotation (RFQ) process, so that the appropriate set of responses can be defined in the proposal. Each of these elements will have a different impact on cost drivers that will ultimately impact the proposed cost.

Working with your stakeholders, it is important to first prioritize what is most important as relates to assurance or supply, quality, and service levels, focusing on the "must-haves" versus the "like to haves." Following legal, regulatory, and safety criteria is not negotiable — these are Go/No-Go thresholds that every potential supplier must meet to even be considered on the bid list. If you go first to your stakeholder or budget holder with the cost criteria, you lose! Unless you can first understand what really needs to be bought, price/cost is not up for discussion. But how do you know whether the "must-haves" are truly necessary. The answer is simple: You pretend you are in kindergarten and you ask the 5 WHYs — why, why, why, why, why — and as you drill down on each criteria, peeling back the layers of the onion, oftentimes the stakeholder comes to realize that what they think they need is not what they actually need, and you open up the discussion for redefining the SOW, which can impact price/cost. So the lesson here is one that was very simply summed up on a plaque that sat on the desk of Robert Kennedy which stated: "Question Basic Assumptions." Most importantly, it assures you that what you end up buying is what you really need!

Procurement may use a form of scorecard to not only evaluate potential suppliers of services during the RFQ process, but also to manage the ongoing relationship after the contract is awarded. Scorecards can be built after the contract is awarded but also defined in more detail in the RFQ response. The weighting of the different factors is also important, and understanding this weighting is fundamental to how the response is crafted.

The RFQ may also include other questions relative to past performance the sales team should be ready to respond to:

- How long have you performed this type of activity?
- Who have you done it for?
- What is the capability you possess to deliver a solution that meets our needs?
- What are the capabilities and quality of the people who will be assigned to perform this work?

In turn, it is essential that a dialogue be established during the RFQ response process for Sales to engage Procurement and understand the drivers behind the outsourcing initiative:

- What is the business outcome you are striving to achieve? What is driving the need for this outcome?
- Why are you asking suppliers to provide solutions for these outcomes? What is the driver?
- What is the reason you are engaged in the outsourcing exercise?
- What is the level of continuous improvement you are expecting after the award is made?

- What are the transformation costs, including the switch-out costs (if there is an incumbent) that need to be considered in this proposal?

- What is the level of pre- and post-award contract savings you are expecting to deliver on the current state?

In many cases, the sales team may not know the exact weights assigned to these criteria. However, these questions can help facilitate an "estimation" of the weights and deliver a more focused and coherent proposal. Asking the listed questions during customer reviews can help the team better understand the expectation.

In some cases, the procurement team running the RFQ may not be fully cognizant of the different criteria that need to be considered. This is often the case especially with a "price-conscious" procurement team that is only rewarded for price savings over the current state. The cost of change is a significant factor that should also be well-understood and communicated in these discussions. This could also span the "political" costs, particularly when the incumbent is favored over any new party by local constituents. In many cases, an incumbent to the contract will try to sell the statement that "you can't do without me, and I'm the only one who knows how to serve you," while the potential competitor will sell the point that "changing over to our system is easy and will be seamless." Neither statement is true.

> The most important element of this process is getting assurances IN WRITING that the team the supplier is proposing to do the work, the "A team," will actually be the team assigned to the account. Real life experience — my (Howard's) procurement team went on a comprehensive request for proposal (RFP) process that insisted on review and approval of the supplier team members doing the work. When we had the final review with the supplier before signing the contract, we sat around the table with the supplier's seven people assigned to execute the software implementation. We looked each of them in the eye, and my boss and I asked each of them if they were on our implementation, and each responded yes. We signed the contract, and when we were ready to launch two weeks later, we were informed by the supplier that most of the people on the proposed team needed to continue serving their current clients, not us. The supplier swapped out six of the seven people on the team and replaced them with the "C" team, not even the "B" team. We were livid, but at that point, other than to escalate to the supplier's senior management (which we did to no avail), we had no other options but to start the implementation project with the C team, which was time and budget constrained due to availability of internal resources and funding in a certain window.

It should also be emphasized that Procurement has a responsibility to fully understand the capabilities of potential suppliers in the process. One executive noted:

"As a result of the RFQ, we selected two different suppliers for two different DCs. We used an identical process, and they appeared both highly qualified based on their respective responses and proposals. One of the suppliers operated flawlessly, and only required two meetings annually to review performance. The other supplier had horrible performance, which required weekly reviews to deal with a stream of continued operational issues."

To bar against the likelihood that the business will "game" the weights to get their preferred supplier, mature supply management organizations will establish the weights ahead of time.

There should be a "referee" who sits on top of the weighting system; in most cases, it will be the company auditor. A good procurement practice will have an audit requirement to define the weights before the RFQ is issued and not change them during the process.

If, as a result of this assessment, it becomes clear that the RFQ performance criteria and weights are not aligned with the supplier's key capabilities, the sales team may make a decision to not pursue the proposal. However, unless these types of questions are asked through engaging the procurement team, the pursuit strategy will not be fully informed, which could lead to a tremendous waste of resources.

Question 2: What are the rating criteria used to evaluate performance after the contract is signed? How are these evaluations carried out? And how can these evaluations be employed to drive retention of the customer, create a renewal, and avoid a new bid?

Quarterly business reviews (QBRs) are part of the operational business responsibility, not the business development team. However, the business development team has a responsibility to participate in these reviews for important customers to be able to "monitor the pulse" of the relationship, as well as to be aware of the opportunity to drive improvement in performance and address shortfalls before they mature into major problems.

Procurement executives in our study emphasized that they ideally want to run QBRs, lead the team, set up the timing of these reviews, invite the key participants, and follow up on the outcomes of the reviews. As such, it is important that key business stakeholders from the customer participate and that the business development lead for the relationship also be involved. Typically, customer business representatives will be involved in scoring the evaluations for cost, service, quality/safety, innovation, and contract compliance. Data collection to "feed" the scorecard may be collected through operational systems outputs, internal satisfaction surveys, external performance metrics, or other sources. The extent to which the business stakeholder is involved in QBRs is a function of how mature the procurement organization is, and reflects the extent to which the right people are engaged and attending.

Not having business or procurement representation at QBRs should be interpreted as a warning sign. If this occurs on a regular basis, there is a good possibility that the relationship may be headed "off-kilter," in that the right level of feedback is not being obtained. It is difficult to manage a relationship if stakeholders don't attend, as procurement personnel may not be fully cognizant of all the issues. On the other hand, not having Procurement at the meeting may lead to a situation where the local business operator is emphasizing operational performance issues, but is not communicating the priorities for ongoing cost improvements and shifting global/corporate level requirements. The post-award contract shift in the RACI diagram (see page 67) suggests that Procurement should facilitate at the local level, while the global category team lead should be informed of the outcomes of these meetings through a global "supplier scorecard." But not emphasizing the opportunities for continuous cost improvement through procurement dialogue is a risk if the focus at QBRs is solely on operational performance. Procurement also has a responsibility to inform the supplier's team if the scorecard has "shifted" and there are changes in the weights being assigned to different elements of operational performance and cost. This can only occur if Procurement is viewed as an "ally" in the relationship and it feels compelled to inform the supplier if there is a shift afoot due to a change in leadership, a change in business priorities, or other sudden shifts in the business.

Perhaps this was emphasized in a recent 3PL company's experience, whereby the performance scorecard was "all green." Both supplier and customer were rating one another on relationship, safety, service, and commercials. The QBR was hosted by the local site client, and there were no indications that anything was wrong. In the next quarter, however, the supplier lost two major operations contracts at two of the customer's sites, and it became clear that local constituents at these sites had not been properly surveyed, were dissatisfied, and had pushed for a change. In general, the statement that "green is not your friend" holds here, and that there should always be an opportunity for improvement identified in a healthy relationship, as the benchmark may be set too low.

This is especially true when it comes to the category of innovation. Executives have told me that about 20 percent of innovation ideas are cost related, but this level may not be properly connected into the true sources of business value. In addition, less than 15 percent of innovation ideas are ever properly resourced and brought to fulfillment. This is because in most cases the return on investment (ROI) is greater than six months. A longer contract-planning horizon would undoubtedly translate into a higher proportion of cost-savings ideas being adopted and implemented. This value proposition clearly needs to go beyond the level of procurement and engage the business in both service-level and cost-related performance improvement ideas. One sales executive noted:

> "We are losing value opportunities by not focusing on the total cost of ownership outcomes of service improvement. Cost is a Procurement conversation, and Sales teams are often not equipped to have this conversation, as they focus more on operational issues. We don't recognize what different people want in terms of cost performance, and it may be an opportunity for us to drive an important source of value."

The implication is that Sales should be educated and trained in the application of total cost of ownership (TCO), as a means to influence both Procurement and business stakeholders in their customers of the potential savings from operational improvements. Some of the issues here may include:

- How do we monetize value from performance improvements?
- How do we quantify in dollars the performance value we are creating and improving on?
- How do we aggregate this savings across our volume of product and labor productivity?
- How do we highlight the financial impacts on working capital, inventory, and other balance sheet items that are derived from our performance?
- What are the primary financial key performance indicators (KPIs) that procurement is focused on, and how are we addressing those?

Many of these issues can be addressed by establishing the proper agenda for QBRs ahead of time. The agenda should span an overall business view but also address performance and cost. An "ideal" agenda that was highlighted by a procurement executive at our meeting was described below.

At XYZ, we only held QBRs with our top 20 suppliers. Below the top 20, there was a six month or annual review held with suppliers. But the format of the meeting with the top 20 was the same every time, and we had a timekeeper to ensure that we didn't go past the two-hour meeting timeframe for each QBR.

- *State of the Union.* What is happening in the business? (*30 minutes*)
- *Where have we been?* An in-depth review of each dimension of performance in the scorecard, and clarification of where deficiencies are noted. (*30 minutes*)
- *What can we do better?* What are the specific actions that need to be taken to address deficiencies in the next quarter? (*30 minutes*)
- *Where are we going and where are you taking us?* What types of innovation and suggestions can we consider to drive not only savings but improved performance? This might include topics such as value analysis, value engineering, productivity improvements, etc. (*30 minutes*)

In some cases, the review of scorecards can produce important insights into deficiencies and assumptions regarding performance that are misaligned. The scorecard may suggest that the supplier is not performing, but it is the role of Sales to come prepared to explain why the performance is lacking, and Procurement should likewise seek to explore the root cause of performance deficiencies.

Question 3: Is there a better way to plan ahead on contract renewals?

The volume of business up for renewal on major contracts can be stressful for suppliers. Similarly, Purchasing is often in the position of waiting until the last minute to renew contracts, and it may be forced to extend the contract date by a few weeks to catch up with the review process. Both Sales and Procurement can benefit significantly by proactive planning ahead of the renewal cycle.

Sales personnel can begin by planning ahead and bringing up the renewal cycle during QBRs, and not waiting until the last minute. Sales account managers need to coordinate with business development personnel and coordinate their activities to ensure that the procurement team can help "sell" the business internally. Again, mature procurement personnel want suppliers to be successful and are relying on them to also help drive down total cost. As such, development of a joint proposal with sales and procurement, facilitated in a working session, can help create a value proposition to renew a contract before it reaches the end of its term.

Customer retention is becoming an increasingly important element of the sales cycle. A senior sales executives notes that:

"We had 93 percent retention last year but still lost millions of dollars. We need to adopt a philosophy of monetizing business development, which is both an operational and business development responsibility. We need to do a better job of identifying account management solutions that drive upside value and growth. What is the cost of a lost customer? We don't really emphasize that enough to both our teams, and think of this as not just account management but sales development! Roughly 30 percent of our compensation for business development is renewal based — so there is incentive to ensure we retain business. But the broader question: Is that compensation extending outside business development, and is the entire business incented on growth of that account?"

One company I worked with, for instance, has a "customer for life" model. One of the upfront criteria discussed when evaluating a customer is to conduct an open business meeting with the customer and get them to openly share "what we like about you and don't like about you." These annual meetings are not a "group hug," but rather an opportunity to candidly assess if there is a good fit and what needs to be done if the relationship is going to be continued.

In fact, it is advised that the procurement category owner and the supplier owner get together before the QBR to set the agenda and also ensure that their KPIs and data align and match. This not only increases the "trust" factor, but also helps run a smoother QBR. Transparency goes a long way. And it also provides a good forum for discussion of payment terms and alternative scenarios for cost savings linked to quicker payment.

The business stakeholders and budget holders can get lazy! It happens all the time: suppliers seeking to upsell and expand their revenue streams come into the business with recommendations to change the current ways of working. But sometimes there is an inherent WIIFM ("What's in it for me?") problem for the business, as individuals may have a personal stake in their job descriptions and activities that may be threatened by the change, so they don't run these opportunities up the chain for approval.

This is where Procurement can really shake the tree. I (Howard) have seen this several times where Procurement holds a *supplier forum* and invites in the top executives from its most important suppliers. Invitations will not be extended to suppliers that do not commit to send a senior level (SVP+) executive to the forum, assuring that decision-makers will be present. Procurement, along with business executives, present the state of the business to the suppliers and usually have a couple of "ASKS" … one is always money, such as a commitment to reduce cost by 20 percent over three years! The funny part is that the suppliers expect this, but the resistance comes from the internal business people that have the relationship with the supplier. It feels as though Procurement is accusing them of not doing their job. I've heard people say, "How can you treat my supplier this way?!"

But Procurement also offers a second piece of the puzzle to the suppliers — submit a "white paper" to Procurement of all the things that get in the way of accomplishing the 20 percent cost reduction; ideas that can be implemented that will improve efficiency, reduce waste, and expand their line of business with you; and their commitment to meet the target if these things are implemented. By doing so, the roadblocks are made public and the business realizes that they must do their part to contribute to this process. Timing isn't everything, it's the ONLY thing, and the best time to take this route is when the business is hurting and really needs a boost.

By the same token, the sales team can also share with Procurement how the customer is responding to their suggestions for improvement. For example, a large oil and gas company procurement team recalls that they were given a list of proposals for improvement and, upon reviewing it, learned that it was the same packet received the year before! Not a single initiative had been taken on any of the suggestions on the list. If a supplier is providing opportunities and the business doesn't pick up on it, then the fault may lie in the lack of follow up, the lack of a business case, or the inability to really sell the benefits.

Procurement is often seeking evidence that improvement is an ongoing priority for the supplier's sales team. A procurement executive notes that:

"I may tell my supplier that I want them at an 8 in terms of performance. But if I go to the QBR and I see that they are at 2.7, which is up from 2.4 last time, and their goal is to get to 3.2 next quarter … that is a great relationship in my book. We are seeing evidence that improvement is a goal for them!"

There is also a tendency for the roles of account representative and operational staff from the supplier's side of the business to work together and be more transparent. Several procurement executives we spoke with emphasized that they would rather hear about the operational details from the local site manager, and that the account representative may often try to "spin" the performance issues. There needs to be strong representation from both parties.

To help drive continuous cost improvement, a number of ideas came up during our discussion:

- Demonstration to Procurement that the redundancy in their operations due to inability to deploy improvements is costing them money.

- Involvement of operational staff from both organizations to define specific project initiatives and project planning.

- Defined continuous improvement roadmaps with performance measures and incentives tied to outcomes.

- Upside and downside incentives for gain sharing and penalties, using both the "carrot and the stick" approach.

Incentives are a great way to drive cost savings, but the experience is that generally this is very hard to do, often due to the complexities with accounting to validate savings. An emerging issue is how to reward suppliers for the value they create, while having a penalty for value destroyed. It needs to go both ways.

A clear approach is needed on how to proactively plan ahead of renewals. Many companies will use Salesforce.com or a similar customer relationship management (CRM) tool to flag executives 14 to 16 months ahead of the renewal expiration. This should set off a series of discussions that target the following approaches:

- Review of service-level agreements and performance against them.

- Current client business strategy assumptions and aligned approach.

- Pricing and terms.
- Projected next steps in terms of contract renewals and project timeline.

The carrot and the stick, or in essence bonus/penalty clauses, may not drive the behaviors envisioned by those who insist on having them in the contract. Why is that? First of all, revenue streams and budgets for cost in a business may be separate accountabilities. Your business stakeholder may be experiencing a growth in revenue, partially or wholly due to the successful actions of a supplier (say, your creative agency), and the people who are getting commissioned on these higher revenues are enjoying the benefit. But that doesn't influence the finance and accounting team responsible for maintaining the budget for that team — all they see are larger payouts to the supplier for its performance, and spend budgets are not normally adjusted upward in a fiscal year with revenue projections. This can cause friction over the supplier bonus issue, especially if the person in charge of the P&L feels that the revenue growth might actually be attributable to other factors as well.

Then there is the penalty side of the equation in the contract, where a supplier is underperforming against certain KPIs and/or SLA performance criteria. It could be on-time delivery percentage, up-time percentage of a system or service, time to resolve issues or process orders, any number of criteria that may be called out in the contract with the goal of improving performance. The penalty might be 2 to 3 percent of the contract price. The last thing I want to see is that penalty check arrive from the supplier — I (Howard) want them to FIX THE PROBLEM, not get money back! But I have seen suppliers that react by saying, "I've fixed the problem by paying you a penalty as called for in the contract, and it's less costly for me to do that than to improve performance to the KPI or SLA."

This has happened, and though you may be determined to replace that supplier or cancel the contract based on breach, that might not be what the business is prepared to do, and the hurdle rate for the cost of change may not justify the activity. There is also opportunity cost to consider — is it worth the procurement effort to do this versus another category pursuit for savings? So be careful what you wish for.

It was notable in our discussions that procurement functions did NOT have a good approach for managing their contract renewal process (generally speaking, even though there are a multitude of contract management apps and modules available in the marketplace). It may be a useful exercise for the sales management team to map out the activities and information that should be exchanged over the year prior to contract renewal that can help drive the renewal to its logical conclusion in a timely manner. The role of sales as an "advocate" to procurement can help ensure that the right approach is followed. An example follows of what an annual contracting plan might look like for a company and the required business intelligence that needs to be collected ahead of each contracting renewal.

This exercise can help the sales team focus on the renewal and work with the business development team to keep abreast of the issue. This can also lead to opportunities to expand the current service offering. In the words of one sales executive:

"We have to earn our wings every day, and we think about renewals and keeping it front and center from the day you sign the contract. If I start thinking 14 months ahead of the renewal, and I take 2 or 3 months to develop a tightly buttoned-up proposal, we will be more successful in creating effective real estate solutions and can think about building a portfolio around buildings. But we need a longer runway to be able to deliver these scaled solutions. If we can eliminate the RFP altogether by adding services that creates an early renewal, that is also a win. I'd rather avoid doing RFPs altogether, and just do renewals!"

Pre-Contract Information Sharing

Process Analysis – Results of Workshop

	Jan	Feb	Mar	Apr	May	Jun
Activities	Scheduling		Forecast vs. Actual			Forecast vs. Actual
	Receiving (all year)					
Business Intelligence Required	Technical Data					
	CoA					
	MSDS					
	Commodity Info					
When is the information required?	Throughout the year					

	Jul	Aug	Sep	Oct	Nov	Dec
Activities		Budgeting	Forecast vs. Actual	Negotiations		Blanket POs
	Receiving (all year)					
Business Intelligence Required	Technical Data					
	CoA					
	MSDS					
	Commodity Info					
When is the information required?	Throughout the year					

It is clear that doing RFPs, even if the supplier is an incumbent, is not in anyone's best interest if market dynamics have been fairly stable. Procurement is involved in a lot of extra effort and time that chews up resources, and suppliers must also provide a level of activity that is not immediately beneficial or provides evidence for improvements. But on the other hand, if there is a proactive approach to regular performance reviews that results in continuous efforts to improve, conducting an RFP isn't needed. If a supplier can make their incumbency so powerful that there is no need for an RFP, then continuous renewals are possible.

In my (Robert's) experience, a large gas company in Eastern Canada maintained a ten-year contract with a single supplier. One of the major reasons for using a market-based approach with a unit-based rate is to ensure the market is competitive. A lump sum bid has advantages in that it drives a competitive quote from the market, but in an environment of labor shortages, it also risks being able to identify a guaranteed qualified workforce for the bid winner.

The lump sum market-based approach was NOT used in this case. The senior procurement executives involved decided that a major disadvantage of this approach is that it provides little true visibility into labor, profit, and overhead rates. An important benefit of their long-term agreement with a single supplier was to be able to monitor rates and drive productivity improvements.

An argument often made for using a unit-based rate is that it reduces the risk and potential to be "over-billed" for change orders, etc. The implicit assumption here is that the supplier is not efficient and is eager

continues on next page

to make changes that result in additional billing. Although a time and materials contract is implicit in the long-term agreement used by this company, there were additional checks and balances in place to increase visibility. First, the company could track delays, workflow, and other elements associated with the work. Second, audits were regularly performed, and when discrepancies were identified (which is always possible), they were rectified. The ability of both parties to be open with one another was at the root of why this relationship worked. When both parties are acting in good faith, there is no room for overbilling or other unethical behaviors. In effect, a good description for this relationship is "trust … but verify!" Suppliers we interviewed in this relationship emphasized the importance of the trust in these contracts.

In the words of a supplier: "We are an alliance. For it to work, you have to have trust. We both feel it is important that we measure everything and find new ways to get better. We measure delivery to customer, and we open up our books completely to have their auditors come in and view our financials. We are proud of the accuracy that we have demonstrated to them. There are productivity items in the scorecard, and we measure everything to demonstrate that we are continually improving. I'd like to see this relationship run for 30 years. It is an open and honest contract, and we work through any issues as they arise. We haven't had to pull up a contract or talk to a lawyer since we signed it. When there is an issue, we work through it collectively, instead of pointing fingers." Another supplier noted: "We have leveraged off what we have created, and this has allowed us to build relationships with other companies in Canada. But this relationship is special. This is the most sophisticated group of people we have worked with — and we are anxious to see the relationship continue for another 13 years! We are able to provide streams of data to our partner that also allows them to operate more efficiently. We are all driven by the same drive to improve. The only Achilles heel, to be honest, is that we shut down for 3.5 months each year … but we are managing that as well."

Question 4: When should the business development sales team turn down the opportunity to bid?

One of the most important elements suppliers seek to avoid involves participation in an RFP when there is a low probability of success. One of the key areas that many strategic outsource providers avoid is the "reverse auction." While reverse auctions are useful for true "commodities," there are too many ways to manipulate price that lead to adjustments to recover margin later.

> "If somebody is new and wants us to participate in an auction, we won't be successful. There are too many ways to manipulate price and come back to it later to recover margin. I first want to know — what is their view of a third-party outsource, and is this a real opportunity or not? An RFP can be just to gather ideas and do nothing. And so we push hard to do an assessment up front, and test whether the organization says we are all in or not. A customer survey can also provide information — if they say they want a lower price, higher flexibility, and we have excess capacity and want you guys to take over our site and charge us less, that is NOT for us!"

Generally, there are several "red flags" that will lead a supplier to explicitly decide NOT to respond to an RFP:

- Is it the right relationship with the client?
- What is our market position and strength of our portfolio relative to the other competitors? If this is an area that is not our strength, then don't pursue it.
- What is our ability to deliver and execute over the life of the contract with this customer in the past?

- Is the customer very price-sensitive to the exclusion of other forms of value? ("We will not be the lowest cost supplier.")

- Do we want to bid and put some hurt on our competitors? (This is generally not a good reason to compete in the RFP, as it is not good for the client.)

- Does the client have data that can be compiled through interviews and templates? If there is low access to data, we can't build a case. However, we may not want to work to collect data to present to the client, which they in turn present to their incumbent!

- Are we just a third supplier added to the bid list? Are they really committed to a change in the incumbent? Or are they just shopping for bids, which they will turn over to Procurement to put pressure on the incumbent for a price reduction?

- Is the customer just looking for a "directional quote" (sometimes positioned as a "hypothetical")? This can lead to confusion, particularly if the scope of work has not been effectively articulated.

- The RFP is sent out with a short time period (less than two weeks), and there is no way to mobilize a well-developed proposal in that period of time. The minimum time required for a typical logistics outsourcing proposal is generally 6 to 8 weeks.

In all of these cases, suppliers must pick and choose RFPs that make sense for their limited business development teams to pursue. These teams are often constrained by design, so as to not have to pursue every RFP and achieve a lower win rate. Many business development groups are expected to complete about 12 major deals in a year, with a 50 percent win rate yielding 6 major deals. But if the win rate goes up to 9 deals to yield 6 wins, the resources can be better focused and allocated efficiently. That means the team can be unconstrained, so long as the right resources are dedicated to the right opportunities.

Reverse auctions, like any other tool in the procurement toolbox, can be a huge driver of value if used in the right manner. Three examples:

1) A "trinkets & trash" memorabilia supplier of lucite milestone awards, trophies, and other "tchotchkes" to a large company had been their preferred partner for 30 years. The buyer was convinced that they were getting "below market pricing" from this reliable supplier, but a procurement transformation was taking place that dictated a change in strategy. The supplier was informed that a reverse auction was going to be held. A week before the auction, the supplier's owner came in to meet with procurement management, offering a compromise: "If you cancel the reverse auction, I will lower my prices to you by 30 percent." Procurement's response to this was as follows: "Sure, just write us a check equal to the 30 percent overcharge that you have been giving to us for only the last three years, and we will call off the auction." Of course, this didn't happen, and the auction proceeded as planned — and resulted in a new supplier being selected.

2) My (Howard's) company was doing major building construction in the UK which, among many things, required a *local area network* (LAN) infrastructure. Procurement approached the CIO and told him that they would source this from approved suppliers using a reverse auction. The CIO was unfamiliar with this type of bidding but agreed to try Procurement's strategy for determining price. The CIO was invited to watch the reverse auction live, and it was a boring affair with little movement until the last two minutes.

continues on next page

Procurement Confidential *continued*

Then suddenly, one of the bidders lowered their price by £400,000 and the auction ended. Curious, to make sure that it wasn't a data entry error on the part of the bidder, Procurement later approached the low bidder to ask about their bidding strategy. The GM for the successful bidder told them the following: "We needed to win this bid, and it was the biggest job that we knew we would get for several years. I went to our head of marketing and asked him how much was in his budget for winning new customers, and he said £400,000. I asked him for the money, saying that if we won this account, his mission would be accomplished. He agreed, and gave us the money to use in the bid."

3) I was standing in line at the airport to check my bags for an international flight when I turned around and saw the CEO of my pharma company standing behind me. I introduced myself to him and told him my role in IT procurement, to which he replied, "Are you doing any reverse auctions?" I told him we were, and his response to me was "Good! We are being forced to participate in reverse auctions in our vaccine business, and I want to make sure that we are doing the same with our supply base."

Each example is different, yet reverse auctions were universally being applied as a powerful tool by different parties to drive toward the lowest price. One company I worked with executed 1,000 auctions in one year. Interestingly though, in only 50 percent of the cases did they select the low bidder. The auction was only to drive toward lowest market price, but the other criteria of assurance of supply, quality, service, and innovation carried more weight than the price in the decision criteria.

Question 5: What is the governance around supplier relationship management?

Procurement Process	Activity	Category Manager SPM or equivalent	Corp. Lead	Contract Owner/ Business Sponsor	Contract Holder/ Business Focal Point
Assess demand and supply	Determine the business needs	A	R	C	S
	Establish clear roles and responsibilities for key personnel	A	R	C	S
	Assess market conditions and risks	A	R	I	C
	Profile current and potential suppliers	A	R	I	C
	Identify value opportunities	A	R	S	C
Develop and select strategy	Develop cost profile/model and identify opportunities	A	R	I	C
	Develop value initiatives	A	R	S	C
	Develop category and sourcing strategy	A	R	I	C
	Conduct peer review	A	R	I	C
	Endorse category and/or sourcing strategy	A	R	I	C
Source and award	Manage sourcing process	A	R	I	C
	Evaluate and award contract	A	R	I	C
	Sign contract(s)	A	R	I	C
Implement contract	Communicate contract details and create alignment	I	A/R	C	S
	Localize contract	I	A/R	C	S
	Prepare systems for automation	I	A/R	I	C
	Operationalize contract	I	A	R	I
	Reconfirm clear roles and responsibilities for key personnel	I	R	A	S
	Conduct contract kick-off meeting and develop CMP	I	R	A	S/R
Execute and manage contract	Commence contract operation, manage contract execution	I	R/S	A	R
	Manage contract performance	C	S	A	R
	Optimize contract (continuous improvement)	C	S	A	R
	Manage commercial impact on contract	C	R	A	S
	Complete contract closure	I	R	A	S

R	Responsible to do or get it done
A	Accountable – must sign off results
S	Provides **S**upport to the responsible party as necessary
C	Must be **C**onsulted on task and results as necessary
I	**I**nformed about tasks and results as necessary

This RASCI is for putting a category strategy and/or contract in place. For strategy selection/FA, the category manager is the CP lead and contract owner. Changes from RACI to RASCI indicated in red.

Understand the Procurement Decision-Making Process

As shown in the figure above, there are designated roles that Procurement plays at different points in their own cycle that may or may not mesh well with the sales cycle. It is important for both parties to understand the decision-rights that drive alignment between procurement, business stakeholders, and suppliers. The role of the different actors will vary before and after the contracting process. This variance is shown in the RASCI chart above, which stands for **R**esponsible, **A**ccountable, **S**upporting, **C**onsulted, and **I**nformed.

NC State University research points to the general best practice that joint ownership of the contract should ideally be assigned to both the business and Procurement. It is generally acknowledged that the business may not have the necessary skills to manage the contract independently, and that Procurement does not have the vested interests of the business in the contractors, so the ideal outcome seems to be "integration and collaboration" of the two functions so that joint ownership occurs.

For instance, one of the most important differentiators of "successful" projects in a recent study was that project risks were identified early during the contract negotiation phase (77 percent of respondents). Early risk identification was found to be a function of getting the right people at the table early on in the negotiation process. The results also indicate that having key stakeholders at the table during contract scoping will more likely lead to identification of project risks and better outcomes. This is especially true for large complex oil and gas projects in which clients and sponsors (especially investment companies) are seeking returns on large investments with multiple stakeholders involved.

A number of other interesting themes were also discovered in our research. For example, many of the companies designated specific roles for contract managers from Procurement to ensure all contract terms are in accordance with the contract, the business contract owner ensured the work was completed according to the scope of work, and a contract coordinator (contract holder, budget holder, demand manager) from the business who was accountable to the contract owner to ensure the daily work was being done according to the plan. What is also clear from this and other responses is that the process must be documented to clearly define roles and responsibilities, because in the end, the contract management work requires close cooperation between the business and procurement.

The major phases of sourcing and contract management as depicted in the RACI chart are as follows.

Assess demand and supply: Procurement/category management should lead the contracting effort by working hand in hand with key business stakeholders to understand the diverse needs of engineering, finance, project management, etc. These requirements should be contrasted and compared to the attributes and historical performance of key suppliers being considered. At a high level, market factors, capacity, capabilities, technology roadmaps, etc., should all be taken into account during this phase. The business is closely involved in helping establish these performance requirements. As conflicts arise, they must be addressed through consensus supported by data and a business case. Again, when determining business needs, it's important to ask the 5 WHYs to truly determine what are "must-haves" versus "like to haves."

Develop and select strategy: Based on the preceding activity, strategy development occurs through a structured Procurement-led process involving sharing of market intelligence, supplier profiles, TCO models, and value-based insights, which are often conflicting. A well-developed sourcing strategy is one that creates and offers options to the business that are data-driven and objective, leading to a reasonable discussion of which priorities will benefit the enterprise as a whole. The challenge at this stage often involves dealing with multiple stakeholder priorities. The business stakeholders are actively consulted and engaged in this data-driven activity. Key risks and KPIs are established and integrated into the "ideal contract" structure and review periods are identified. This phase requires "active" engagement of the business, although the business may not believe this is their "responsibility" at this stage.

Source and award: The sourcing activity and contract negotiation is largely led by Procurement, but business stakeholders must be involved to communicate KPIs and articulate contract requirements clearly during this period. Any misunderstandings must be resolved and clarified with all parties involved. Risks are identified and discussed with the supplier, and means of reducing risks through clear communication roles and responsibilities are established. This was a clear differentiator of successful complex projects in a JSCAN study identified.[1]

Implement contract: During this phase, the transition begins to shift from Procurement-led to business-led. A big part of this effort is around communication of change, implementation, automation, project mobilization, and clarifying roles and responsibilities, as well as performance expectations. Any misunderstandings between what the contract states and what suppliers/ stakeholders expect must be addressed (although they should have been properly addressed in the previous stage ideally).

Execute and manage contract: At this stage, the business takes over and runs the agreement. Procurement should be activity involved at major contract review periods to bring commercial clarity in the revision of demand or specification/service levels, alterations in KPIs, and ensure the contract and supplier relationship is running smoothly. Procurement involvement may occur through a local procurement supplier manager, who will report outcomes from reviews up to the centralized category management team. However, the business takes accountability over the contract during this phase. Any other issues that come up must be resolved immediately, rather than at the end of the contract period.

However, there are several best practice guiding principles that are the caveats to this process. Based on my (Howard's) interaction with many different procurement contract managers and

---

1 Handfield, R., Primo, M., and Valderes, M., "Effective Relationship Management In Oil & Gas Projects: Insights from Procurement Executives," *Journal of Strategic Contracting and Negotiation*, volume 1, issue 1, pp. 1–27, April 2015.

executives, I believe many of these issues have yet to be fully integrated into most procurement processes.

- Collaboration and integration of various functions and the business in the early stages of the contract development steps is required. The business may claim to be "too busy" to be involved, but as eventual owners of the agreement, they have a responsibility to send their best people to these early meetings and help shape the contract requirements and KPIs.

- The cross-functional contract management team need to have a multidimensional approach to address and gain continuous improvement of all the key value levers (demand management, specification control, risk management, KPI management, Health, Safety, Security, and Environment (HSSE), etc.). In the automotive industry, much of this approach is driven by a "target cost," established by an independent "cost engineering" function that serves as the basis around which to make decisions in other areas of technical specs, materials, etc. In the typical oil and gas or life sciences environment, the challenge is to overcome the need to "over-spec" requirements as opposed to using industry-standard specs, and these may need to be challenged to meet fitness for purpose requirements.

- End-to-end participation of the key people involved must occur. If parties are not involved, they cannot complain when the outcome is not successful. Roles and responsibilities must be clear, and a "check the box" mentality will not suffice. This is especially true when it comes to defining key performance indicators.

- Balance of global and local business engagement. It is important to have a global perspective of the product category, and the supplier and the site within that global category, but contract involvement and execution must come from a local team. Centralized category groups that do not understand operational conditions are not going to create the right contractual outcomes.

- Competent procurement organization and staff. In organizations that do not have a mature procurement function, the procurement group may not be up to the task, and the business will form a separate group that will operate independently to get the job done!

- Need for ongoing meetings and continuous improvement initiatives with suppliers/contractors. Quarterly reviews of KPIs must be taken seriously and not simply by "checking the box." Corrective action plans must be put in place to address issues, of which there will never be a shortage. These meetings should be bilateral, in that suppliers should be encouraged to provide ongoing feedback on customer-related issues that are driving up cost or increasing complexity and are non-HSSE related. Continuous TCO improvement opportunities should be followed up on by the customer and adapted, with savings shared with suppliers to incent ongoing activities.

Although this discussion illustrates the "ideal" state of how governance should occur around the relationship, the fact is that there is considerable variance in the manner in which this takes place across organizations. It is therefore incumbent on a good sales team to explore the relationship of the decision-maker to procurement and understand the roles that each plays in the decision. The "ideal" view is portrayed in a procurement strategy known as "category management," which involves having Procurement as a facilitator of the business roles. The formal nature of putting all the decision-makers on the same team, and making them responsible and accountable in front of the sales organization, is still many years away in many organizations and is a function of the maturity of the supply chain function. It is also important that the right people be put into these roles, and that they show up for the meetings. Business leaders may also send people who are not fully responsible. Understanding the nature of the dynamics and players involved is key for the sales organization to understand, and they must be able to have their fingers on both the business stakeholder and the procurement facilitator's pulse.

One of the biggest mistakes made by Sales is believing that the local site manager has exclusive control over the decision. There is almost always a global decision-maker who may be driving the decision, and if one or the other is not represented, there will be disjointed decision-making and this will not lead to a global decision.

In such cases, there is merit in being able to pull analytical insights from across the organization that pulls together not just delivery issues, but cost and opportunities for cost savings, too. In particular, there is a need to be able to deliver advanced analytics that create insights into TCO. This is a capability that has become increasingly valued by Procurement.

When there are major differences in cost and price estimates in a new RFP situation, there is generally a reason for that gap. This may be a logical reason relative to the competitor's market position. For instance, perhaps they have a backhaul that is empty and are willing to take on a route or business to cover their fixed costs. A second reason may be a difference in the interpretation of the statement of work, or a difference in the labor base cost or the facility cost. So there is a need to engage with Procurement to derive increased disclosure at the right level of detail, even if the bid is lost. Too often, however, Procurement will only state the price differential that the other supplier won the business at ("You are 40 percent too high — you just are!") without giving any detail or explanation why. This can result in disqualification from the running. But there are also stakeholders who don't want to see you disqualified and understand what the performance requirements truly are. So there may be internal training across business functions required to help people understand what the full requested work really entails. This means the sales team must be fully cognizant of the data behind the presentation as well. To be effective, it's critical that the sales team have a strong relationship with the procurement entity, not just the business stakeholder.

Development of a relationship map is important to understanding the role of different stakeholders.

Unfortunately, the roles are not always mapped out well. Sales should focus on planning ahead of the RFP and work with Procurement to help them also understand the business needs and challenges. This can lead to the proper timeline for preparation, data analysis, and understanding of the issues to be proposed at the time of the renewal.

> **Question:** What is the biggest mistake that Procurement makes?
>
> **Answer:** People in procurement tend to be good negotiators, but they don't fully understand the business requirements that are valued by the users and therefore negotiate for all the wrong things! The end result is they put out contracts that the business ignores, and Procurement somehow still publishes the "savings" from the contract.
>
> Having the business users define the SOW and deliverables is essential to success in the process, and without clearly defined RACI/RASCI roles and responsibilities, the process will fall on its face. Collaboration within the business is a "must-have."
>
> The real challenge, though, is that each user in the business may want things that are at cross-purposes, bespoke to their area, and in doing so, overcomplicate things and build in unacceptable complexity that costs everyone in the long run. There needs to be a higher-level executive sponsor from the business for the sourcing process who can make the call to override all requests in the SOW or deliverables to meet the company's end-state objectives. Without this, even buying and negotiating for the right things can lead to failure and underperformance in the contracting process.

Part of the opportunity may also involve engaging in "risk sharing" agreements, whereby incentives are created to drive cost improvements and operational performance. Procurement is increasingly bringing stakeholders (physicians, engineers, project managers) onto category teams to engage them in the operational issues that matter to them. But this is not always the case. In many companies, the category manager (working in the central office) may have little to no interaction with operational managers at the business or at sites. So it is imperative to talk to both, and if required, bring them together into the same business meeting to improve their alignment. The "commercial" owner may be Procurement, but the "operational" owner may be the business, so mapping out these roles and speaking to both may be an important component of the relationship development process. Too often, discussions solely with the business will focus on service, performance, and safety. But in Procurement, it may be solely on price. Conducting a RACI exercise that lays out the procurement process and the stakeholders, with a view to the ownership of the procurement relationship, can be an eye-opening experience for the business development manager charged with managing that account. Many of the operational specifications and requirements may come from the business or engineering design team, while the category team will impact the commercial elements of the relationship. Focusing on one or the other stakeholder exclusively can create a false impression, and in some cases, can result in missing a bid package or opportunity to renew. The mistaken assumption in many cases is that "Procurement are the gatekeepers" and not an integral part of the process. They are often believed to have a limited view of the engagement, and their power as a decision-maker is frequently underestimated. On the other hand, Procurement can act as a facilitator to promote sales across the organization into other business units, and QBRs can be used as an opportunity to cross-sell in the business.

Procurement also has a responsibility to change the nature of the sales relationship and to ensure that all decision-makers are brought into the process. The facilitator (Procurement) and influencer (business) need to work together to render a unified decision. Procurement is not the brains and legs — they are the spinal cord. If Procurement is doing their job, information should be flowing throughout the organization.

Question 6: How can Sales and Procurement work through difficult terms and conditions?

After the sales team has been awarded a deal, the sales process is not yet over. The contract still needs to be negotiated. And in some cases, the contract contains onerous terms, including unlimited limits of liability. In some cases, the contract is part of the RFP process. If this is the case, then the team should initiate the contract review process early in the RFP process to avoid delays later in the process.

Discussions relative to terms on the contract should focus on how the risk architecture is structured and where the risk is perceived to lie in the work to be performed. Some attorneys are very good at fleshing out these elements in contract reviews. If Procurement can work to offer the stipulated terms and conditions on the front end of the RFP — stating the standard terms and conditions for logistics, limits of liability, etc. — they can be reviewed early. If they are indeed contentious, legal teams can begin conducting discussions early, particularly if there is a high likelihood of a positive outcome. If the terms, however, focus primarily on scope and pricing, there may be no need for legal to get involved at all. In most cases, lawyers will not get involved unless there is corporate policy or an esoteric requirement; otherwise, there may be no need for their input on operational perspectives of the contract.

Initiating the process of review of the T&Cs at the beginning of the RFI/P/Q process is a best practice. Insist on suppliers getting the proposed red-lines of the contract to you when they submit their bids. This not only expedites the process, but gives you warning as to who will be willing to work with you to drive acceptable terms and who will not. This avoids a lot of wasted effort on the back end, and the possibility that you may choose a supplier with whom you can never come to agreement, requiring you to start the bid process all over again.

We all know that boilerplate T&C discussions can be laborious, time consuming, and not really add any value in the end. Contracts are not for when things go right — they are for when things go wrong, badly. So to make this process less cumbersome and more relevant, in the bid process, tell your suppliers that you expect them only to red-line the 3-4 clauses that are most meaningful, and if they red-line the whole document, their bid will be automatically excluded. Get people to focus only on what's really important and brings value to the equation, and represents a fair sharing of risk. After all, what is a contract but an agreement between two or more parties to share risk and return.

A preemptive conversation on legal terms and conditions before a customer pursuit is also an activity that the sales team should engage in. The legal language will vary significantly based on industry risk; energy and chemical companies tend to have much stronger legal language due to the stronger liabilities they have. This is especially true if the contract contains onerous terms such as "unlimited indemnification." In such cases, there will need to be a cap negotiated, and a standard document will cover the typical limits of liability on major events in a preventive fashion. Procurement will typically try to engage the supplier using "their" contract, which will of course favor their organization. But getting involved early is especially important, as Procurement may not be willing to side with the supplier in a legal battle. This can result in unfortunate outcomes when the award is made, but the contract terms prevent a go-live from happening!

In most cases, if the legal teams are standing between your company and the business, they know that time is ticking, and it is in their best interests to put the agreement into place. Legal can be your business advocate if they are involved early, especially if caps on limitations of liability are involved. Getting to an agreed-on position regarding a liability risk is usually a proactive activity that both parties want to get settled. In general, getting lawyers involved as little as possible is the goal.

Nevertheless, it can take time. A large pharmaceutical company took eight months to agree on legal terms, and in this case, both legal teams were very stubborn. However, legal is responsible for signing off on the business risk, but may be more flexible if Procurement or Sales is willing to sign off and accept the risk. That may involve an internal negotiation with the legal team, who will state their dislike, but the officer has to accept that going forward with that potential liability outstanding. This again emphasizes the importance of proactive, early management of the relationship that should be addressed early in the renewal process. Contentious language should be brought forward as early as possible. Prolonged contract terms negotiations can start the relationship on the wrong foot from the first day and result in adversarial relationships. The same thing goes for indemnifications and businesspeople who "color outside the lines," and proceed with these outstanding items; they may face a potential legal issue down the road. For example, DHL sold a company and indemnified the company regarding drivers being considered employees, not contractors, and this bubbled up three years later as a $100 million liability.

Lately, the number of terms requiring legal review are expanding. In addition to indemnification and limitation of liability clauses, cybersecurity concerns are driving closer adherence to company's obligations regarding protection of intellectual property, work product, data privacy, *personally identifiable information* (PII), and what happens in the event of a data breach or ransomware incident. GDPR (General Data Protection Regulation) legislation in Europe has put significant penalties in place for companies who don't comply, and fines can amount to as much as 4 percent of their global revenue!

Using external counsel is also considered a generally bad idea by both Sales and Procurement. Even though internal legal teams may be tied up, an external counsel will show up wanting to show their value and will seek to "bog things down," especially if they have little experience on these types of contracts and don't understand the operational conditions. This can significantly deteriorate the relationship.

Many suppliers have a history of using rigorous safety standards and protocols aligned with those of their key customers. A lot of time is spent on contracts consumed in the development of exhibits in each contract, as almost every point has to be documented with a KPI. Having a detailed contract with details spelled out is to the benefit of both parties and may catch some procurement people by surprise.

On the other hand, procurement is moving more toward national contracts with fewer, larger suppliers. For large volume purchases, a standard contract is needed to minimize intervention by the sites.

Conclusions

This chapter has identified many of the complex interactions and discussions that need to take place to drive mutual value between Sales and Procurement. The most important feature of collaborative contracting as we've discussed is continuous, transparent, and open communication between the parties. Many of the frameworks, structures, and tools discussed in this chapter can serve as the scaffolding to ensure the right types of communication are underway — but in the end, it is also about having the right people and the right personalities to manage buyer–seller relationships. We explore this issue more as we delve on in the book.

Chapter 5:
The "Ask" of the Procurement/ Procure-to-Pay (P2P) and Supply Chain Organizations

(and why they are not usually aligned to the strategy of the company)

P2P and supply chain organizations are being asked to perform a growing portfolio of services that take exceptional effort and talent to execute, have significant impact on operating margins, and yet are not truly aligned to the strategy or the organizational structure of the company and the way it does business. This chapter explores the disconnect between sourcing and supply strategies and company success. We look at Finance's role in determining how procurement functions are funded and structured, and how the *financial planning and analysis* (FP&A) budgeting process often does not sync with Procurement's category management mission and objectives or align it with the company's metrics for success.

When I (Howard) first made the jump early in my career from Finance to Procurement, I received a lot of comments questioning the wisdom of my doing so and the lower status that it would bring. An MBA from a top 10 business school was a wasted asset in this reactionary function, or so I was told. After all, Finance was looked up to as the strategic engineers that drove P&Ls, balance sheets, cash flow statements, M&A (mergers and acquisitions), and capital expenditure decisions that drove the stock price and reputation of the company in the *Wall Street Journal*, while P2P was just a bunch of order-placers and grunts. ... Finance flicked its wrist, and P2P got to writhe in pain from being at the tail end of the bull whip.

Compare that to what I was initially doing in controllership — setting budgets, then tracking variances to budgets every month and reporting them, then making monthly budget forecasts based on variances to budget, then quarterly forecasts and variances to budgets, yada yada. We would publish these to our department heads and the general managers who had P&L responsibilities for the product lines, and you know what they would do with them? Absolutely nothing. It was meaningless because it didn't tell them anything that they didn't already know.

Fortunately, I moved on from that into capital expenditure and risk analysis where I was preparing financial packages with projected returns on investments (ROIs), net present value of cash flows, risk/reward scenarios, and other critical information for the board to make decisions on whether or not to approve major capital projects. This was exciting, at least, and felt important, but there was still an element of this that didn't fulfill my needs — I was an analyst, not a decision-maker.

So for me, I saw it as a simple proposition: Procurement (called *Energy & Materials* by this company) was the only job in the company, other than Sales, where I could walk into work every day and say that I'm not leaving until I make a large dollar impact on the bottom line. There was something very exciting about that, being an official agent of the company, empowered to make decisions on what to buy and with whom, and at what price and how that contributed to the building of the company's plants and products that generated revenues from customers. Also, I could put more of my MBA finance skills to work in procurement than I ever did in finance. I had to analyze commodities and trends, analyze suppliers and their strengths and weaknesses and supply chains and their future prospects, then analyze my own company to understand our products and services and how the third-party supply base could help us achieve our short- and long-term goals. It presented a combination of analytical and strategic skill challenges that excited me. In addition, there was the legal side of the work with *terms & conditions* (I had also applied to law school but didn't go down that route) and it satisfied my penchant for getting into the nitty gritty of contract law and negotiations. To me, it appeared to be the perfect profession that would both challenge me intellectually and satisfy my professional goals.

I will tell you right now that I have no regrets about becoming a procurement professional, despite all of the sourcing and supply chain nightmares that I endured. If you want to be a player in the game, you've got to get into the battles and fight them. I had to work cross-functionally throughout my career with every part of the business. Being in operations in many ways enslaves you 24/7, but in virtually every function in the corporate world, if you want to differentiate yourself and be successful, you have to be willing to get in the line of fire.

A Day in the Life of Procurement

In Procurement, I always started out doing the basics, as we should. First things first — we need to know what we are buying, how much and from whom, and is it meeting our business requirements? Who is at the controls, making the buying decisions? Does past buying reflect future needs? What is the spend profile, direct versus indirect spend, and is it global/international spend versus regional/local spend? Is Procurement being brought in on the front end of sourcing processes to help buy at competitive market pricing, or at the tail end to push the paper across the finish line and get purchase orders issued so that suppliers can get paid? Can cost increases be passed on to the customer, or is the end product or service being sold subject to market pressures that limit pricing flexibility?

Then we have to address how we will measure our performance. As one CEO used to tell us, "If you're not keeping score, you're only practicing" (he was a former world-class tennis player). So we start off with defining our procurement metrics with savings, the worst of all procurement metrics (with the exception of all other procurement metrics), and we hope that it drives the right behaviors, not the wrong behaviors (as one supply chain executive once told me, "Good luck with that!"). Then we ask ourselves, is the goal to deliver P&L savings, market savings, benchmarked savings, savings to budget (ugh, like budgets have any relevance to the market), cost avoidance, total cost of ownership (TCO) optimization, ROI, net present value of future cash flows, free cash flow (FCF), working capital preservation, value engineering, cycle time first to market with innovation/new product offerings, risk reduction, process efficiency improvement through Lean Six Sigma that eliminates waste and saves time and resources, or a combination of all of them? Some are tougher to quantify than others, and you need someone in Finance to validate it all or else you won't have any credibility.

Regardless of how you measure performance, it may not be seen by internal budget holders/ decision-makers as part of the delivery of the company strategy. Therefore, Procurement is often brought in on the back end of sourcing decisions so as not to interfere with the supplier prefer- ences of the budget holders but merely to optimize a price and delivery concern and facilitate payments to suppliers. As long as Procurement doesn't abuse the supplier and sour the relation- ship, it's cool. If they save some money against the budget, that's cool too because they will use that to spend on some other stuff they want to buy.

I mentioned budgets, and yes, I get convulsions thinking about it. But most companies run on flawed budgeting processes, and very few apply zero-based budgeting to the process (an exception being private equity, where ruthless cost cutting can be the cultural imperative, driven by leveraged buyouts that saddle the company with enormous debt loads and a need to cover the interest payments on the debt). Budgets grant managers the "right" to spend the company's money, and the incentive is rarely to return that unspent money to the business. Budgets are a control measure that companies use to plan their P&L and return to shareholders and can be ratcheted up or down during a year depending on the performance of Sales in generating revenue in line with sales projections and quotas. But they also act as the enemy of demand management, encouraging unnecessary spending when times are good or on plan, and in my humble opinion, are the bane of all high-performing organizations. What relationship does a market price have to a budgeted "price last paid"? It says nothing about what something should cost, only about what you paid for it last time.

But some procurement organizations align their goals and objectives solely around their stakeholder budgets, seeing that as fulfillment of their mission and the path toward achieving recognition as a "trusted advisor to the business." If your objective (and culture) rewards you for answering every request to "Jump!" with an answer of "How high?!" and then you proceed to do whatever your stakeholder/budget holder asks you to do, then congratulations. As we stated in Chapter 3, just don't call yourself a service organization, because you haven't added any value to the equation — you're just a servant organization. But who am I to knock that if your reward structure reinforces that behavior?

What I Learned

The first thing I learned was that if you wanted to be a true value-added partner to the business and not a servant, you will never have enough time or resources or perfect data or processes and systems to do the job as it's meant to be done. You will always be overworked, understaffed, stressed out, and stretched beyond capacity if you try to work every contract and every bid in your category and execute your category strategy and run your supplier relationship management (SRM) with your key suppliers the way it is meant to be done, and then apply a metric to it to measure the impact. Nobody in Procurement is over-resourced, ever! You have to make a choice: Do you run your job, or does your job run you? Too often, I made the wrong choice, as you probably do on occasion.

How is the procurement function actually budgeted?

The procurement budget is often set to a benchmarked cost standard that pegs it based on a percentage of total revenue or total sales, general, and administrative (SG&A) costs. For example, some studies showed if you spent more than 0.64 percent of company revenue on a procurement function, it was below "world class" efficiency. Another standard has to do with head count ratio per dollar of spend. A general rule is that you need to allocate $20 to $25 million of spend per SMs/GCMs to manage the company's spend appropriately. In this, you also need to consider if you have the right balance between SMs/GCMs and those who supported them in Operations and analytical roles, SRM and Supplier Diversity. Normally, you don't want these "overhead" costs within the procurement function to amount to more than 10 to 20 percent of the total procurement budget. The people at Hackett Advisory Services are great at accumulating such data and helped to create these standards.

So why are procurement functions usually under-resourced to do our jobs as a value-added service organization? Why does it feel like pulling teeth to get funding to fill head count, invest in systems that would consolidate data and aid productivity and improve our cycle time for running RFI/P/Qs and the SMP? Why are we competing for resources with all other functions when we can demonstrate that a buyer could/ should generate savings at 3 times their salary, a sourcing manager (SM) at 5 times their salary, and a global category manager (GCM) at 7 times their salary? And despite the increased number of responsibilities that Procurement has been handed, why isn't there a commensurate increase in head count to handle it? Because no matter how much you save, Finance will usually treat procurement as an overhead cost in its budgeting, no different than the accounting/controllership function, or the quality function, or the accounts receivable function. Very few procurement functions get incremental budget based on its savings generation capabilities unless sponsored by the C-Suite as part of a major transformation effort for the company.

But the job of the SMs and GCMs in value-added procurement functions keeps growing and growing. Not only are we responsible for generating savings (however measured), but we became responsible for also running the SRM process and finding ways to leverage the global spend footprint of the company. Then we became responsible for supplier diversity, and not just using diverse-owned businesses (minority — Black and Hispanic, woman, veteran, disabled veteran, LGBTQ+, HUBZone) but also qualifying them as suppliers, getting them added to bid lists, and mentoring suppliers through the maze of company processes and systems.

Then we became responsible for *environmental, social, and governance* (ESG) monitoring of our supply base to make sure they weren't using subcontractors that used child labor, or mined minerals from forbidden sources, or weren't on a terrorist FACTA list. We were responding to the Board and shareholder pressure to reduce and track progress on the carbon footprint within the company and within its supply base, and operate in an ethical manner, including the use of diverse businesses. Our supplier diversity work fit neatly into this, but then we were also asked to negotiate all sorts of protections into our contracts. We had to tighten up our T&Cs to make sure that we weren't violating people's data protection rights (the EU passed GDPR legislation in 2017) or exposing the company's intellectual property or work product ownership to those who might steal it. We had to address potential cybersecurity intrusions, insisting that our suppliers (and their lawyers) agreed to unlimited liability if any of these things should happen, and be properly insured (and track their *certificates of insurance* to make sure they were renewed annually). This almost doubled the cycle time to negotiate contract red-lines and get signoff approvals. We were always expected to make sure that our supply chains were secure and that availability of supply in accordance with our business needs was guaranteed, but never have we faced such a challenging time as this with simultaneous black swan events of pandemic and war.

As if this wasn't enough, we were extracting data manually into spreadsheets to try to come up with accurate spends by function or department with the suppliers for SKUs and services that had a thousand differing descriptions of what was being supplied to us. Somehow, we are supposed to consolidate all of these data (yes, data are plural) and turn it into a coherent sourcing strategy. Of course, data are always backward-looking, so it told us what had happened but didn't inform us on whether those spend patterns would be repeated, which takes endless meetings with stakeholders in the business to understand their future plans. Then we have to do stakeholder mapping to know who will support our efforts, have influence in making change possible, and are going to help us with implementation.

Procurement steps on its own toes — rules of engagement and who owns what

When you do all of this planning and set out to execute the strategies, there are the Procurement disputes of category definitions and lines of demarcation that need to be drawn so that SMs and GCMs aren't fighting over who manages which spend and strategies and suppliers (larger suppliers often tend to supply different goods and services across a number of categories and geographies and functions). There is a lot at stake, because savings cannot be claimed by more than one individual without distorting the reporting of procurement value generation to stakeholders and Finance. What happens if the desktop services strategy includes laptop hardware, core software images, telecommunications capabilities and a service contract for warranty repairs — those may be four separate SM roles in the IT procurement function but requires a unified approach and ownership to maintain the execution of the desktop strategy. How about when the marketing categories includes data systems that "belong" in the IT procurement space — who gets to lead it, and who has to follow and support? (By the way, marketing C-Suite executives at many companies have higher data and systems spends than CIOs and CISOs at many companies now). There are too many examples of these cross-category overlaps to mention, and guess what — category definitions have to keep changing as companies look toward digital solutions as part of their ability to deliver services. As we "pivot to the cloud," we aren't buying hardware, per se, but *software as a service* (SaaS) and subscriptions instead. Capital SMs are being informed that what they buy may no longer be capitalized and will now be expensed instead — do their category responsibility and role (and performance measures) change with it?

Once you get around these rules of engagement of who owns which categories and how they are defined, you have to sort out who manages which suppliers and which stakeholders (who also might have multiple asks of the procurement function in different categories but don't want to deal with seven different procurement people). You also have to figure out how to deal with changes in personnel, either in your own organization or in the stakeholder organization, especially if there are reorganizations ongoing in the company (and there always are). We talk a lot nowadays about having more efficient systems to help us do all of this work better, and some of the plug & play digital tools are really helpful, but if all of these changes result in constantly having to plug new information manually into these apps, it creates a lot more grunt work just to keep the systems updated. Living with a large, multi-module upstream-to-downstream procurement system and having a group that represented 10 to 20 percent of my head count running it because of all of the systems problems that generated work for my SMs/GCMs (accounting, invoices, payments, SOX (Sarbanes–Oxley Act) controls, etc.), I always felt like we were working for the system as opposed to the system working for us.

On top of all of this, someone will come up with the idea that this procurement work should be outsourced to companies that can do the work cheaper and more efficiently than the internal procurement organization. If they are not cheaper, they can offset that by generating higher levels of savings because they have more category expertise than the internal SMs/GCMs — they are able to apply that expertise across many companies and have a database of what represents highly market competitive pricing. They also may have better procurement systems in place for managing the entire life cycle, from purchase requisition to RFI/P/Q to award of contract to contract adherence to final invoicing, issuance of receivers against invoices and payment. I should know — I was one of the consultants used in this manner for almost five years; I also managed the outside consultants who were brought in to work side by side with our own SMs/GCMs and acted as variable resources to help bolster the team, get them kickstarted, and educate the SMs/GCMs on the categories.

The problem, of course, is that these are short-term solutions unless you want to make it a permanent outsource of the function, which some companies choose to do (then bring it inside after a few years when they get sick of paying the high prices for these services). Then there are the stakeholder and supplier complaints that come with the territory, and who will deal with the delivery and payment disputes, and whether receivers were issued for the services that trigger the payments, or quality issues at delivery, or monitoring and managing the KPIs and SLAs that were supposed to improve quality and service. How about handling the last-minute end-of-quarter or end-of-year purchases that functions want to make to use up their budgets so they can justify at least that much allocation for next year's budget? Somebody has to do this (*whether* they should do this is another matter), and the one mistake that you can count on is that companies will never spend enough money for the resources required for the governance of the outsource relationship. It never happens!

Working at Cross-Currents Within the Company

Whatever we do and however we are organized, we are always working at cross-currents within the organization because of some very simple truths:

- Finance funds by project and function, not by global/international/regional/local categories.

- Nobody who has a budgetary, P&L, or project responsibility will voluntarily take a hit to their budget, P&L, or project funding for a category-sourcing strategy that creates winners and losers, even if it benefits the corporation as a whole.

- Savings reporting works at cross-purposes if Finance grabs all of the budgetary and project-funding savings generated by Procurement because it leaves nothing to the budget holders for when things go wrong, and they have to cover overruns.

- There are situations in the company where the only way to make an impact is to change what exists, even if a great category strategy has been put in place. (Can you imagine a new marketing director coming into a position and saying, "I'm going to do exactly what the last person did in this job."?)

- Running cross-functional sourcing teams is difficult, as many on the team from the stakeholder functions may have a different agenda from Procurement. Teams tend to gravitate toward what I call "lowest common denominator" solutions in which everyone gets what they want, which leads to smaller, incremental wins, as opposed to pushing the envelope. There is little desire for the stakeholders to take on added risk and institute changes, even those that can lead to breakthrough solutions (huge wins of 30 to 40 percent cost reduction) if it means creating winners and losers on the team. To do this right, everyone on the team needs to "lean into discomfort, and get comfortable in that uncomfortable place," but what is their incentive and reward system for doing so? It probably isn't even part of their performance objectives, which tend to be directly associated with other functional activities.

- Instituting new processes, onboarding new suppliers, and giving Procurement a seat at the table in this decision-making, especially in "third rail" categories such as HR benefits, legal services, creative agency selection, preferred airlines and hotels and car rental companies (people want their loyalty points for personal use from business travel!), real estate leases and facilities management, and all IT categories of spend means either a perceived or real loss of power and authority for the budget holder or stakeholder that runs the function.

- Procurement people are often being asked to do all of this without the change management and leadership training required to help people "lean into discomfort," and often don't have what is referred to as the "soft skills" to be successful at this. In addition, many of those SMs and GCMs assigned to the work are working with people cross-functionally that are two, three, or four levels higher than them in the organization at the senior director, executive director, and VP level.

A Simple Truth

In fact, there is one other simple truth that puts Procurement into a cross-current with the stakeholders that they support that makes the job so difficult. It's the equivalent of saying to them, "I'm from the IRS and I'm here to help you." They don't believe you! The IRS (Procurement) is not here to help them build up their budget, expand their organization, and broaden their span of control, and that's the WIIFM ("What's in it for me?") they are looking for. Sometimes, Procurement tries to respond by colocating its resources in with the function or department as a confidence-building measure and in the spirit of teamwork. We know that by embedding within the function, we can learn a lot more about the category specifics and stakeholder needs, improve responsiveness, get access to data, and develop the knowledge that can help us develop more robust buying strategies which satisfy our stakeholders. But we also run the risk of our SMs representing the interests of the stakeholder over the interests of the procurement function. This plays into the whole centralization versus decentralization argument and striking the right balance between having local knowledge and applying global best practices.

Very simply, we are talking about what are perceived by others to be power struggles and a fight for control, and there is very little confidence from the stakeholders that the procurement person will really care about the levels of quality and service and innovation that can be derived from favored suppliers in exchange for lower cost. Besides, the stakeholder is the expert in the category, not the SM or GCM assigned to it (at least not initially). Then comes the issue of executing the change of supplier, and the resources required to execute the change, monitor the performance to new KPIs and SLAs that might be established in the contract, and there will always be disputes and misunderstandings that will need to be mediated in the process. Who will do that work, and why is Procurement taking my life that was running so smoothly and turning it upside down on me, creating all sorts of stresses and dissatisfaction within individuals on my team?

When you look at all of this and what Procurement is being asked to do, and is expected to meet and exceed all goals that are set, there is one other big disconnect: How does this tie to the strategy of the company (unless that strategy is simply to operate within budget)? The answer is that, oftentimes, it does not. In my last experience leading global indirect procurement for a software company, the company published 28 metrics for success in the marketplace, and Procurement's mission tied into only one of them: operating profit. One of 28 — why bother? That's when we knew we had to change the strategic vision and mission of the procurement function. It was a matter of relevance. This wasn't the first time I had felt this.

A way to better align Procurement with the strategy of the company is to become revenue focused

In order to become relevant, we needed to get laser-focused on what the procurement organization could do to facilitate and drive **revenue growth** in the business and make it actionable and noticeable. The things that mattered to our executives were the efficiency and effectiveness to our salesforce, the faster rollout of products and updates from R&D, the rollout and commercialization of new products that were acquired through licensing and M&A deals, getting existing customers to renew their purchases, making sure that existing customers were not abusing our licensing and were properly trued-up annually, and helping our customers pivot to the cloud and move from on-premise licensing solutions to hybrid cloud SaaS subscription service offerings. In addition, this redesign of our products was resulting in massive growth of one expense category that was impacting our gross and operating margins: the use of public cloud compute and storage space. Wall Street was measuring our company's success by looking at the growth rate in SaaS-based revenue, free cash flow, and *annual recurring revenue* (ARR).

In addition, we took on a strategic role that others in the organization could not take — we became the air traffic controllers of the complex environment in the technology space that thrives on "coopetition." While you must always firewall negotiations on what you are selling from what you are buying, and with whom, we saw Procurement as uniquely positioned to keeping the company informed of the strategic nature of these relationships and to let the left hand know what the right hand was doing. Our major suppliers were in many cases also our major customers, but also in some cases actual or potential competitors to our business. It's the equivalent of the Apple–Samsung relationship, where they constantly sue each other for patent infringements on smartphone technology, but Apple also sources $2 billion in smartphone parts from Samsung. Procurement supported our sales, marketing, strategic alliances, R&D/engineering, finance/M&A and technology CIO/CISO functions, so we saw what was happening across the entire playing field. Nobody was better positioned in the company to play this role, so we made it part of our offering to the stakeholders to become the air traffic controllers in this complex space of "coopetition." Yes, it took time and resources (and upgraded skills) to pull this off, and I had to make trade-offs by giving up other funded positions to go down this route. But most importantly, it gave us a relevance to our stakeholders that they had never experienced before, and a relevance to ourselves that we were filling a void that the company needed filled.

Tracking procurement categories and projects that supported these efforts became a focal point of our long-range strategic plan as an organization, and we tracked how we contributed to revenue growth in all of these efforts. We made it our lead headline in our communications with the business. We didn't stop doing all of the other things — we just made sure that we were not positioning ourselves as a control/budget-oriented organization based on "Savings R Us," "Negotiations R Us," or "Contracts R Us."

Earlier in my career, shortly after joining SmithKline Beecham, a large multinational pharmaceutical company, I got the feeling that cost was only relevant to us in Procurement. Nobody else seemed to care. Now it's one thing to feel it, but it's an entirely different thing when your CEO says it! As a function trying to grow and establish its roots and relevance, we set an initial annual savings target, probably in the range of $150 million. We were instituting a five-stage sourcing management process and working at forming cross-functional category teams when the company announced it had made a settlement with the federal government, agreeing to pay $450 million for running unnecessary lab tests and overcharging for the tests as well (of course, we did not have to admit guilt). The CEO included in the announcement, to assuage shareholders, that the $450 million one-time penalty payment was "immaterial." From that one statement, I easily derived that what we were doing as a procurement function, to drive savings at one third of that amount, could also be considered by the company to be "immaterial." It was a deflating moment. We had defined our purpose and existence in the context of "Savings R Us," but no function in the company had bought into it as a strategy.

Procurement functions and the leaders within the function are also guilty of the WIIFM of trying to expand their budgets and organizations and grow their span of control. Why not? This is how most managers get rewarded and get their jobs upgraded in publicly traded corporations.

It's a reality of life. Human nature guides us to do whatever is in our best interests. Heck, capitalism itself is based on this very real tenet. I got a lesson in this when I once applied for a director position under a CPO. The CPO was setting up a new strategic sourcing organization and he had mapped out three direct reports with different category responsibilities in his organization chart. When I interviewed with him, I told him that he could save some budget money if he hired me because I had experience running two of the three category groupings. He immediately rejected that idea (and me), explaining that would reduce his "span of control" if he only had two directors reporting to him. I was such an idiot not to see that; I had totally forgotten about the WIIFM.

So how do you leverage the global spend footprint of the company to maximize the company's profitability, drive growth in revenue and operating margins, and simultaneously reduce Procurement's budget/cost to operate and improve user satisfaction and experience while aligning the function strategically to the company goals? It's a tall order, to say the least. CPOs need to rewrite the playbook, but it requires a huge change in both the culture of Procurement and how Procurement's role is perceived by the organization, which we will cover in Chapter 8. New technology and lighter plug & play apps and systems are also part of the answer, and we will cover that in Chapter 11 (bad dual entendre, I know). But as stated in an earlier chapter, if the CPO has a different WIIFM, it will most likely take the form of a wash-rinse-repeat cycle.

Chapter 6:
Organizing and Understanding the Procurement Organization

Background

Following a working session with Procurement and a group of business development executives held in January 2017, it became clear to me (Robert) that there was a need for both *business development* (BD) and operations managers to better understand the position of Procurement in organizations, which has dramatic implications for how the sales process needs to unfold and how the business relationship should be designed over the life of the contract.

This chapter provides guidelines around **a decision process** that identifies the dimensions of supplier–customer relationships that calls for the right tactical and strategic actions to "retain" an existing customer and to grow the account. The framework for the tool is shown below. The variability of characteristics of procurement in the organization results in significant differences in how to build the interorganizational relationship.

Using the Tool

We developed a framework embodied in a tool that helps organizations determine how to interact with the procurement function.

- The tool requires executives to answer a series of structured questions that will result in a dialogue around the current status of the relationship with the customer.

- In some cases, you may not be able to confidently answer a question and you are asked to use your "best judgement."

- For some questions, you may require access to other market research on the focal firm in question, which can help in providing additional guidelines and insights.

In this chapter we explore the following:

- How procurement plays a role in the award decision, as well as how operational roles need to be integrated into this approach effectively.

- Guidelines on whether a particular business opportunity is worth pursuing further and the associated barriers that may exist if the decision is to move forward.

- When required, identify the need for additional market research early in the development of the business opportunity.

- Recommended strategies and tactics for sales executives to follow.

Several important outcomes are essential to building solid interorganizational relationships:

1. ***Educating Procurement about your company***. Education of procurement leaders on supplier capabilities will lead to improved positioning and credibility within customer organizations. Specifically, Sales needs to be more proactive in engaging Procurement in discussions to shift their perception that your company is a "leveraged" item, implying that it is a commodity. This is the first primary barrier to overcome when working with Procurement, as individuals (even category managers) may not be aware of the full range of your capabilities, nor fully understand the scope of work involved in the product or services. Education of procurement will ensure that scopes of work in bids consider all relevant factors, that the key stakeholder requirements are embedded to allow an "apples to apples comparison," and will ensure that you have a fair shot at winning and/or retaining the customer account.

2. ***Procurement's role in the sales cycle***. The stages in the contracting cycle need to be fully understood, along with the shifting roles and responsibilities that occur throughout this process. If you wait until the request for quotation (RFQ) comes out before beginning your target account research, it is too late. Understanding of the relative power of Procurement in the decision cycle is imperative. Development of this knowledge requires collecting information from multiple participants inside of the organization. Elements such as the criteria used for evaluating bids, the level of satisfaction with the current performance, prior experiences with your company at other locations, the mindset and philosophy of the CPO, and multiple other factors requires greater understanding and research earlier in the cycle. A general rule of thumb that emerged is this: "The minute you sign a contract, you begin preparing for the renewal or the new bid."

3. ***Performance measurement and analysis***. Once the role of Procurement is understood, there also needs to be an understanding of their specific goals, both within their category management structure, their cost targets and portfolio, upcoming business strategies, capital renewal cycles, and other activities going on within their business. Understanding these factors will play heavily in determining the key success measures that will determine customer satisfaction levels as well as driving new business opportunities within a 6- to 12-month window. In particular, the development of new metrics that capture major wins in reducing the total cost of ownership (TCO) will require a structured approach to data collection, performance analytics, and report generation to support current accounts, but also build a portfolio of "wins" for use in new client account engagement.

Decision Points

Instructions: For each decision point, read the description of the decision points involved in the strategy development process. These definitions can be interpreted and discussed by the business development team, as they may not be inclusive of all characteristics of the organization, but in each case the team must answer every question embodied in the tool. If the team is unsure, then employ a default value closest to the situation. The unit of analysis in this case is the **specific business unit** associated with the customer (not the entire enterprise). The reason for this will become apparent.

Decision 1: What is the tenure of your company with this customer?

- **<3 years** — If this is a new customer, then it is imperative that this decision process be followed. A customer evaluation checklist may be employed to determine whether the customer should be actively pursued. However, it is likely that your company has not yet established a strong history of performance even if it is an existing customer, as three years is a relatively short period following signing of a contract. There is a strong likelihood that the customer will put the contract out for bid if it is an existing customer. In such cases it is more important than ever for your company to connect with Procurement, unless there is already a strong relationship in place. If you have had the firm as a customer in the past, then you are essentially starting all over again at day 1, as the personnel and leadership has likely changed in Procurement.

- **>3 years** — This suggests that there may be a good relationship upon which to build. However, if the relationship is only with one division or operation, then you may not have a strong representation yet within the company. In other cases, the CEO or executive suite may have changed, or a recent acquisition has changed the nature of the board, which has led to an increased focus on cost cutting. In either of these cases, the goal here would be to leverage the existing relationships but also begin the process of learning more about Procurement and its relationship to the business.

Decision 2: What is the organization's procurement maturity in the customer's transformation journey?

Every organization today is seeking to transform their procurement function and can be viewed along a spectrum on this journey. Prior research conducted by the team suggests that the following spectrum can be used in mapping the target account's progress. (Further details of the Procurement Leadership Transformation Accelerator tool is provided in the Appendix.)

SC Maturity Levels versus Savings Opportunities

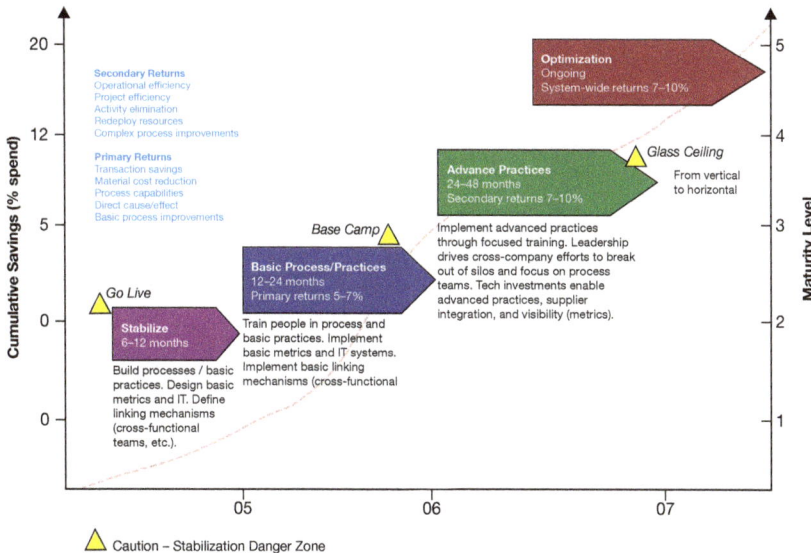

Outsourcing example:

- **LOW (Maturity Stages 1 and 2)** — The business unit has an internal operation, or is in the early stages of outsourcing transportation, warehousing, or customer service processes. The business unit in this case may have a high level of resistance to outsourcing due to job losses, and there may be significant change management and transition activity associated with this event. This category should also be used in cases when there is a single business unit that has internally managed logistics operations, even though you may be doing business with another division.

- **HIGH (Maturity Stages 3 and 4)** — The business unit in question has a significant history of working with third-party providers, whether it is you or another party. Managers may have a track record of KPIs and cost measurements available to review. If it is already an existing customer, the goal here would be to retain this customer by building a strong business case.

Some of the questions that may help stimulate discussion include the following:

- What is the organizational hierarchy in Procurement around your category that you fit in — is he/she a category manager, director of sourcing (transportation and related services), and CPO?

- Who are the members/roles of the cross-functional team responsible for implementing strategic sourcing for your category?

- Do they have a formal strategic sourcing program?

- Are they organized around spend categories?

- How much do they spend on your category?

- Is the spend category fragmented or consolidated?

Decision 3: What is Procurement's influence on the decision? (Low, High)

- **Low** — Procurement is not a mature function, and as such does not have a great deal of influence on the decision. One way of assessing this is relative to whether the organization has a strong category management process in place, which is more likely if they have a high level of procurement maturity.

- **High** — In high maturity organizations, Procurement may essentially "control the purse strings," and therefore has a major influence on the decision. However, the degree of influence is assessed in Decision 4.

It is also telling to explore where Procurement reports to in the organization (see Chapter 10). Who they report to will have an influence on the bias that exists in the Procurement department.

For example, at a large CPG (consumer packaged goods) company, Procurement reported to Finance. The only measure of performance was *purchase price variance* (PPV). This was also being driven by the CEO. But is PPV really the best measure to reward Procurement?

Procurement is always thinking about cost savings, year over year. But is this really a true measure of competitiveness? So Procurement will have a budgeted amount for, say 4.5 cents per unit for a product, when the current price is 4 cents. They are able to hammer the supplier and get them down to 4.2 cents, so Procurement declares victory and says they saved their organization a lot of money — 0.3 cents per unit! But is this really savings?

In our opinion, this is the wrong way to measure procurement. In our collective experience of more than 70 years working in procurement, we have never met a procurement person who has ever missed a cost savings target! Why is that?

Instead, Procurement should be focused on the competitive advantage they deliver to their company, vis-à-vis their competition. This idea extended back to a meeting I had with a chief procurement officer (CPO) and his chief financial officer (CFO). At an informal dinner, the CPO half-jokingly asks: "Sales guys get all the limelight. Here I have delivered more than one billion dollars of savings and I don't get the same respect. Why is that?"

The CFO had a great answer. Sales organizations are always measured on revenue growth and achievement — but they always have a second dimension, which is market share. If you grow your top line by 30 percent but your market share drops, someone else is growing faster than 30 percent. Procurement will only get respect if you have a dimension that is the equivalent of market share.

So, "savings" is the same as revenue growth; however, what is Procurement's equivalent of "market share"? Saving $100 million is great and that might have represented a 3 percent reduction in the company's cost structure, but what if the competition had been able to achieve a significantly higher reduction in that same year? Would that not erode the competitive advantage of the company?

But how can one find out how much competitors are spending? From a benchmarking perspective, every company would love to know exactly what their competitors spend on each raw material/service. This is the "holy grail." But as the saying goes, don't let great be the enemy of good — and should we strive to benchmark the unattainable?

One way is benchmark cost savings through a measure of the COGS (cost of goods sold). This includes all production items — packaging, raw materials, manufacturing costs, logistics, etc. In most cases, COGS can be derived from annual reports and can be done on an industry basis. Let's look at a simple industry: beer. If we extract COGS from annual reports over a period of time, say from 2011 to 2015, and compare them across competitors, then the COGS (Standardized) of Six Competing Beer Companies chart (next page) is produced.

COGS (Standardized) of Six Competing Beer Companies

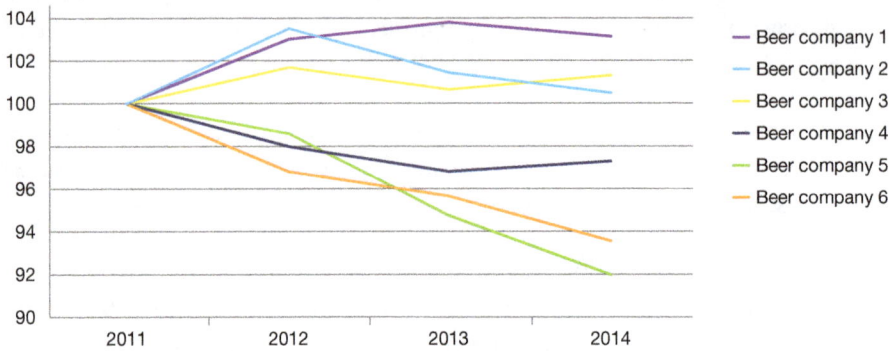

If you take 2011 as the baseline year, each of the companies would have a different COGS/revenue ratio, but let us normalize this and assume everyone starts at the exact same point: 100. As you can see, some companies end up below 100 in 2014 and some end up above. If revenue had stayed constant, three of these companies are actually spending more on COGS (per $ revenue) in 2014 than they did in 2011! However, the annual reports of these three companies has a write-up in which they talk about the massive savings delivered by Procurement. This dichotomy leads to cynicism on the true impact of procurement.

This same analysis can be applied across industries and, in general, research shows that half are doing really well and half are not. It is not the intent to explain the differences — the world is changing in many different ways; markets change and some firms may be impacted more — but everyone is operating in the same world. Ultimately, if sales is measured on relative advantage (generally market share in marketing), then procurement should be measured on cost competitiveness as well relative to the market.

If best procurement practices are followed, this can actually drive some improvements in supplier relationships. If you move to a model where the supplier makes a decent margin, cost management can be a much more open model. Japanese procurement organizations rarely change suppliers; they have long-term relationships, and while they certainly hold the supplier's feet to the fire to get a competitive price, it is open-book and there is a guarantee that the suppliers will always be making a decent margin — the supplier will invest in productivity and pass on the margins. This competitive advantage is what Procurement needs to be focused on.

In our opinion, Procurement is still too focused on price — but the biggest issues are specifications and demand. The price you pay per unit, how many units you buy, and what kinds of units you buy are the key parameters. By focusing too much on price, Procurement is not paying attention to whether they are buying the wrong things and are buying too much of them, which will impact cost. Every time one company went to the market to get the best prices on a product, they found they had the lowest price. But their COGS competitiveness was low. This was because they had 10 times the number of SKUs per $1 billion of spend — making it difficult for suppliers to work with them. Procurement needs to think about local optimal versus global optima. One bad spec, and you can get a local optima — but the real cost savings comes with the right cost specifications! COGS benchmarking can help expose these types of issues.

Decision 4: What is Procurement's role in the decision? (Do Not Manage, Influencer, Gatekeeper)

- **Do not manage** — Procurement is not actively involved in developing the request for proposal (RFP) and is only tangentially involved in running the bid or renewing the contract. In such cases, the business unit may operate in a decentralized environment. Note that it is easy for the BD team to assume this is the case, as there may not be significant precedent for Procurement involvement. In less mature organizations, the sourcing decision will be more ad hoc, will be typically led by decision-makers in the business unit, and the textbook accelerate approach of working through coaches at a local level makes sense. A buyer or senior buyer may be present.

- **Influencer** — An important foundational issue for sales personnel to understand is the relative level of procurement maturity within the organization and the extent to which the organization has developed a category management structure. This involves developing deep insights into the target account's internal organizational structure. An increasing number of organizations are going through procurement transformation initiatives and are seeking progress toward a more centralized, structured procurement organization.[1] If the company has a strong centralized category structure, it is important to understand the role of Procurement in the organization throughout the contracting cycle and how much influence they have in the supplier selection decision.

- **Gatekeeper** — Procurement is a gatekeeper generally in centralized or "center-led" procurement organizations. A center-led organization (see Table 1, page 100) generally appears in organizations with a more mature function. Understanding the governance structure and the procurement relationship with business unit stakeholders can provide important insights here and may require using a RACI or RASCI chart with your contact to really understand the clarity of the roles. Center-led organizations are supposedly allowing business units to operate independently but may have "category managers" to lead the outsourcing or contract renewal process. The RACI or RASCI chart can lead to appropriate discussions with the right people in the procurement organization structure beyond the immediate stakeholder to help educate and inform others in the organization about the supplier's capabilities. Second, it can lead to improved understanding of the governance structure for upcoming contractual negotiations and the size of the "prize" that exists across the network. Third, it can lead to important insights on business priorities and critical success factors that can lead to the right operational metrics that become important during the contracting cycle. Center-led organizations are tricky to navigate and may well depend on the personal philosophy, mindset, and culture of the CPO (see next page).

---

1 Dr. Handfield has developed a database of procurement maturity for the Fortune 500 – these elements will become available to DHL sales as a source for market research on procurement maturity and current organizational structures. The website for accessing this data will be made available in the pilot approach.

Some of the roles you might encounter when discussing procurement people in the organization include the following (please see Chapter 10 for a more in-depth discussion of this topic):

- **Chief Procurement Officer** (CPO) — May generally report to Finance (CFO), but rarely reports directly to the CEO. If the latter, Procurement is generally higher on the influence scale.

- **Category Manager for Logistics** — A category manager is in charge of sourcing the entire category, generally across the organization. This is a reliable signal of a mature procurement organization seeking to centralize their spend. They are likely going to be the gatekeeper in this instance.

- **Supplier Relationship Manager/Contract Manager** — Generally tasked with managing the contract. May only be around during the quarterly business reviews (QBRs) but will likely have a strong influence on the decision of whether to renew. They may report to the business C-suite or to the corporate executive.

- **Senior Buyers and Buyers** — Generally located within the business unit; their role is largely transactional in nature. They may be involved as influencers if they are on the team. Generally, however, they do not have a strong influence on the outcome.

It may also be useful to understand the overall structure of procurement and whether they are "centralized," "decentralized," or "center-led." A brief description, as well as advantages and disadvantages of each, is shown in Table 1.

Decision 5: Example — How does Procurement at the target view the *third-party logistics* (3PL) category, value (Performance, Resilience, TCO), or cost/price?

The level of influence may also be determined by how an organization views a category, such as the 3PL industry within their category portfolio. If the organization has a strong or developing category management structure in place, Procurement will conduct a category segmentation assessment. This can help address several key questions that are important to consider using the category segmentation and organization assessment, shown on the next page.

This category segmentation tool is derived by answering a number of questions that require the 3PL to "put themselves in Procurement's shoes." In so doing, it provides a realistic assessment of the extent to which the 3PL is considered a truly strategic partner. In the segmentation example that follows (next page), the procurement organization considers the 3PL category an important strategic category and would more likely focus on performance related to TCO, inventory turns, and other strategic measures.

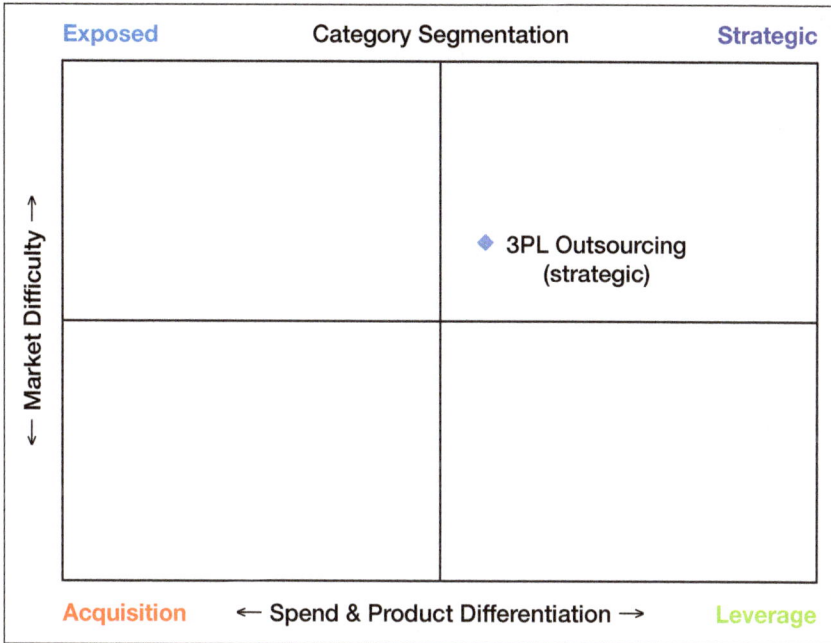

Exposed   Category Segmentation   Strategic

← Market Difficulty →

♦ 3PL Outsourcing
(strategic)

Acquisition   ← Spend & Product Differentiation →   Leverage

In the diagram below, the supplier segmentation framework also provides an indication of whether the 3PL company being evaluated is viewed as a strategic partner versus a "commodity." In both cases, if the 3PL finds that they are not in the strategic quadrant, they may be subject to bids, reverse auctions, and other "arms-length" bidding approaches. Understanding the criteria for performance evaluation is also key. If possible, the team should also understand the "scorecard" elements, and then develop preliminary insights into how they are weighted.

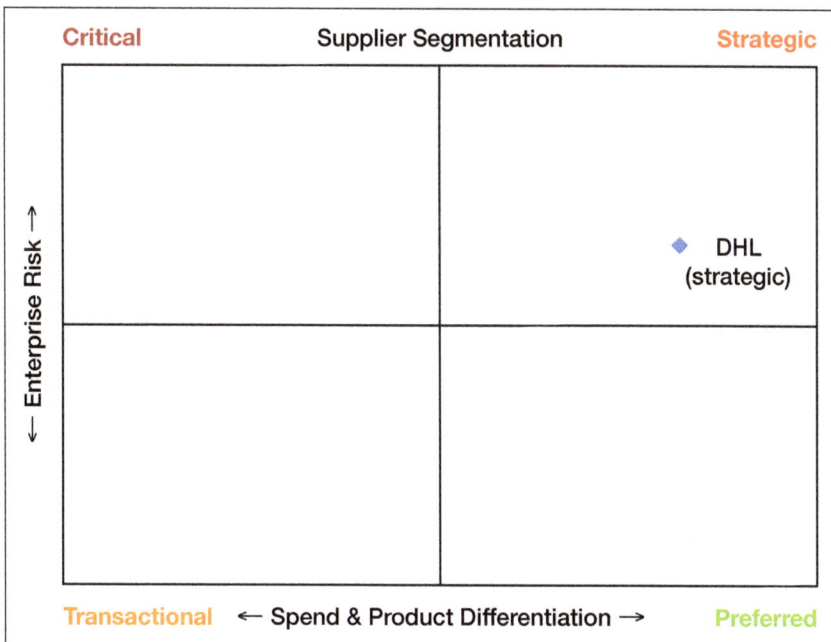

Critical   Supplier Segmentation   Strategic

← Enterprise Risk →

♦ DHL
(strategic)

Transactional   ← Spend & Product Differentiation →   Preferred

Analysis of these frameworks should lead to reflections on the part of the team to consider the following questions, which can lead to the appropriate strategy or tactics:

- Is 3PL value potential high or low?
- Is 3PL complexity/risk high or low?
- Is 3PL a critical (strategic) or leverage (commodity) spend category?
- How can you influence your customer to view its 3PL (in this example, DHL) as higher complexity/risk to push it into the strategic quadrant?
- Do the strategy, tactics, and actions fit the descriptions (critical or leverage)?
- Which sourcing tactic(s) are being used with the 3PL category?
  - Strategic partnership
  - Long-term contract
  - Price contract
  - Blanket order
  - Spot buy
- Do they view 3PL as relationship or transactional focused category and how does this affect you?
- What is their savings target?
- Is 3PL a high savings, easy-to-implement spend category? Or have they already exhausted all of the "easy savings" targets?

If Procurement views 3PL as a commodity item that has low complexity and low risk, it is not likely to present a suitable opportunity for a company like DHL to compete. The remedy in this case is either to further educate Procurement on the details of the statement of work (SOW) required and ensure that the individuals who are decision-makers in the organization structure are informed and aware of these requirements. Also, understanding the priorities of the category manager and the key metrics that determine success for this category, including cost targets, will allow the team to deliver a much more informed business case. This is further assessed in Decision 4.

- **Acquisition/leverage quadrant: the primary emphasis will be on cost/price.** In some cases, the prevailing measure for performance is lowest cost, and performance may not be emphasized or well understood. This is not an ideal fit for DHL, especially if the emphasis is simply on price per unit. However, if DHL is able to educate Procurement on a business case focused on TCO, they may be able to influence the decision-maker appropriately. In particular, the operations team must be sure that they are quantifying the cost savings and productivity improvements that are being passed on to the local business on a regular basis, updating the record, and ensuring that BD is aware of the cost savings that has already been delivered over the life of the contract.

- **Strategic/exposed quadrants: the primary emphasis will be on performance.** In such cases, it may be beneficial to ensure that the operations team is not only measuring performance but can work with the procurement team to understand the "weights" on each of the different performance criteria. Procurement may have a scorecard with different weights on different elements of performance than the local business unit, and it is important to establish what those elements are. Developing a performance scorecard can be a useful exercise to fully understand what criteria are being evaluated in the current business and whether these criteria have changed recently or will change in the upcoming RFP. There may even be an opportunity to develop a "two-way scorecard." If understanding is low, then the team should seek to develop insights by creating their own "scorecard" for how they believe the customer views the 3PL category overall, as well as this particular target activity.

Strategies and Tactics

The BD team should go through these five decision-making steps and use a number of different combinations to come up with a characterization of the current relationship with the customer. Here, we have identified relevant strategies and tactics that may be employed, as well as commercial considerations that may need to be discussed with your Finance team and possibly General Counsel.

CASE STUDY EXAMPLES

The following examples are adopted from the workshops run by Rob Handfield and are intended to be used as examples of how to use the tool. Participants should go through each of these cases, identify the different dimensions of the relationship as they pertain to the tool, and develop their own plan of work. (These may be reviewed to ensure knowledge and proper application of the tool.)

Case Study 1 – Example Account: Daimler and its 3PL, DHL

Daimler is a big global customer — if DHL could grow their account, they would provide a strong point of leverage for growth. There is a lot more to play with them — and the relationship with Germany is of some value — but the auto guys and the truck group are very sophisticated procurement managers. Daimler has a very structured and rigid procurement process. Once a provider is "qualified" by the business owner, Procurement drives the ultimate selection. Many (former) potential coaches are reluctant to provide information and refer to Procurement for all information.

What is the current relationship status? DHL has a very strong relationship with one division: the business owners at Daimler Trucks. DHL is respected by the business owners at Mercedes-Benz but the relationship is much more distant. Procurement at both organizations respects DHL and is highly motivated to include us in all pursuits. However, they are rigid and by the book when it comes to working strictly with Procurement.

What is the relationship with Procurement? Inside information has to be obtained before the RFQ process. Once an RFQ is released, Daimler goes on *lockdown* and all information is funneled through Procurement. Business owners are very active during the qualification rounds and will participate in detailed technical reviews and even visit supplier sites. Some of the more motivated coaches will even advise DHL how to deal with Procurement and provide feedback as to competitive offers. Once finalists are qualified, Procurement *owns* the selection process. Their primary motivation is lowest cost and favorable contractual terms. All providers that are finalists are considered able to perform the business to satisfaction if selected.

Governance Issues: Different divisions of Daimler are more willing to work with a favored supplier. The more the division is controlled by Stuttgart, Germany, the more rigid their procurement process. Mercedes-Benz in Vance, Alabama Manufacturing is the closest to Stuttgart and is the most rigid. DTNA Aftermarket is the farthest from Stuttgart in terms of relationship and the most willing to bend the rules.

Target Approach: This is a customer where understanding the procurement governance model is critical. TCO, innovation, ongoing cost reductions, and understanding the role of Procurement versus stakeholders are essential to success with this target account. And innovation is key, as Procurement knows their business very well and so they will buy at a price level that is tight and competitive but not crazy. They are also prone to cyclical and economic environments — and when it is down, they are more likely to demand cost reductions. So price of admission is ongoing improvement and cost reduction, but be prepared to adapt if the economic environment dips. Working a RACI or RASCI chart with this account could help to identify stakeholders in the business and establish greater engagement with Procurement. However, understanding the process and cycle of Procurement's activities and bids can provide improved reparation and analysis that develops a TCO approach.

Tools to Adopt:

- TCO: To identify cost opportunities in response to cost down requests.
- RACI or RASCI: To understand how Procurement works with the business and assigns roles in cross-functional teams and develop coaches.
- Scorecard: To understand elements considered in bid evaluation and important sourcing processes and policies before, during, and after gaps.
- Category segmentation: There may be different strategies that the Procurement organization is adopting for different product segments and business units.
- Porter five forces/market intel: Understanding upcoming acquisitions and outsourcing activity will be important. In particular, the 3PL distribution center (DC) activity in Memphis may be a candidate for outsourcing.

Case Study 2 – Target Account: SC Johnson (SCJ) and its 3PL, DHL

This project summary documents how the SC Johnson company has renewed its long-standing decision to make DHL the provider of choice. Ultimately this decision was made based on SC Johnson's belief that DHL has always been and will continue to be the leader in operational and executional excellence.

What was the relationship status? DHL has had a positive and substantial relationship with SCJ for more than 18 years. The majority of the activity has been in North America, where DHL has run all seven of the existing SCJ distribution centers (DCs). These operations were run in a very consistent and highly productive fashion through a close collaborative effort with the customer. Systems and processes were customized to support the SCJ businesses, and the sites were managed as a network focused on continuous improvement and the sharing of best practice. Over the years, we extended our service offering deeper into the SCJ organization, allowing our counterparts within SCJ to focus more on their products and customers. DHL had consistently delivered year-on-year savings to SCJ in a cost-plus environment and enjoyed a very positive relationship.

What was the relationship with Procurement? As time passed and their leadership evolved, they became less engaged in the day-to-day business, leaving that effort to DHL. This created a knowledge gap regarding the details of their own supply chain, and Procurement in particular became disconnected from understanding the details of the business. The DHL operating team remained consistent and continued to drive improvements into the business, but the SCJ business owners lost perspective on how our service levels and costs compared to other service providers in the industry.

In 2011, SCJ made a key acquisition that changed their business profile significantly and resulted in increased cost to serve based on a new level of complexity. The new SCJ leadership team found itself having to explain budget gaps that it did not understand and could not rectify. While DHL adjusted to the new profile and become more efficient, the impact of the new products and profile caused SCJ to take actions that were more focused on cost than service. This sometimes-conflicting focus between cost and service became a more regular occurrence, which eventually led to a change in the DHL account team. While we maintained a solid service level moving forward, SCJ determined that at contract end, the entire network would be put out to bid.

DHL worked very closely with SCJ during 2014 to assist in the RFP process. At this time, we also planned and developed our network bid response while continuing to run the entire network in a flawless fashion (DHL's perspective) resulting in a budget savings to SCJ of over $1 million. The bid process was long and hard and resulted in an SCJ decision to award the entire network to a competitor based on a perceived savings of $5 million annually. These savings would represent a 19 percent decrease in the overall revenue in the network, while for 10 years, we had historically saved 2 percent year-over-year. We were skeptical of the proposed rates and sent SCJ formal communication suggesting they may not have fully vetted the solution. Nonetheless, the change was announced with a long lead time requiring Excel to remain in operations for an extended period beyond the existing contract term.

Target Approach: This is a customer where understanding the changes in leadership and their view of 3PL as a "leverage" category was important. Their new procurement team clearly did not fully understand the requirements, and the RFP that went out did not have a proper SOW.

The transition phase included a revised short-term contract and several changes to the rollout plan. This taxed our operating team and put our operating sites at risk relative to performance. While the rollout was occurring, members of the SCJ team began to change and we started to hear of operating challenges being faced by the new provider. As performance got worse at the two transitioned sites, our team stepped up and actually took on additional volumes at the remaining sites that we still operated. At the same time, we started to develop a very positive relationship with some of the new leadership team at SCJ. When the rest of the site transition dates neared, the remaining old guard at SCJ was steadfast that they would make the transitions despite obvious issues with service and cost with the new provider. The DHL team remained confident that ultimately SCJ would see the mistake they had made and revert back to them as a significant and loyal partner.

Tools to Adopt:

- TCO: Establishing and quantifying the total cost of the contract would have created more of an "apples to apples" comparison for SCJ and could have potentially avoided the RFP.
- RACI: To understand how Procurement works with the business and assigns roles in cross-functional teams. As the new organization evolved, it was important to ensure that leadership and Procurement were aligned.
- Scorecard: To understand elements considered in bid evaluation and important sourcing processes and policies before, during, and after gaps.
- Category segmentation: There may be different strategies that the Procurement organization is adopting for different product segments and business units.
- Porter five forces/market intel: Understanding upcoming acquisitions and outsourcing activity will be important. In particular, the 3PL DC activity in Memphis may be a candidate for outsourcing.

A leadership change was made at SCJ shortly after, and our team was asked to meet with the new leadership team. In that meeting, we met the new team, some of whom we knew from the past, and the tone of our discussions changed abruptly. They apologized to us for what they had done and asked if we were willing to reestablish long-term operations at the remaining five sites. The new team expressed a great deal of confidence in us and admitted that SCJ had misjudged the value we brought to them over the years. We started commercializing our new agreement going forward and worked to establish long-term plans.

This provides an excellent example of perseverance and capability as a provider of choice. In addition, it suggests the importance of continually influencing leadership and Procurement that outsourcing logistics is NOT a simple commodity type of relationship.

Appendix – What is the Procurement Leadership Transformation Assessment (PLTA)?

The *procurement leadership transformation assessment* (PLTA) measures the "current state" of a procurement function in an organization, along the trajectory of increasing maturity, from functional efficiency (PL1), cross-functional cooperation (PL2), supplier collaboration (PL3), and network coordination (PL4). It is important to realize that the assessment is not just a questionnaire but a framework and a model that forms the basis of improving the supply chain processes, as developed by Dr. Ian George. Combining this with the assessments developed by Rob Handfield and collected through *machine learning* (ML) technologies, the assessment provides a static representation of an organization's maturity in its supply management transformation based on "publicly available" information, and allows the enterprise to compare itself to other companies in its industry as well. The MBL algorithms apply keywords to collect details on the Fortune 500 companies, and then develop insights into each firm's procurement strategies based on currently available public information. It is a high-level assessment, and it requires additional validation to be used in the context of a one-on-one customer engagement. The aggregation of accelerator and analytical assessment has resulted in a program that changes the dynamic of transformation in favor of internally developed capabilities.

The chart on page 87 shows the progression of an organization along these dimensions measured through the PLTA. Note that the nature of metrics also changes at each phase of transformation. In the early stages, the focus is on year-over-year price reduction. In PL2, the focus becomes more on total delivered cost, comprising the cost of logistics, service, etc. In PL3, the metrics focus on TCO, including end-of-life and customer impact cost. In the final most advanced stage, metrics focus on value delivered to the organization. As discussed in our other research, Procurement begins working with sales associates in their supply chain to coach and create innovation and revenue generating opportunities, using capabilities that do not lie inside the walls of the buying company. This is the most advanced, and we believe, the greatest potential contribution that Procurement can make in the future. Yet very few organizations are at this level today, and when they do come close, it is not always clearly defined how these contributions are rewarded, as the organization is part of a network and value may be mutually shared across the network.

The PLTA assessment provides an answer to the questions "how far along are you relative to your peers in your procurement transformation journey?" and "which processes are lagging compared to your peers?" This is effectively a "snapshot" in time. It is not designed to provide an answer to the question "how should the procurement process be improved?" Transformation is intended to be a follow-on activity delivered through a membership/network structure.

Another attribute of maturity is the governance structure of Procurement. As shown in Table 1, procurement may be a centralized, decentralized, or center-led structure. In general, more mature organizations are moving toward "center-led" structures that seek to combine the benefits of both the centralized and decentralized models.

Table 1: Centralized / Decentralized / Center-Led Governance Structures

	Advantages	Disadvantages
Decentralized Procurement	A decentralized model of procurement, where each business, functional, or geographic unit is responsible for its own purchases, has a number of advantages. It empowers individual business units with autonomy and control over their process and design decisions and improves their overall satisfaction. It speeds up process and issue resolution and allows your organization to take advantage of expertise in the local market.	Does not allow leveraging of corporate spend or alignment of business objectives with those of the larger organization. May result in poor coordination between business units. Procurement, when decentralized, uses inconsistent tools and processes for decision-making, which calls into question their professionalism and actual contributions to the business.
Centralized Procurement	A newer, centralized model of procurement, where all acquisition goes through a single, central organization, has many advantages. First of all, unlike the decentralized model, it allows you to fully leverage your corporate spend across the enterprise and drive standardized sourcing processes throughout the enterprise.	Lose extensive knowledge of individual supply markets and consumption patterns afforded by local supply market intelligence. There is a risk of losing knowledge about local supply markets — not all centralized procurement organizations fail at this.
Hybrid Model Procurement	Provides a procurement center of excellence (COE) that focuses on driving corporate strategies and category strategies, best practices, and knowledge sharing, while allowing the buying and transaction activities to occur in the business units. Centralized procurement organizations are more likely to establish COE resources that help decide whether to buy according to a global, international, regional or local strategy, and what categories of spend should be treated that way. If regional or local strategies are appropriate, it devolves them to individual business units to execute them with Procurement guidance using standardized methods and approaches.	Allows decisions to be made independently by the business, but allows COE to influence decisions with facts and analytics.

The final variable to consider for sales is the level of influence that the procurement team may have on the decision. In a highly centralized environment, procurement may have strong influence on the decision and may lead the decision through a structured category management process. We have labeled this as a gatekeeper role, which means that Procurement will ultimately make the final call on awarding the business. If Procurement has less of an influence in a more decentralized organization, then they will play the role of an influencer — which means they may have some say in the decision, but ultimately the business stakeholder will make the final call. Depending on whether the primary criteria for decision-making is Cost or Value, sales may elect to use a variety of different tactics, which are shown in Table 2. Understanding these these types of parameters in a target organization is critical for Sales to understand.

Table 2: Procurement Influence on the Decision

Procurement influence on decision	Role of Procurement	How does Procurement view 3PL?*	Scenario	Strategy/Tactic
	Influencer	COST	Strong relationship with business stakeholder. Unlikely that Procurement will be decision-maker given that they have low influence and low maturity.	Continue to work with local business stakeholders, but offer to meet with Procurement if they would like to be involved. Seek to educate Procurement on 3PL market.
	Influencer	VALUE	Strong relationship with business stakeholder. Unlikely that Procurement will be decision-maker given that they have low influence and low maturity. They may be consulted during the RFP process as they have good understanding of market intelligence. Likely they will emphasize cost in this case.	Continue to work with local business stakeholders, but offer to meet with Procurement if they would like to be involved. Given that procurement understands 3PL markets, they may have more influence in the near future.
Procurement Influence **LOW**	Gatekeeper / Decision-maker	COST	Historically strong relationship with business stakeholder and coach. Procurement may be seeking to gain influence over decision, but historically has not been involved. Watch out for potential new leadership at CPO level who may be seeking to build influence across the company and want to be involved. Even where Procurement influence is low, they may be asked to use a procurement tool to house and run the RFP process.	Continue to work with local business stakeholders, but offer to meet with Procurement if they would like to be involved. Seek to educate procurement on 3PL market and, in particular, emphasize performance metrics and history of strong track record.
	Gatekeeper / Decision-maker	VALUE	Even though Procurement is not yet mature, they may have a mandate from Finance to develop cost savings. It is critical that you understand what target is (annual percentage) and identify how it is being measured. The procurement team may have some strong 3PL experts on their team – get to know them. You may be able to help them understand the TCO value equation. Higher level of procurement control of the RFP and sourcing process, as well as the strategy that is agreed to be executed.	Schedule a research meeting with business stakeholder and invite Procurement to the meeting. Prior to the RFP, ensure Procurement is aware of the evaluation criteria at the site and the required capabilities for any new provider. If they are knowledgeable, they will appreciate the input. Invite Procurement to capability review; ensure that if there is a procurement council for multiple businesses, you have an opportunity to present and help them understand the criteria.
	Gatekeeper / Decision-maker	COST	The strong relationship with your business stakeholder may be at risk as Procurement may have new leadership and have become the gatekeeper. Their low understanding of 3PL services could lead to a risk of outsourcing through RFP to low–cost lump sum bidder.	Danger zone! Educating Procurement on the key criteria for awarding the 3PL outsource process, the impact on the cost and TCO is imperative. Procurement's lack of maturity and understanding may result in loss of the account without warning if steps are not taken.
	Gatekeeper / Decision-maker	VALUE	The strong relationship with your business stakeholder may be at risk as Procurement may have new leadership and have become the gatekeeper. The good news is that Procurement understands the criteria; thus, you may be able to influence them.	Cautionary zone! Understanding procurement's cost savings targets, especially for the 3PL, part of the business, is important. If 3PL is not a significant part of their overall business, it may likely be relegated to a simple bid – if criteria are not well established.
Procurement Influence **HIGH**	Influencer	COST	Procurement is starting down the path of building category teams for 3PL but is not yet mature. They may change during the next business cycle.	Conduct category review with business stakeholder, invite Procurement, and begin to foster relationship.
	Influencer	VALUE	Even though Procurement influence is low, they may have strong knowledge, perhaps through initial outsourcing of the 3PL category, and may have strong internal cost data.	Conduct category review with business stakeholder, invite Procurement, and begin to foster relationship. Emphasize tools that can provide procurement insights, demonstrate capabilities, and influence with technological features that driver lower TCO.

* HIGH strategic – VALUE vs. LOW leverage – COST

Chapter 7:
Putting the Procurement Team in Place

(or "People are not your greatest asset … people are your ONLY asset!")

This chapter focuses on what it takes to assemble a high-performing procurement team capable of navigating the complex internal and external landscapes within which Procurement must operate to be successful, and what differentiates those teams that do from those teams that don't! Of course, this assumes that Procurement wants a strategy-oriented team and not a tactical one, and every salesperson needs to know which one they are dealing with. This chapter helps provide clues to identify which is which.

The statement made at the start of this chapter — "People are not your greatest asset … people are your ONLY asset!" — is, for me (Howard), an understatement. Let me tell you why I came to this conclusion 25-plus years ago when I first started managing a team of IT procurement experts at SmithKline Beecham. Having been handed the assignment to lead this small team of six people, I told my boss, Willie Deese, that I knew nothing about the IT category. He assured me that neither did half the people in IT, and not to worry, I would learn. The fact was, he had an opening on his *procurement leadership team* (PLT) that needed to be filled, and I think he saw me as a loyal and capable asset in building the type of team that he wanted to lead. He needed more focus on the *how*, not the *what*!

Leaning into discomfort

I came quickly to the conclusion that I had to "lean into discomfort, and get comfortable in this uncomfortable place" (I'll credit Murvin Lackey, one of Willie's trusted lieutenants, for that thought). IT Procurement was a place where everyone on my team knew 10 times more than I did about the various categories of laptop, server, and mainframe hardware; enterprise and desktop software, middleware and licensing; telecommunications and telecom services; and outsourced IT services and contractors. We were spending at least £300 million (at that time, equal to $480 million) annually in the categories on a global basis. Not only that, but I had to represent the procurement function on the CIO's IT management team (ITMT), giving me both a permanent seat on the ITMT and a dotted-line relationship to the CIO. To be honest, I was in over my head and scared shitless.

But I recognized that my team members were also in an uncomfortable place, knowing they needed to bring me up to speed on everything they were doing. They knew I didn't understand even a fraction of it, yet I had to push these issues forward at ITMT meetings for their approval of the category and sourcing strategies. They had to get me to a place where I could at least talk the talk, if not walk the walk. There was a lot at stake for them, as their success now depended on me. It was going to take some time, and there would be mistakes and bumps in the road as we went down this process. And yes, I was also given the feedback that I was being "wishy-washy" and lacked strategy in my decision-making, because I truly did not know what I was doing!

> But this is how you grow in Procurement — taking on new categories of spend, researching the complexities of the category, benchmarking best practices that others are doing in the category, studying your internal business needs, studying your supply base and its capabilities, then developing a strategy on how you should source your needs from that supply base, and selling that strategy into your stakeholders (or better yet, getting them to participate in the process of doing the analysis and development of the optimal sourcing strategy with you, and having them take some ownership in the strategy). Once the strategy is agreed, you have to execute the strategy and the contracts and start your supplier relationship management (SRM) process to optimize what you've done.

Later in life, I had the pleasure of listening to a lecture by *New York Times* Foreign Affairs columnist Thomas Friedman, who emphasized that the most important skill today is one of "learning how to learn." He cited examples of why this skill is more important in these fast-changing times than having specific subject matter knowledge, which can be easily accessed, researched, and transmitted (and with ChatGPT will become easier than ever, though accuracy will always be an issue). I wish I had heard this 17 years earlier, because it was good advice.

We were still in the dark ages regarding data gathering methodology on what the company was spending and on which SKUs, with which suppliers, by which departments, over varying budgets over varying periods of time. The systems were inadequate, and we were instituting a procurement process and category sourcing management process (SMP) that had not been fully vetted or widely accepted by the company. Stakeholders and budget holders had most, if not all, of the decision-making authority, and Procurement was just getting started in its transformation. Regardless, just a year into this, my IT procurement team was blowing the doors off of all of our savings metrics and measures of success. Was my leadership responsible? Not on your life! I had no clue what our strategies should be, as I barely understood the complexities of the categories. It was then that I came to this conclusion: "People are not your greatest asset … people are your ONLY asset!"

> I dare you to challenge this statement. If you can point me to a high-performing team comprising great processes and great systems but run by mediocre people, I will be floored. I have never experienced or seen a high-performing team with that makeup. In fact, I have found a number of examples of the inverse: high performing teams made up of great people that exceeded all expectations despite working with terrible data, outdated systems, and poorly designed processes.

I get sick and tired of listening to HR types declare that, at their company, "People are their greatest asset." It's a joke, and it's meaningless. They are the first to immediately resort to layoffs and cutbacks when it looks like quarterly numbers are not going to be met. They position people to be an "asset" that can be traded off for other assets (mostly operating margins and EBITDA), and they can easily be classified as "one-time nonrecurring restructuring costs."

When I say that "people are your ONLY asset," I truly mean it and believe it. Nothing replaces high-quality, knowledgeable, motivated, driven members of your team that constantly exceed all objectives and overcome all obstacles laid before them. Nothing! They are the only asset of any value to a high-performing team or organization, and they are not to be thought of as a trade-off for anything. How one can rationalize a decision to reduce the number of sourcing managers in a headcount reduction exercise when that sourcing manager (SM) is delivering value generation equal to 5 times their salary (and benefits, possibly) is beyond me. It's simplistic, bean-counting nonsense. I've had to deal with this time and again throughout my procurement career, and it has never made sense to me. Maybe it's my MBA in finance training that has me thinking more about decision metrics like *return on investment, internal rate of return, payback, free cash flow*, and the *net present value of future cash flows* as opposed to budgets and impact to the next quarter's P&L EBITDA, *net profit*, and *earnings per share*.

Recruiting the High-Performing Team — Become a Salesperson!

Okay, I'm getting off my soap box at Hyde Park (West London is fabulous, by the way), so let's delve into the real discussion of what it takes to put in place a high-performing team, assuming that's what you really want. The first thing, and I can't stress this enough, is to give talented people a reason to come and join you, and money will be a smaller part of their decision criteria than you think. They are not in sales for a reason (okay, that was a knock on Sales, I admit it). But people who lead procurement functions or groups within the function need to think and act like sales and marketing people if they are going to build up high-performing teams. They need to be able to paint a vision for candidates about why this place is the best place for them, now and in the future. Candidates need to be motivated by the possibilities of what can be, and what success and reward will look like. Otherwise, you will just be filling positions with people who want a job, and this does not create high-performing teams.

People are drawn to companies and functions based on how they perceive their role will be in this setting, and whether they will be able to manage their responsibilities, have decision-making authority, have opportunities to grow and advance in the job, have an impact on the success of the function or the business, and have opportunities to be recognized for their successes. One of the things that I learned at M&M/MARS was that you shouldn't interview people just to fill the open position, but also to fill the next level position. If the candidate was not considered capable of being a candidate to advance, they shouldn't be brought in to fill the current role, period (as you will see in Chapter 8, "Culture Eats Strategy for Lunch")!

Of course, all of this assumes that the people who are doing the recruiting and interviewing (usually the hiring manager) are the best people suited to do so, and this couldn't be further from the truth. Some people are just more perceptive than others when reading into a candidate's true intentions and skill sets, and whether they will be a good fit for the team. There is so much innate bias in the process to bring in people who are exactly like you, and while the term *diversity* may be misused in this context, creating a diverse team is a driver of success. But what do I mean by *diverse* (in addition to cultural, gender, and ethnic diversity, which has always been a big plus on my high-performing teams)?

You Cannot Put Square Pegs into Round Holes

There are so many different contexts for what makes up a diverse team, far beyond gender, national origin, disability, or minority status, and the first thing that I always look for is *subject matter experts* (SMEs) versus *best athletes*. Some categories of spend lend themselves more to one versus the other. When it comes to the various IT categories, logistics, and sometimes marketing services like creative agencies, I have found that SMEs tend to do better. SMEs love being the experts in their field and doing the deep dive with their business stakeholders.

If you want big successes in your procurement team, focus all of your best SME resources on the IT technology categories, especially software. Why? For the same reason that Willie Sutton gave for why he robbed banks: "That's where the money is." Software companies operate on very high gross margins, often times 80 percent or higher. Salespeople up and down the chain in software are authorized to give up a percentage on the sales price to get you hooked as a customer, as they have plenty of margin to work with and are trying to get your account to become an annuity of maintenance or subscription payments going forward, i.e., *annual recurring revenue*. The difference between good software deals and bad software deals is huge, so huge that my IT procurement teams generally had savings rates that were 3 times higher than any other category of spend in the company. By the way, if you are offered a 75 percent discount from list price and you negotiate an 80 percent discount, you have just reduced your cost by 20 percent (do the math).

But when it comes to many of the third-rail categories of business services such as legal, HR benefits, or management consulting, or more traditional services categories like contingent labor, executive search and recruitment, or facilities management, I have found that best athletes do well. Best athletes can apply transferable procurement skills and principles of analysis and process thinking across all of these categories in a logical and coherent manner. As they make the deep dive into the subject matter, best athletes learn just enough to be dangerous, where they can talk the talk. They love waking up every morning hoping that the day ahead will be different than any other day they've had, and they look forward to climbing up the steep learning curve of category knowledge required to perform. They also love working multiple categories at the same time, giving them time during the day to refresh their stream of thought.

The SME discussion also extends to whether or not you can take someone from the business who has expertise in the field, and convert them into a commercial (procurement) person. Sometimes you have no choice — SMEs can be difficult to find! SMEs from outside of procurement may have a better chance of success than a best athlete who has to quickly ramp up the learning curve and develop the necessary level of subject matter expertise. I have seen it work, and I have seen it fail (miserably), so I look at it as a strategy of last resort. It also depends on whether you need someone who can deliver a quick win, or if you have the time and luxury to deliver a longer-term category management solution.

Within all of this talk of SMEs and best athletes, you have a thousand other "diverse" variables that get processed relating to where people are classified according to their personality profile. Yes, we are talking Myers-Briggs and DiSC and Herrmann Brain and any number of other proprietary systems out there that try to figure out whether we are control freaks, or innovators, or rule followers, or aggressive risk takers, or cautious "analysis paralysis" types, or facts and data oriented, or extroverted or introverted, or any combination of these traits. When it comes to "square peg, round hole" discussions though, I have found that the style by which people work is informative but not necessarily a determinant of success. CEOs can be introverts or extroverts. Global category managers (GCMs) and SMs with varying personality traits have successfully worked in a variety of situations. What is important here is that each individual GCM or SM is astute enough to consider the various personality traits of their internal stakeholders and their supplier salespeople, and that they know themselves (their own traits), and they recognize that different people respond differently to different stimuli, approaches, and circumstances. You can have any of these traits and be successful as a GCM or SM if you are self-aware (an extremely valuable trait).

When leaders in the procurement function discuss staffing needs and head count and organizational and reporting structures, they rarely spend enough time talking about obtaining these diverse balances within the team — balances of SMEs and best athletes and people with various personality traits and backgrounds. They look at each position individually, hoping to find the best candidate for the job who invariably looks like them, talks like them, thinks like them, and acts like them. It's human nature. We gravitate toward what we know because of the comfort level it brings us. It's Maslow's *Hierarchy of Needs* that we cater to. We are all guilty of this.

Do chief procurement officers (CPOs) want people on our teams who will take orders and do what they say ("Yes-men"), or do CPOs want independent thinkers who will pursue facts and data, align people to a common cause, make decisions, and execute? You will be surprised by the number of "leaders" in the company (and CPOs) who actually want Yes-men, people who will not threaten them or challenge their thinking, or worse yet, their role! Some people cannot stand the thought that people below them might actually know more than they do about a category or subject — in their minds, it makes them look weak, and dependent upon others — and that's not a comfortable position for them to be in. It makes it very difficult for some CPOs to take credit for the successes that happen below them when they think this way. I will come out and say it: There are many great CPOs out there, but some CPOs fit this description. And how can you argue with that style of leadership and management when it results in personal success for them in their climb to the top of the procurement heap? Some people are just good at politics.

In the end, leaders should be judged on the turnover rate in their functions. The bottom line is that turnover is expensive, and on exit interviews you learn that people don't actually leave companies, they leave their bosses. You don't actually work for a company — you work for a boss — and when you realize that you have become the square peg in the round hole, it's always best to leave than to continue to be a misfit. Remember, nobody in this world gets to choose their parents, but sometimes you get to choose your boss!

Soft Skills

Whenever I have talent discussions with leaders in the procurement field, the term *soft skills* always comes to the fore. How do we get people with the soft skills necessary to achieve procurement success — facilitation skills, team leadership, communications, managing up, encouraging others to adopt your goals and make them their own, and most importantly, change management skills and processes. Even more than analytical skills, which have historically been a skill gap in procurement, the soft skills necessary to create change and achieve breakthrough results are the biggest differentiator in the success of the function.

When it comes to recruiting procurement people who have, or who can develop, the soft skills needed to be successful at running global category strategies and cross-functional SMP, we get dragged back to the personality trait discussion. Leaders in the procurement function, when filling SM positions in their organization, are looking for good negotiators above all else. They see this as the most important core competency, and they couldn't be any further off the mark when doing so. As mentioned earlier, the biggest mistake that procurement people make is not one of being poor negotiators; it's one of not knowing their true business requirements, and not asking the 5 WHYs to better understand their business needs, so they end up negotiating for all of the wrong things for their stakeholders.

People with soft skills tend to ask the right questions, clarifying questions that do not threaten their stakeholders, but follow the Stephen Covey habit of first seeking to understand, then to be understood. In seeking this clarity, the stakeholders also go through a metamorphosis and a willingness to question basic assumptions, which then leads to an openness about looking at solutions that are not restricted by the preconceived notions of the function. The team can then be freed to stretch the original boundaries of its team charter and set higher goals for changing end-to-end processes that generate much higher levels of value for the function in quality and service and innovation, and eliminate waste and drive efficiency — all of which lower the total life-cycle cost of the service and give their function a competitive advantage. These joint cross-functional successes get publicized and take on lives of their own, and then others want to join in on similar adventures. Excitement starts to build, and a new dynamic and culture arises as they see that the procurement function is no longer a control function focused on "Savings R Us," "Negotiations R Us," or "Contracts R Us" and can be a *trusted advisor to the business*. Other than that, there is nothing at stake here for Procurement.

The bottom line is that procurement team members will never get a seat at the table or be considered *trusted advisors to the business* without developing these soft skills. Why is that the case? (And Sales needs to know this.) Because when it comes to indirect categories, in most organizations, Procurement is not the decision-maker — the primary budget holder holds the "D." But procurement people who are effective at applying soft skills can change the dynamic with their budget holders to let them run the process as it should be run, and they can lead the user team through the change management steps that give them the leverage and the confidence to make big changes. If Sales sees a Procurement-led team operating in this strategic manner, watch out and get your "A" team into the game because you are in for a big challenge.

Job Qualifications

I have probably helped write more than 100 procurement job descriptions (JD), reviewed more than 1,000 resumes, and interviewed several hundred people for positions over my career, and HR always insists on having some nonsubjective "must have" qualifications listed in the JD. There are legal reasons behind it to assure that you are not discriminating against qualified applicants, and to make sure that nepotism is not influencing your decisions. I get it. We always insisted that SMs and GCMs had college degrees, and graduate degrees were an extra bonus, and a certain number of years of experience in the function, depending upon the position. We wanted to see people with concentrations in business subjects, analytics, or even STEM that could be applied to specific category expertise. This gave us a level of comfort that their background was a good fit for the work we intended to throw their way. This was bullshit and couldn't have been further from the truth.

If you want someone on the team who (other than being a great negotiator) was capable of driving a well-defined SMP along a facts and data–driven logical approach, go look for someone who majored in philosophy, whose core principles are based on the application of logic. If you want someone who has the soft skills to analyze the motivations and WIIFM ("What's in it for me?") of cross-functional team members from across different functional silos and geographies and lead them in a change management process, go look for a psychology or anthropology major. If you want someone who is great at communication for helping the team coalesce around a shared vision and mission and get your stakeholders to see that, get someone who majored in English or creative writing or literature. If you want someone who is willing to get down in the mud and wrestle with unruly stakeholders who are unwilling to share data and are circumventing the approved procurement process, get a street fighter from a public university that scrapped out a degree through community college while working three odd jobs to support themselves. Again, stop looking for you! Think about all the pieces that need to come together of complementary skills and diverse backgrounds that end up forming high-performance teams. Think about how these people can "share and build" with one another while challenging one another in a collegial way.

A growing number of universities around the globe are establishing or have established Procurement and Supply Chain bachelor's and master's degree programs now, and these students are looking for career opportunities. This was not something we used to see. This is especially true for students who come from East Asian countries where there are developing economies, and people have great respect for the roles that Procurement and Supply Chain play in their country's growth and development. They bring with them some analytical approaches and skills that help question basic assumptions about what is being done, and why.

In Chapter 8, "Culture Eats Strategy for Lunch," we will discuss how all of this comes together. People with the right qualifications can be taught how to "manage up" and deal with people that are several layers above them. I know this because I have never found a successful procurement organization that didn't master this skill. We will discuss the concept of *boundaryless behavior*, and how end-to-end process thinking and empowering people to act is essential to forming high-performing teams. This and more are necessary for success, but if the culture is not right, it will all be tactical, unsustainable activity that will be caught in an endless cycle of rinse, wash, repeat.

No matter what the qualifications may be, it's the intangibles that usually define success often reflected in the soft skills. Some of those intangibles include traits like:

- *tenacity*, and the unwillingness to take no for an answer;
- *curiosity*, always driving a need to understand more and learn more;
- *courage*, and the willingness to smash through the brick wall that has been put in front of you instead of dancing around it;
- *respect*, for the responsibilities of others and seeking out an understanding as to why they do the things they do;
- *humility*, being aware of your own limitations and faults and not trying to hide them;
- *active listening*, always having your antennae up and sensing not only what is being said, but the emotions that accompany the spoken and written word; and
- *speaking from the heart*, expressing what you really mean and not talking from the head or in cliches.

Chapter 8:
"Culture Eats Strategy for Lunch"

The Culture of the Procurement Function Isn't Everything — It's the ONLY Thing!

The impact of corporate and departmental culture on accepted behaviors, reward systems, and prioritization of activities should be set above any category strategy, sourcing management process, systems, and operations. It is reflected in all procedures and organizational structures and how decisions are made (or not made), and the culture is designed to reinforce the status quo. If you ever wonder why companies adapt whole change management processes (I have worked with three different ones in my career), it's because they know how difficult it is to change a culture and its ways of working. There are always winners and losers in this battle, but in the end, it's the culture that dictates success or failure of the function in its mission to support the corporation's goals.

The point here is that the culture of the procurement function and how that meshes or reflects the culture of the wider corporation or organization that it supports can vary greatly, and measures of what is success (and how success is rewarded) within these cultures will ultimately determine whether Procurement will mature and reach its ultimate goal of becoming a *trusted advisor to the business*. The strength of corporate culture is often underappreciated by procurement people as they interview for jobs, focusing instead on the position title, salary and bonus, number of direct reports (if any), geographic scope, spend influence, category assignments, reporting relationships, and career path to future positions (how many people say they want to work on the tactical stuff, not the strategic stuff?). But in the end, true job satisfaction will greatly depend on the corporate culture and whether it reflects your particular value system and encourages behaviors in line with your own comfort level.

I (Howard) have worked in every procurement culture imaginable, including but not limited to the:

1. collaborative, democratic, process-driven but hierarchical multilayered culture;

2. culture of hierarchical brutality where the only accepted way of working is to beat people over the head, lie, steal, and breach contracts with the supply base, and expedite delivery of parts to the assembly line to prevent line stoppages;

3. culture of a flat, delayered, and empowered function where decision-making was pushed down to people working at the "coal face," the lowest level; risk-taking was actually rewarded (including failures!); and the only measure of success was to prove that you were doing better than the market and your competitors;

4. culture of pretending that you were rewarding people for employing best practice tools like *global category management* (GCM), multistage sourcing management process (SMP) and supplier relationship management (SRM), but in the end only rewarding savings claims, however measured, and those who did whatever it took to have the savings booked against their name were the ones who were rewarded;

5. culture of actually rewarding people using a balanced scorecard for employing best practice tools like GCM, SMP, SRM, meeting *supplier diversity* targets, and scoring high on customer satisfaction surveys along with meeting aggressive savings targets;

6. culture of an outsourced procurement function applying best practices in GCM, SMP, and SRM while managing and teaching a smaller in-house procurement function to do so; and

7. culture of boundaryless behavior, where the members of the procurement team were encouraged to challenge one another in a "share and build" environment, share critical and complementary instantaneous feedback with one another to help accelerate the process, and look at all challenges as business problems, not procurement problems, that required multifunctional, end-to-end process thinking and solutions.

Guess which cultures were my favorite (if you guessed #3, #5, & #7, we are on the same wavelength). They were actually very uniquely different cultures and positioned in three very separate types of industry — #3 being M&M/Mars (now Mars Wrigley), one of the largest multinational, private family-owned conglomerates in the world; #5 being Merck, one of the largest global publicly traded pharmaceutical companies in the world; and #7 being Citrix Systems, which was then a $3 billion mid-sized slow growth but profitable publicly traded software company that prided itself on democratized decision-making and work-life balance for its employees (but was recently privatized, merged, dismantled, and converted into a highly debt-leveraged private equity entity called Cloud Software Group, whose culture has taken a 180-degree turn).

Culture Example #3 – M&M/Mars

When I first joined M&M/Mars in 1989, there were things about the culture that had me drawn to them at first instance. There were five principles at Mars, and all 26,000 Mars associates around the world knew them by heart and actually used them to guide their decision-making. Today, in 2024 there are 140,000-plus Mars associates in 80 countries around the world, and the same five principles haven't changed one iota — *quality, responsibility, mutuality, efficiency*, and *freedom*. Any time I bump into a current or former Mars associate, we can look into each other's eyes and those same five words come spilling out of our mouths. Now you probably think that it's a cult, right?! To some degree, all corporate cultures are asking you to buy into their "cult" (wait a minute, is the origin of the word *cult* from the word *culture*?).

My allure toward Mars and its alignment with my own personal values was instant. Nobody in the company, not even the family owners, had an office. You could not have a partition around your desk more than three feet high, eliminating all barriers to communication. It didn't matter what your position or rank in the company was, you could just wander over and talk to people you needed to get your problem solved. Most meetings were spontaneous, the result of people bumping into one another in the walkway to and from the cafeteria. The concept of "calendaring" was not the overriding way to get business done.

If you worked in the manufacturing plant making M&M's or Snickers, or Starburst, it didn't matter — everyone, from the plant manager to the finance director to the HR director to the commercial procurement manager, wore a white uniform with a hairnet and a bump hat every day so that no one would be unable to enter the plant to fix a problem.

There was no "procurement" function; we were called "commercial." We were responsible for sourcing all raw materials, plant equipment, and services to run the company, and people respected what we did as an essential part of meeting *net sales* and *return on total assets*, two measures that were tracked weekly and resulted in adjustments up and down to our base pay every 28-day period! We hedged and traded all agricultural commodities and foreign currencies that impacted our operations, and we had huge discretion on our trading positions (though we could never be "net short" — after all, we were in the business of making candy, snacks, and ice cream and always needed to have inventory of commodities to produce product). When it came to our relationships with the supply base, *mutuality* was a principle that we adhered to. Yes, we worked with our suppliers to achieve a lower market price than any of our competitors, but we never did anything to them that we wouldn't want done to us. We had to base decisions on mutuality of benefit to our stakeholders.

When it came to the market forces in which we had to compete, we got monthly reminders (aside from having our pay increased or decreased) that we had to make, distribute, and promote the very best brands, whether they were M&M's, Snickers, Milky Way, 3 Musketeers, Twix, Skittles, Starburst, Combos, or Dove chocolates or ice creams. Every day, they put out trays of our candy for us to sample and comment on the quality of our products; but once a month they put out all of our competitors' products instead with a simple message — this is what you're up against in the market and you better be better than this! If not, make it so.

This is why *commercial* did not have a "savings" metric — it was immaterial. The only thing that mattered was whether we were doing a better job of buying, hedging, trading, and sourcing of quality ingredients than our competition, and coming up with ways to track and measure against that. Our metrics were totally **market-focused**, not budgets or price last paid. We invented a concept called "neutral cover" — how much contractual protection (how many months out) should you have on a commodity or service if you were neither bullish nor bearish about it — and then take a position that reflected our view. For example, I saw patterns regarding corn prices over the years that suggested if I had four months of contract cover (for corn syrup purposes) to meet our production requirements and always kept it at four months, I would probably break even through longer-term cycles of growing season and harvests; for soybean oil, I had six months. So I took bullish and bearish positions against that neutral cover and tracked how well I did against that metric. We assumed that our competition would do their hedging to meet neutral market conditions, and we traded around that to beat the competition. How did I do? I was positive three of the four years that I was hedging and trading, so not bad.

All eight of us traders — grains & oilseeds (me), sugar, foreign currencies, and cocoa — sat in a big semicircle that emulated a trading pit on the floor of the exchange, and as we went about our business, we also walked around to talk with one another to exchange ideas about things that seemed to work in one market versus the next or creating algorithms to support our activity. It was so collaborative! We kept an equanimity about us, never getting too excited about a big up day when we made a lot of money, or a big down day when we lost money, and we supported each other. We knew we had one thing in common — our gains and losses were reported to the Mars family every morning in a computer run that was distributed to their desks — and the last thing we wanted was the dreaded phone call with a request to change our position. I also collaborated with my trading friends at the Mars Pedigree petfood business, as they were also hedging corn and wheat for their products, and we had to be sure that the Mars family wouldn't see us trading against each other — I couldn't be long on my corn position while they were short on it! We hedged for different businesses with different price points, margins, price sensitivities and business cycles, so it got a little tricky, but made the job more challenging and enjoyable.

When it came to larger global issues of our impact on commodity farming practices, or tariff legislation, or user health and preferences or environmental concerns, we actively engaged to help drive change. It was a dictate over 30 years ago to ship everything by rail that we possibly could in order to lessen the carbon impact of greenhouse gases in the environment. We tracked over 30 years ago the trends in global warming and how that impacted climate and sea surface temperatures which led to the El Niño–La Niña climate cycles and caused flooding and droughts in food production areas, as well as the spread of bacteria and fungus that could ruin crops. I worked with a team of climatologists, meteorologists, and agronomists on studying whether we would have surpluses or shortages of materials due to varying climate conditions, and whether sourcing and production of cocoa beans, or oats, or wheat, corn, or soybean oil or palm oil or sugar needed to change to meet environmental concerns. When trans fatty acids were discovered as part of the hydrogenation process for oils, we immediately had R&D working at changing our formulations to be able to duplicate our production processes without changing the character of our products and brands. Some 25 years after I left, Mars Wrigley was working with indigent, women farm workers in India to provide them with microloans to grow mint for its gum products in a sustainable manner on small plots of land that would give them the financial independence they sought in a male-dominated caste society.

Culture Example #5 – Merck

Fortunately in my career, I had the experience at Merck where the procurement function and all of its efforts at category management got tied into the strategy of the company, and I learned that it was possible, even in Big Pharma. It helps to start in a bad situation where whatever you do will look good by comparison — the lowest performing procurement function in the industry in 2004 with a "savings" rate of 1.4 percent of spend. But it also helps when the following conditions are met:

- The company had three consecutive years of no revenue growth, failed drugs in Phase 3 clinical trials, and was looking at revenue falling off the cliff with the expiration of patents on a few blockbuster drugs;

- There was a sponsor in the C-Suite who recognized that there must be a change and a willingness to recruit talent from outside, fund a global transformation, and break all cultural norms that had existed for 100 years (it didn't hurt that he was also promoted to CEO less than 1.5 years later);

- A procurement leadership that was brought in from the outside that would not give in to "flavor of the month" strategies and was determined to set a strategic path to bring in the needed resources, processes, and systems to execute the change; and

- A procurement leadership that worked across functions throughout the company, with Finance, HR, IT & Business Systems, Legal, and Corporate Communications that was willing to do what it took to accomplish the task, and led from the front by assembling resources to do it together with them.

The process started by understanding the basics of *first things first* — how do we know what we are buying, how much and from whom, and is it meeting our business needs? Who is at the controls? Does past buying reflect future needs? What is the spend profile, direct versus indirect spend? Are we touching all of the categories of spend (answer — Procurement was involved in only 52 percent of the spend, and much worse in the indirect categories, which represented 70 percent of the total spend)? How much of the spend was being managed on a global, international, regional, and local basis, and how much of this had to change to properly leverage the global footprint of the company?

But underlying all of this, most of all, was culture … a 100-year history of "my way or the highway," "not invented here" syndrome, and no recognition that years of stagnant growth and a growing cost structure were the jaws of death for a company. People were content to put their heads in the sand, do what they always did, pretend that any attempts to create change were just passing fads and annoyances, and that all would right itself over time — "this too shall pass." They were on a burning platform, and they didn't know it! They had no idea there were two courses of action — either burn to death or jump 100 feet into the ocean below and hope you survive. The benefits and reward systems continued to support these old behaviors, so why jump?

When I first arrived at Merck to help lead the change management process for the global procurement transformation, I walked around to talk with many in the procurement function — dedicated, loyal people who loved the company and its mission for drug discovery and development, and they loved their jobs. I asked them how many years they had been there, and the answers were stunning — 20 years, 25 years, 30 years! Then I asked them how long they had been dealing with a specific supplier in their category and always got the same answer — 20 years, 25 years, 30 years, **but we always get "below market pricing!"** Wow!! A savings rate of 1.4 percent of spend and they always get "below market pricing" without ever making a supplier change … you can't make this stuff up (well, maybe they were actually getting 2.8 percent savings because they weren't touching half the spend in the company).

We knew that some members of the procurement function would not be up to the task of making the changes we would be demanding of them, so we had to do an HR-led assessment of the team. I like to refer to that process by the name of one of my favorite movies — *The Good, the Bad, and the Ugly*. It didn't take long to discover the *ugly*. I interviewed a member of the IT procurement team who was buying certain software for the manufacturing team. He started bragging to me about the great discount from list price that he had negotiated for his stakeholder for the purchase of some licenses for their operations. Okay, that's nice. Then I asked him about what had been negotiated for the ongoing annual maintenance payments on the licenses. His response nearly knocked me off my chair. "I didn't care about that," he said. "I let them charge whatever they wanted. That comes from a separate IT budget, not my stakeholder. I'm not responsible for that." The only thought going through my head at that instant was, "Do I have the authority and power to fire this man on the spot?" Later that night, as I discussed this conversation with my leadership over dinner, I came to realize that he was only doing what he was being asked to do, and he was being rewarded for doing what he did. They said "Jump," and he said, "How high?" How much more could you ask of an individual? I scheduled a follow-up interview with him, during which I was going to inform him that he should be looking at other opportunities, but he beat me to the punch and informed me that he had decided to retire and move to Florida. I congratulated him and wished him luck, and I walked away with a sigh of relief that my job had just been made a little easier.

The supply base was more astute though, and they could see the change coming from our procurement leadership faster than the internal employees did. We notified the top 100 companies of direct spend, top 100 companies of indirect spend, and top 100 companies of European spend that we wanted their senior leadership to attend supplier forums, and if an SVP or higher didn't show up, they weren't invited. They knew what was coming, and the demand to lower their costs by 20 percent over three years (with 7 percent immediately) was no shock to them. They had seen and heard it before, and they knew that they had to be prepared to respond. As we've noted in earlier chapters, the biggest pushback came from our own internal stakeholders who told us, "You can't treat my supplier like that." They felt threatened because we gave all of the suppliers the opportunity to submit *white papers* on what had to change internally in their relationship with the company to help facilitate cost reductions that could help them reduce their pricing to us. We were asking them to tattle on all the people who had designed their jobs around these supplier relationships and created checkers who would check the checkers and all kinds of other waste in the system. The stakeholders were scared.

Getting back to "below market pricing" without ever changing suppliers, we challenged the assumptions. I gave an earlier example in Chapter 4 of where we informed the supplier of 30 years who provided all of the service awards, trophies, Lucite memorabilia of special events, and other "trinkets and trash" that we were going to hold a reverse auction for the category. One week before the reverse auction, he came into our offices, begging that we call off the auction in exchange for him granting us an additional 30 percent price reduction! Are you kidding me? You want us to call off the auction? How about first bringing us a check for the equivalent of 30 percent of everything that you sold us for the last three years, then maybe we'll call off the auction. Of course, that didn't happen, and this supplier lost the business. We had to let everyone know that we were serious about change, and examples had to be made.

But the real test of the global procurement transformation came eight months into the process when Merck announced that it was withdrawing Vioxx from the market, its blockbuster anti-inflammatory drug, because of reports of heart-related hospitalizations and deaths that started coming in from the field. The stock price dropped 30 percent that day, and it was one of the gloomiest days in the office in my entire career. We knew that not only were we hurting some of the very patients that we sought to help, but we were also losing a blockbuster drug and had opened ourselves up to multibillion-dollar lawsuits that could threaten the very survival of the company and its 30,000 employees. We were about to launch the next wave of the procurement transformation and needed funding to do so, and it would have been an easy decision by the *executive leadership team* (ELT) to can the whole thing. But they didn't and instead recommitted to go ahead with it. And I know why.

Our sponsor, Richard Clark, president of Merck Manufacturing Division, brought in Willie Deese from GSK for this transformation for a reason, and that was to **lead a cultural revolution within Merck**. He saw it as a necessary step in its future existence if the company wanted its name to continue to start with an "M" and end with a "K." It was about Procurement being at the tip of the spear to force this 100-year-old culture to change. We needed a company that acknowledged the realities of the changes that were coming in the pharmaceutical industry and what was necessary to both survive it and thrive in it. If we didn't get our costs under control, the jaws of death would consume us.

The Board must have seen it too, as seven months after Vioxx, they named Richard Clark the new CEO and elevated Willie Deese to take his place as president of Merck Manufacturing Division (with Procurement reporting up through him). Four years later, and with $2 billion in documented Finance-approved procurement savings, the company survived its $5.6 billion Vioxx settlement (plus what had to be another $0.6 billion in legal fees). I can honestly say that I felt like Procurement had been aligned to the strategy of the company. Ken Frazier was the General Counsel that led this legal effort to save the company, and he later became CEO of Merck, and one of the most respected CEOs in the country.

As stated earlier, during Richard Clark's tenure as CEO, he was trying to force a cultural change across Merck, and he knew he needed to start with his own executive leadership team. Procurement was setting an example of the radical type of change that was needed, and I heard him say, "We need to change the people, and if that doesn't work, we need to change the people." After about six months, he knew Plan A to change the people wasn't working, as he saw little of the cultural movement that he needed from his ELT. It was still a "this too shall pass" attitude. So he went to Plan B and changed the people, replacing half of them and putting in a new outside boss above them. It was a bold move, but when you're on a burning platform, it's amazing how many people will just stand there and hope the fire goes out or pretend it doesn't even exist.

Procurement — "the tip of the spear" of a cultural change management initiative

Change management is always difficult in corporate circles, and it has to be led from the CEO and the ELT if it will ever have a chance of succeeding. But all category management and application of SMP to major subcategories of spend is largely an exercise in change management — getting people in cross-functional teams to expand the scope and boundaries, looking for business solutions through the third-party supply base that can drive breakthrough results. It is difficult work! It means leaning into discomfort, and getting comfortable in uncomfortable places. It means challenging the status quo and team members outside of Procurement to take risks that are not even aligned with their own personal objectives against which they are evaluated and measured. But if the CPO can lead a procurement transformation that aligns with the cultural and strategic imperatives of the CEO and the ELT, Procurement can be "the tip of the spear" for the CEO to test out elements of the cultural change that is required in the company. For Procurement's SMPs to be successful, it needs to do it anyway, so why not align with the higher-level strategy and help lead the way?

As I've said before, savings is the worst Procurement metric, with the exception of all other Procurement metrics. While we had strict savings rules at Merck that had to be validated by stakeholders and Finance for anything above $100,000, we also made some changes to encourage the right behaviors by the SMs and GCMs. If we didn't have a last price paid to benchmark against, we developed a market-based or benchmark savings that was fair and would reflect the hard work done by them to achieve not only competitive pricing, but recognition of Total Cost of Ownership (TCO) optimization over the life of the buy that included its maintenance and other lifecycle costs. We created incentives to come up with the business solution that was right for the company, not just a Procurement metric. We differentiated between P&L savings that would come out of budgets and savings that could be kept by the budget holder as an incentive to cooperate with us, help us lead the efforts, optimize the solution to their business problems and give them some WIIFM ("What's in it for me?"). In escalating markets, we tracked cost avoidance though we didn't report it as savings, and we gave credit to the achievement of those avoidances in reviews, especially if the SM or GCM could demonstrate that they saved cash from going out the door. By doing so, we eliminated the need for competition between SMs for category assignments that had higher savings potential — everyone was going to be rewarded for hard work.

Capital projects were given separate treatment for market competitiveness, as each tended to be unique, and we considered depreciation impact on the P&L, and value engineering ideas that reduced the amount of capital that needed to be spent or would result in lower ongoing maintenance costs. When it came to lease versus buy decisions, or whether it was better to get into longer term 3- to 5-year agreements, we gave credit to following years and the benefits that it provided versus market realities. We set expectations and measures that reflected the desired end result, whether it was:

- setting up market competitive catalogues that gave R&D researchers choices in what they needed to buy; or

- working with contract research organizations and investing in processes or systems that would speed the cycle times of clinical trials to help us bring drugs to market faster; or

- working with HR Benefits to find new solutions that lowered the cost of employee contributions to the medical plan and the cost of their prescription drugs; or

- working with the salesforce on optimizing their lease car cost, reliability, and maintenance; or

- optimizing the recruiting process for finding and onboarding new salespeople (due to turnover in the industry).

Procurement was there to drive competitiveness and solve business problems, not procurement problems. It was hard work, but by going about it the right way, the savings machine went into perpetual motion mode and satisfied the company's need for optimizing its spending. Wherever we could find ways to substitute, reduce, avoid, or eliminate the need to spend with a different solution, we took the credit it deserved. Elimination of unnecessary spending is 100 percent savings! You can't do better than that.

There were also some more contentious elements of this change management process, like adopting some GE-type tactics of creating a totem pole of all workers by performance, and then zeroing out the bottom 10 percent from all bonuses and inflation/salary adjustments. This also made it easier when the time came for thinning out the organization during layoffs and applying a performance layer to the process. I found this to be somewhat brutal and at times unfair, as we were constantly rewarding people and also letting people go throughout the year in procurement based on performance, and we weren't given credit for having already eliminated poor performers when they applied this as a corporate-wide initiative. I had heavy objections to this and let it be known.

I also saw that not everything that we were doing as procurement — to be the tip of the spear to lead cultural change at Merck — was taking hold in other functions. I began to see more of a "do as we say, not as we do"-type attitude taking hold in other leadership teams. As a 400-person function, trying to lead 30,000 people in a cultural change has its limits. I finally left Merck at the end of 2008, and inevitably, new cycles started to take hold with a huge merger with Schering-Plough, new procurement leadership, new priorities, and new challenges. There is nothing more constant than change.

Culture #7 – Citrix Systems, Inc.

Boundaryless behavior — what is that? For me, it was a cultural revolution that redefined everything that I ever thought or knew about how corporations work. It was by pure happenstance that I bumped into an old friend 30-plus years after he had mentored me in a youth group in high school, only to find out that he had become a high-powered consultant who was guiding change at GE under Jack Welch's leadership. Ron Ashkenas had written or coauthored several books, one of which was *The Boundaryless Organization*. This was the book that changed my life, my entire approach about the impact of culture in the corporate world. Companies could no longer be successful as hierarchical organizations and needed to move toward speed, flexibility, innovation, and integration to survive in the fast-paced environment that was coming into being.

I first became aware of looking at corporations as biological beings when I was introduced to Professor Russell Ackoff, professor emeritus of Management Science at Wharton. Already well into his 80s, he introduced me to the concept of each corporate function operating as a biological organ in an ecosystem, and how organs adapted and interacted with one another for the survival of the body in which they lived in the ecosystem of which they were a part. Ashkenas took this to the next level, exploring how functions within the corporation needed to "span" their boundaries in order for both them and their corporate bodies to survive in an ever-competitive world. Boundaries are a necessity because without them, organs like the heart, brain, liver, kidneys, etc. (each representing a function in the body) need boundaries to prevent them from melting into an amorphous mass! But for these organs to function properly, they don't need to break boundaries, they need to "span" their boundaries through the exchange of liquids, chemicals, electrical currents, and nutrients. Their boundaries needed to be firm but porous (maybe allowing for osmosis) in order for the functions to survive and the corporate body to survive.

Ashkenas talked of four types of boundaries that needed to be broken, or spanned, in the corporate world in order to be successful:

- *Hierarchical levels*, breaking the tyranny of the vertical, status-driven boundaries of rank;
- *Horizontal boundaries of interunit divisions*, breaking various functional silos and business units driven by specialization, expertise, and socialization that exist within the corporation (finance, marketing, sales, procurement, supply chain, accounting, IT, etc.);
- *Boundaries between internal versus external organizations in the environment* that separate customers from employees and the supply chains that make up the landscape of the communities in which we live; and
- *Geographic boundaries* of different regions, markets, cultures, social practices, mores, and time zones.

From all of this, and borrowing from all that I learned and liked (and disliked) about the cultures in which I had operated, I asked for and received at Citrix a clean slate to form a new global strategic sourcing organization. This included a new centralized "Procure-to-Pay" (P2P) structure (working hand in hand with accounts payable) operating on a single multimodule upstream-to-downstream P2P system on a global basis, employing a five-stage SMP to run our category management strategy. **But more importantly, I informed my visionary boss (the controller, no less!) that all of this was going to be grounded on a culture and philosophy of boundaryless behavior.** She did not necessarily agree with or understand this, but she gave me the latitude to work it, which is all I asked for.

The essence of this culture was to work in a "share and build" environment where people always said "yes, and ..." instead of "yes, but ...", where everyone took the stripes off their sleeves and worked as a team, where critical immediate feedback was freely given as well as complimentary feedback, and where making mistakes while pushing the envelope would not only be supported but encouraged and rewarded as long as it wasn't hidden. We would accomplish so much more if we worked this way, shared the success, and took measured risks based on facts and data than if we operated on fear and a CYA attitude (do I really need to spell out what that acronym stands for … I think you know). But talk is cheap, and I had to show that we would walk the walk, not just talk the talk.

So in setting up the organization, I appointed an up-and-coming talented young man in the UK as my chief of staff, showing that we would find a way to operate across geographic boundaries as a global team. The very first "screwup" happened one month in regarding the conversion of some temporary labor in Turkey into employees, and I immediately backed my team 110 percent throughout — they saw that nobody was going to be thrown under the bus on my team for what was perceived to have been a Procurement mistake (though the fault really lay with HR). I trusted a young woman on the team to lead a sourcing project on janitorial services, as I refused to sign a contract for a 2 percent increase (based on an increase in the minimum wage) — she restructured the statement of work (SOW), uncovered multiple duplicate charging errors, put it out to bid and achieved a 23 percent price reduction with the same supplier! Then I sent another big signal to the team as we were changing our office location: I gave up my office to sit in a cubicle alongside everyone else and let the team use my office as a meeting room on a first come, first served basis. Stripes had to come off the sleeves. Of the eight members on my procurement leadership team (PLT) that I appointed, three were members of the LGBTQ+ community. Our PLT so trusted each other (a number of them were actually part of the interview process that led to me being appointed in the role), they openly admitted who had pushed for me and who had pushed for an alternate candidate and why (there had been 30 candidates in all). This brought us even closer together.

We brought in some great talent and upskilled the talent that we had, but it was the culture of boundaryless behavior that drove all of it. In working cross-functionally as we set up category management SMP teams, we let them know that we were going to lean into discomfort until we all had butterflies in our stomach about what we were going to do next — only then could we know that we were pushing the envelope and exploring breakthrough solutions. Those solutions were to improve the entire, end-to-end (E2E) process, not the procurement process. Our goal was to solve business problems, not procurement problems. We were going to act in a boundaryless manner, and we needed everyone's help to achieve that. This was our cultural imperative that would guide our thinking and our actions.

Citrix had a culture of very democratized decision-making, so this was not anathema to them. They also had a culture of respect, and if you had a specific job function, they assumed that you had the authority and expertise to perform in that job. But they also had difficulty coming to a decision and executing decisions, and once decisions had been made by consensus, nobody was actually sure who had made the decision, leaving no accountability. We had to work on this to get our siloed functional partners out of this cycle. This really got tested when an activist investor,

Elliott Management, got involved and started forcing some radical changes in the company. But for us in Procurement, they couldn't have come at a better time, as we were pushing for radical changes ourselves through the launch of a wave of SMPs.

Timing isn't everything, it's the ONLY thing, and with the help of some outside consulting procurement resources, we had more hands to run more SMPs and a corporate dictate to help the company restructure and take $200 million out of its cost structure. Procurement was targeted to help with $45 million of that, which was twice as much as had been done in any previous year (we were only 1.5 years into our transformation and were still building out the systems). A year later, and with $82 million in procurement savings validated, we had pretty much blown away our commitment to Wall Street. We wrote up our experiences and submitted applications to Procurement Leaders, a global organization of procurement excellence, and were informed that we were named finalists by their panel of judges in three categories! In May 2017, we were named the winner of the Cross-Functional Transformation Award — developing strong internal relationships. In just 3.5 years, we had gone from being a decentralized paper-pushing organization to a globally recognized leader in procurement excellence. Category management and multistage SMP and a full suite of Ariba tools were only pieces of the puzzle, though; our culture of boundaryless behavior made this possible.

Takeaways on Culture

From my viewpoint, **Procurement must first change its own internal perception of what it wants to be** before the stakeholders can trust that the change is permanent and sustainable and in their best interests (there's that WIIFM again). How you see yourself has to change before you can expect others to see you in a new light, especially if your goal is to be seen as a *trusted advisor to the business*. If you see your role as one of *control*, as one as "Savings R Us" or "Negotiations R Us" or "Contracts R Us," you will be relegated to only solving procurement and supply chain problems, not business problems. **You cannot expect to have the business see you as a strategic partner if you yourself do not see yourself as one or act in that manner.** Running cross-functional SMPs with *team charters* and *source plans* will make no difference to them if all they see you focused on is a savings outcome. They will know your motivations and incentives for what you do and how you act based on your culture as a procurement organization. There is no hiding from it.

The key to ending this cycle of behavior (cycle of violence, in my view) is instituting a culture where all the right key performance indicators (KPIs) are established and measured, and the wrong behaviors are no longer rewarded. Savings can be a positive measure in a truly balanced scorecard, especially if the team achieves alignment with the strategy of the company, and it becomes part of that strategy without compromising best sourcing practices. Some of the balanced scorecard measures I have used to motivate the right behaviors have included focused measurement on percent of spend where early involvement in the sourcing process with the stakeholder functions was achieved (by one measure, we saw value generation for early involvement come out at 3 times the return compared to late involvement); an ROI measurement of the time and resources dedicated to a SMP; and the cycle time for bringing about the changes that are sought. One can add weightings to procurement SMPs that reflect the level of difficulty and complexity to make the desired result a reality. The willingness of the team to "lean into discomfort" can also be a weight in this balanced scorecard. Did the team avoid "team-speak" and challenge the organization to move away from "lowest common denominator" solutions that make everyone feel comfortable but never move the needle? All of this can be part of a balanced scorecard that reinforces the culture that you want to project to your procurement organization, which will then be viewed differently by the stakeholders whose trust you are trying to capture. Only by changing the culture can you be guaranteed a seat at the table where the budgets are controlled and the real decisions are made, one or two levels below the C-Suite.

You've got to set the right KPIs, measures, and objectives to make cultural change.

Example 1: In the 1980s at Air Products & Chemicals, Inc. (APCI), they were having issues with a lot of lost time accidents and workers compensation claims at their manufacturing plants, and road accidents with their drivers of liquid oxygen and nitrogen tank trucks. They called in the safety experts at DuPont to do a review of their operations, who came back with numerous recommendations to not only employ safer practices in their standard operating procedures (SOPs), but to also emphasize a culture of safety in the company. Two changes really stood out. First, all general managers now had 50 percent of their bonus based on their lost time accident reporting at their plants. Second, any employee injured in a car accident while on company business and not wearing their seat belt had to first report into the president of APCI to explain themselves before they could go back to work. The company then went 6,000,000 man hours without a lost time incident.

Example 2: When I first joined Citrix Systems, Procurement had been switched from reporting to Operations to reporting to the controller and head of Global Shared Services. For some reason, people were spending hundreds of hours compiling documentation of contracts and purchase orders to meet a KPI that showed that the function was achieving a metric of 75 percent of "spend under management" that Operations had set. In reality, virtually none of this spend was actually being managed under a category strategy or even competitively bid. It was a useless, meaningless metric, and I immediately put a stop to it.

No matter what business I have worked in, and which you work in, someone will be out there criticizing your very existence: chemicals — you poison the environment; defense — you help kill people; confectionery — you are the cause of mass diabetes and other health issues; pharmaceuticals — you charge exorbitant prices that force people into debt; software — you are destroying people's jobs and livelihoods. I am proud of each of the industries in which I chose to work, but I have not always been proud of the corporate and procurement culture within which I had to operate. In the end, it has always been true that my job satisfaction came more from the "how" than the "what" was accomplished. It is a simple truth: "Culture Eats Strategy for Lunch."

Chapter 9:
Understanding and Segmenting Your Supply Base

To create improved supplier relationships, it is essential to understand that not all suppliers will merit the same types of relationships. For this reason, it is important in the early stages of supplier relationship management (SRM) to fully understand the context and nature of your supply base, and to segment the suppliers in order so that different levels of resources can be allocated to different segments, based on risk, opportunity, and potential for improvement. This process is described next.

Understanding Your Supply Base

A comprehensive understanding of spending patterns in the business is a function of the enterprise's ability to capture data in a meaningful way. The importance of conducting a thorough analysis of spend was emphasized in a dated but still relevant interview with a Big Three automotive executive who recalls how this first came to light in the 1970s during the dramatic run-up in petrochemical prices.

In the 1970s our company was facing over $400 million of economic exposure impacting transportation costs, resins, chemical feedstocks, and other parts. I interviewed buyers and tried to get an idea of which parts were made of what material, and the relative level of exposure they had to oil prices. As this wasn't very accurate, I sought to understand where the raw material was coming from in the third or fourth tier of suppliers based on the types of plastics. But how could I get all the parts and consolidate them in a way that made sense to measure exposure? The only way I knew how to do this was to dive down into the bill of materials and review the commodity description that the part code was associated with. Although there were thousands of part codes, I was able to work it down to 200 specific groupings of parts and compared this to the buyers assigned to each part. And then I compared this grouping to a list that should be the buyers for each part. This allowed me to look at the "deck" of the current buy for a commodity group. I started by looking at no more than 10 commodity groups, and looked at the production buy across these commodity groups. With the data organized this way, I was able to see that I could consolidate the number of suppliers by commodity, the value of the buy for the group, using data that no one had ever seen before. I could then start to see how many commodities I was dealing with, and was able to reload the commodities to a smaller group of buyers with broader respon-

sibilities that might cover more than one commodity. I also had to consider the complexity and workload required for a buyer to cover a single commodity group, and sometimes had to split it.[1]

This example illustrates why understanding spending patterns can lead to other insights on how to better organize internal governance over spending categories of parts and services. The discovery made by this automotive executive in the 1970s applies today, although the spend analysis systems have evolved from the environment of computer punch cards this individual had to struggle with. The important lesson here is that analysis of spend data needs to be combined with business conversations to derive a full picture of who is responsible for the sourcing decision, which suppliers are part of each point of origin for sourcing, and the commonalities and differences that exist.

This discovery does not necessarily lead to immediate recognition for Procurement's authority over sourcing decisions. In many cases, the mechanics of moving toward *source to pay* represents a major change for organizations in the early stages of procurement transformation. One executive recalls that "when I showed up at meetings on budget and technology planning, people at the meeting looked at me and asked 'Where did you come from?' and 'How are we supposed to work together, and what will the outcome be?'" This requires sourcing executives who are sophisticated in their approach to engaging stakeholders and are knowledgeable enough on the commodity to be able to have the right conversation demonstrating expertise and professionalism. Remember how in Chapter 2 a cabinet buyer was assigned to buy a commercial lighting system because it was contained in a cabinet.

Using the right platform for a dialogue with the line of business stakeholders should align on terms that are not necessarily directly associated with driving cost savings. In many of the financial services companies we met with, the primary driver was around risk exposure due to stricter OCC (Office of the Comptroller of the Currency) guidelines around measurement of supplier risk. This is in large measure due to the 2008 banking crisis, and compliance is not an option. This platform can be used as a means for also building a spend database and beginning the process of stratifying suppliers based on operational and business risk, as well as exposure of customer data in the supply chain. This was described by a chief procurement officer (CPO) at a large global bank:

> *At the highest level we have a risk segmentation around concentration of data privacy risk, and an elaborate segmentation around the inherent service a supplier provides as well as the overall stability of the vendor's inherent risk. But we also consider the balance of trade they have with our core partners. We collect four levels of risk which in turn dictates its own level of governance and management. Tier 1 is the low spend low risk, which involves no assessments. Tier 2 is higher risk and we rely on self-assessments. But Tiers 3 and 4 involve much more due diligence by our risk officers and take much more time.*[2]

---

1 Interview of Steve Zimmer by Rob Handfield, February 2014, https://scm.ncsu.edu/scm-articles/article/the-origins-of-category-management.

2 Interview conducted by Rob Handfield, March 2014, https://scm.ncsu.edu/scm-articles/article/using-spend-analysis-to-understand-supply-chain-risks.

Understanding Your Supply Base

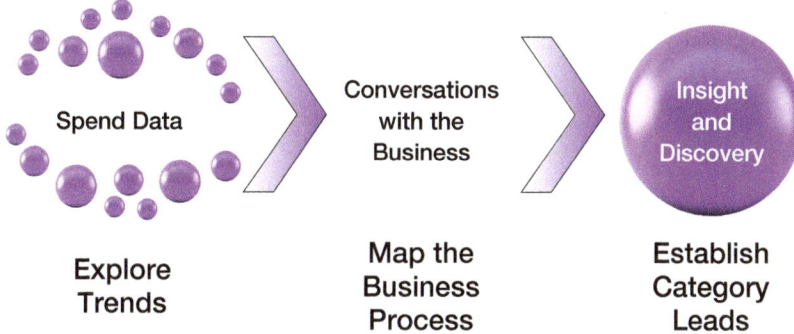

Spend Data

Explore
Trends

Conversations
with the
Business

Map the
Business
Process

Insight
and
Discovery

Establish
Category
Leads

Phase 1: Map Business Processes

Direct conversations through on-site engagement with the line of business is the most direct and effective means of understanding how sourcing processes are occurring today, as well as understanding how the sourcing need evolves and is expressed to suppliers. As an example, one large financial services organization found that corporate offices were buying art to decorate interiors. A total cost of ownership (TCO) analysis revealed that interior design consultants were directing the spend with suppliers, but that the cost driver for art was the cost of framing and transportation and installation not the value of the painting or graphic itself. This in turn generated a different analysis of suppliers that resulted in a different set of outsourced relationships with delivery providers that generated significant savings. Understanding the buying channel currently used and evaluating it against alternatives often leads to a different set of decision frameworks with different sets of suppliers than originally considered by stakeholders. This can be accomplished by assigning sourcing managers to work closely with lines of business, to move beyond the static spend data and understand the patterns of consumption to identify root causes of unexplained variances.

Supplier registration processes need to be designed around sourcing engagement processes, which track the supplier life cycle. This begins with the supplier registration process, which establishes the supplier's profile, capabilities, and service offerings. The next phase occurs when a request for information (RFI) or request for quotation (RFQ) generates more information on supplier capabilities and additional price, volume, and operational business risks. The contracting phase leads to additional details on pricing volume, general terms and conditions (T&Cs), and approaches, leading to ongoing vendor performance against the contract. Often, this is documented into supplier scorecards, and over the Procure-to-Pay (P2P) cycle, invoices and payments occur, which are folded into the ongoing spend analysis. Payments need to be matched against contract prices and performance requirements, and a reconciliation occurs. When a vendor is terminated, the contract is closed out, but the data must be retained over time. If one looks at the entire set of transactions that must be organized, maintained, and cleansed over time to allow reporting and ongoing sourcing analysis, multiplied over millions of vendors across multiple languages, the challenges of tracking and managing spend analytics becomes evident.

Supplier Registration and Life Cycle Analytics

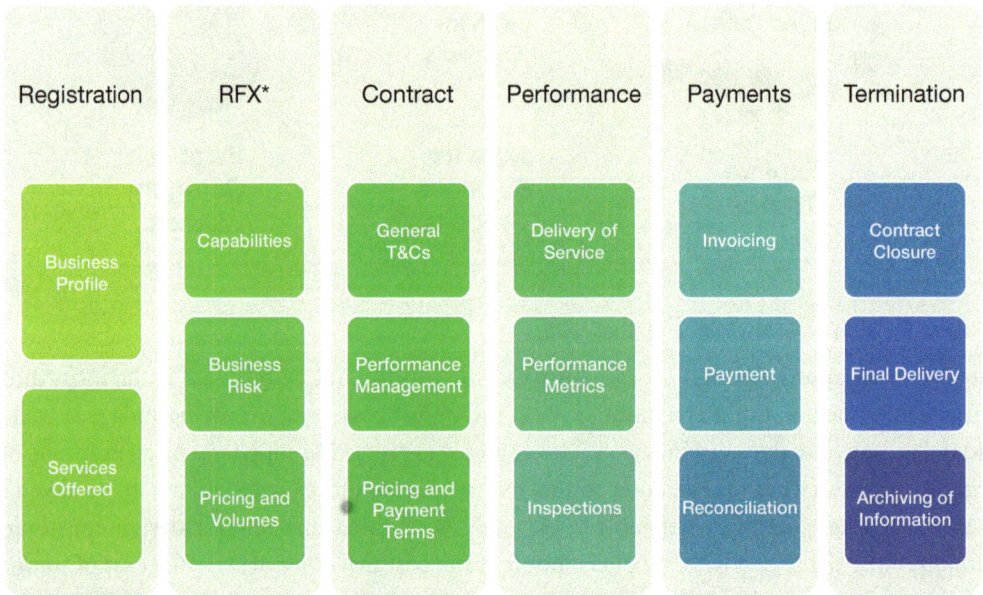

Registration	RFX*	Contract	Performance	Payments	Termination
Business Profile	Capabilities	General T&Cs	Delivery of Service	Invoicing	Contract Closure
	Business Risk	Performance Management	Performance Metrics	Payment	Final Delivery
Services Offered	Pricing and Volumes	Pricing and Payment Terms	Inspections	Reconciliation	Archiving of Information

Source: Doug Hague

*RFx is an abbreviation used for a process that may involve one of three things: RFI, RFP, or RFQ.

Another insight derived through sourcing analysis is to understand the contractual engagement pipeline for sourcing deals. For example, one financial service company is building a database of contracts, monitoring those set to expire in 180 to 365 days, to identify which ones require early preparation and engagement. Some of these may include large service contracts (examples include relocation services, marketing campaigns, etc.). In some cases, these deals are occurring within a single business unit, and it becomes important to engage with the parties early to establish a consultative approach to helping them develop sourcing options that meet the business need.

When the HANA platform was developed by SAP, it enabled a cloud-based spend visibility database (such as Ariba) to drive faster performance, scalability, and speed as well as eliminate traditional database requirements for a legacy database. As shown in our survey analysis (page X), the variety of tools being used to support spend analysis and supplier segmentation analysis varies, with only a minority of companies using an established spend analysis tool, such as in Ariba. Over a quarter of firms still have no formal SRM-related tool or methodology to support analysis of the supply base.

A lot has changed in Ariba's approach to supplier life cycle management since 2014, but unfortunately it was accompanied by a series of module delays happening multiple times. Ariba isn't the only one to go through this. When you offer a full suite of modules for all aspects of the P2P, supplier and contracting life cycle from upstream to downstream, the complexity created in making the system work for you in a meaningful manner becomes exponential. As I (Howard) like to say, "The tool doesn't work for you … you work for the tool," and your cost structure as a P2P organization reflects this. The same goes for trying to institute an *enterprise requirements planning* (ERP) system. Virtually every ERP systems project that I have experienced has failed on budget, timeline, and functionality, even when the best people in the company and the most reputable integrators are brought on board to run it. I had a CIO once tell me that 75 percent of these large IT projects will fail. Why is this? Very simply, it's the law of big numbers (you know, statistics and math!) — as you increase the number of people involved to make it work, the complexity of the tasks, coordination, and communication rises exponentially. That same CIO had two very simple solutions to this: 1) don't do big IT projects; and 2) when you do big IT projects and they start to fail, as they will, throw fewer people at it. Politically, neither of these will get you promoted in the corporate world, which also lies at the heart of the problem. You have to go after the projects when the money gets allocated for them or you lose the funding, and because of the size of the multimillion-dollar investments, failure and scaling back is not a politically acceptable option — you have to get to a point where you can declare victory after moving the goalposts.

There is a solution now to all of this in the digitization of procurement, which we discuss in Chapter 11. A number of SRM and many other procurement apps for running sourcing and auction events, or managing the long tail spend of smaller suppliers and other functionalities, have been developed that are more "plug & play" and can connect into large ERP systems using simple application programming interfaces (APIs). They require limited training for the users and are easy to install, but it requires a decision by leaders of the function and Finance to write off major investments in existing full suite modules and admit that technology has moved on. Like people used to say to me, "Good luck with that!"

An excellent example of real-time spend analytics is Siemens, a €50B global company with multiple divisions and an €8B building controls division. Siemens began its journey by focusing on data governance, beginning with core data on customers and then focusing on establishing quality data for systems operating in different areas. This required developing regional governance by area, using Hyperion to create financial reports, as well as project management tools used by offices executing projects at universities and hospitals, etc. The initial goal was to make sure that the team interconnected data from different places while addressing data quality. Some initial disputes arose regarding whose data went into the data mart first. Finance wanted Hyperion data for financial analytics, whereas Operations wanted the project management spend data — so the team had to go through a reconciliation process. An important component of the rollout was the development of institutional analytics, that is, analytics that have a common standardized look and feel. To enable this, Siemens adopted QlikView as their visualization standard. In many organizations, analysts spend weeks establishing their "end of quarter" spend analysis charts and graphs. The goal was to enable an executive to generate exactly the metrics and charts they wanted, anytime, with a "push of a button." Siemens achieved this goal, creating a platform that allows all senior executives to press a button to produce a real-time spend analysis anytime, not just at the end of the quarter. One executive emphasized that this capability, more than any other, allowed him to completely change the way he managed the business, as he didn't have to wait until the end of the quarter to see how he was doing against his budgets.

Phase 2: Establishing Category Leads

For categories that cross multiple business units, the effort to build a consensus among different groups is more challenging, but the opportunity is often greater. This begins by understanding the individual within the business responsible for developing the strategy, and how each point of view on requirements differs across the lines of business. Finding opportunities for consolidation of supplier spend will vary, and in some cases, will be very difficult to do through a conference call with 10 people! Still, low-hanging fruit can be discovered through these conversations that provide a very easy solution, leading to a starting point for taking on the tougher categories of spend.

In some cases, external hires may be required with prior experience and capabilities in the category of focus. For example, a large insurance company recognized that they needed category specialists to understand the current state and provide advice to lines of business on sourcing options:

> *"We had to hire an IT specialist to work with the IT group to assist in building their IT category strategy. Travel was a similar story: We didn't have a focus around travel and recognized that to develop great travel deals we needed in-depth skills, and hired an individual who is now going out assessing process, tools, and skills on this team to ensure we can make the leap to build a comprehensive travel category strategy. The procurement solutions team works optimally when we have those with good procurement experience and good functional experience. So for our marketing category, we hired advertising agency people and taught them procurement. That has its challenges, but the benefit we got from that ability to build a TRUSTED ADVISOR function was invaluable. We are doing passive recruiting for more marketing people on our team because we feel we have solid procurement experience but need the marketing experience."[3]*

Financial service companies are also moving to establish a "service relationship owner" to manage risks from an operational perspective. This approach recognizes that a center-led approach is not able to manage all the risk with outsourced relationships. These positions are designated to act as an intermediary between those who manage commercial contracts and risk. Companies have also sought to employ third parties to conduct some level of risk monitoring of credit scores, turnover of executives, and other dimensions that can provide updates to supplier profiles.

Developing an understanding of key supplier characteristics, buying channels, spend analysis, and capabilities is fundamental to building relationships and establishing criteria for segmentation of the supply base. It also serves as the basis for establishing communication with suppliers and establishing Procurement's position as the driver of relationships. An important change here is designating individual category owners who become the coordinators for spend decisions when it crosses multiple lines of business, or indeed within a single business.

This is especially the case for other industries such as healthcare that are in the early stages of supplier management and have outsourced much of their spending to third-party "group

---

3 Interview conducted by Rob Handfield with insurance industry CPO, January 2014.

purchasing organizations"(GPOs). In so doing, they have created intermediaries between the purchasing organization and suppliers and have created barriers that allow suppliers to sell directly to clinicians (e.g., "physician preference items"). This is beginning to change as hospitals are creating new category management leaders responsible for surgical goods, information technology, pharmaceuticals, and other categories of goods and indirect spending items. One hospital leader noted:

> "I have made my sourcing category leaders responsible for their own contracts. Many hospitals require lawyers to go through their contracts, but we have learned that lawyers only take com-mercial direction from administrators in the past. Category leaders can track the life cycle of a piece of capital equipment, and begin to think about the long-term service, parts, and warranty costs, which is often overlooked in these contracts, and often where suppliers make their highest profits. We have sought to simplify the relationship, where sourcing leaders are responsible not only for sourcing, but for value analysis, capital spending in that category, contract management, and supplier performance management. Many hospitals today are just happy to be involved in entering the purchase order, without understanding why it is so important to be involved in the earliest stages of supplier engagement. There is also an important cultural change in educating suppliers and introducing them to the category leader who will be their only point for engage-ment from this point forward."[4]

These discussions show that prior to launching any form of SRM initiative, there is a need to fully understand the discipline and variation in current procurement behaviors across the organization. The discipline involves beginning to understand and build better data on activities suppliers are conducting, that leads to insights to establish the right type of business driver Procurement is asking suppliers to deliver to. A full understanding of spending leads to a natural pattern of product and supply clustering that is unique for every organization, and it forms the basis for establishing category team leaders who can specialize in delving into these relationships further. A category leader can then conduct deeper category analysis studies and mine other levels of data that relate to supplier life cycles, which in turn leads to discovery of cost drivers, spending patterns, price analysis, and deeper understanding of supplier capabilities.

Supply Base Structuring and Measurement

Engagement in the sourcing process is only the beginning of SRM. As category leaders begin to fully understand the nature of spending not just within the business unit but across the enterprise, suppliers begin to fall into a number of different clusters or "segments" based on a variety of criteria. In our research, we identified a number of criteria used to build out a supplier segmentation framework that becomes the basis for establishing the appropriate type of relationship that will drive the highest return to the business.

Organizations may never develop 100 percent visibility into all buying channel transactions, as the number of buying channels (purchasing system, p-card, e-catalog, or others) may prevent detailed understanding, particularly for services and indirect procurement areas. However, the

---

4 Interview conducted by Rob Handfield with hospital CPO, March 2014.

level of insight should be directionally correct and provide a basis for establishing a structure around the types of relationships that exist. Thirty years ago, Peter Kraljic's *Harvard Business Review* publication[5] (1983) identified the need for Procurement to establish "portfolio" analysis structures using a 2 × 2 matrix measuring spend volume (low–high) and supplier importance/risk (low–high) (see Figure 1). His key message was that Procurement should focus more on high-value and high-risk supply items and that these called for "supply management" rather than "purchasing management."

Figure 1: Portfolio Analysis

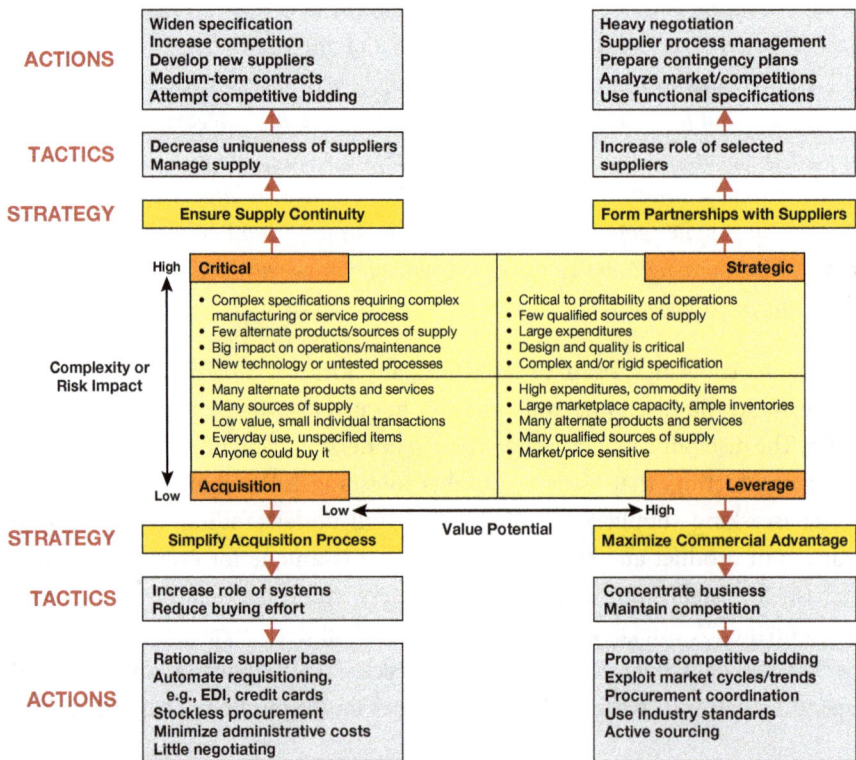

Source: Bozarth and Handfield, 2017

In our study, we found a number of different approaches to measuring and segmenting the supply base, which often varied across industries and criteria. These are covered in more detail on the following pages.

Segmenting Suppliers by Risk (Financial Services)

"Models are always wrong, but sometimes useful. Proxy data is based on an initial assumption and we refine that assumption over time. Risk can't be refined, but we can refine our assumptions about it."

— financial services supplier analytics executive

5 Kraljic, Peter. "Purchasing must become Supply Management," *Harvard Business Review*, 1983.

Supplier segmentation around risk to the business is often the primary means for segmentation in the financial services industry and insurance industries, as we noted earlier in the prior section. For example, one large financial services company has segmented and created five tiers around enterprise exposure and business impact. This is initially done by spend, and as new deals emerge, these are used to update spend measures based on aggregation and concentration risk. These interfaces with the business also provide input as to the criticality of suppliers from a customer-facing impact perspective in the event of a failure or data security breach. The top tier are strategic suppliers that touch a majority of the business, a second tier that stores, hosts, and processes key data elements, while the bottom tiers represent minimal risk but have varying levels of impact and spending with the business. The tiering also drives a cadence of supplier monitoring events, which may include a variety of checklists that assess various dimensions of performance.

A common problem that spans all segmentation methodologies involves creating an understanding of where a supplier sits from an enterprise perspective in the tiering structure. To that end, companies seek to document the procedures for segmentation, and publish materials on the company website to establish expectations for supplier expectations in each tier. This helps alleviate surprises when suppliers are engaged in sourcing decisions by the business.

One company developed a template that is used by the business to help them understand this. It asks questions such as what documents are applicable for the vendor (source code escrow, data security policy, other security policies, etc.) followed by a lengthier survey that goes out to suppliers who do their own self-reporting. A disadvantage is that financial services are dependent on the accuracy and completeness of their supplier's responses to these requirements.

An important challenge in segmenting by risk is data quality. Ensuring data quality has more to do with the skill sets around a supplier database but involves more than just checking to see if data elements such as NAICS codes are correct. Ensuring that people entering the data aren't using four-digit random numbers for NAICS codes, for instance, involves interesting approaches to data management.

For many companies, segmenting by risk involves conducting the right types of analysis on data that may not currently exist about suppliers you don't know you are using! Some of the types of risk analyses include information security, business continuity, subcontracting risk, globalization risk, reputational risk, regulatory risk, strategic risk, performance risk, and financial risk. Establishing the proxies for these forms of risk involves a good deal of assumptions around behaviors and how processes are operating, and whether employees are following the process. This once again mandates a need for closer dialogue with stakeholders as an important component of this process. In financial services, OCC regulations are requiring banks to have a better understanding of who subcontractors to tier 1 contractors are and what they are doing. This is difficult to build into a contract — are we able to go inspect a subcontractor, and what type of information is needed to know whether or not they have been subcontracted?

A secondary element of risk segmentation involves stress testing the portfolio to disruptive risks. Which suppliers will be impacted by hurricanes or major breaches of software such as Windows, and how will you communicate if computer connections are down? Financial services are increasingly being asked to analyze many different types of disruption scenarios (e.g., London and New York have power outages concurrently!) and thinking about the possible levels of interactions and associated exposures is becoming an important component of supplier risk segmentation and management.

Our survey suggests that the majority of organizations (58 percent) conduct an annual due diligence/risk review on key strategic suppliers while others only do when there is a contract renewal (17 percent). Given the importance of risk on organizational business continuity, our opinion is that biannual or quarterly risk reviews may be appropriate given the strategic relationships and the approaches identified by best-in-class organizations.

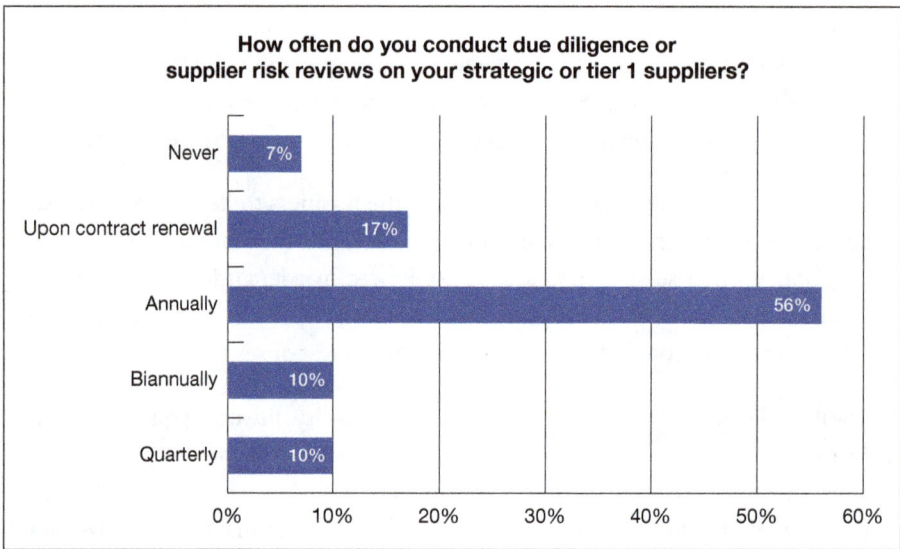

How often do you conduct due diligence or supplier risk reviews on your strategic or tier 1 suppliers?

Category	Percentage
Never	7%
Upon contract renewal	17%
Annually	56%
Biannually	10%
Quarterly	10%

Such approaches will rely on increasingly complex analytical solutions. Information and analytics will play an increasingly important role in understanding and managing supply chains. Informed decisions on supplier segmentation require data architecture quality and flow, and connecting all of the required sources of data to establish a risk portfolio will require ever-more levels of information transparency, which is the goal of reporting. For example, one financial services executive stated: "My goal is to commit to having stakeholders display the information they need in 15 seconds or less. But to do this means I need to have the data quickly, but it also has to be data that my internal customers can trust. To achieve this, I need to establish the right data architecture and flow to ensure that information is time-stamped, and is the data being provisioned correctly in data warehouses and drive the right analytical sandboxes, or be able to join it virtually."

Risk and its definition to a company will vary based on your line of business. During the pandemic, supply chain "assurance of supply" risk became a top priority due to its impact on both costs and revenues for companies. However, even bigger risks have emerged in the areas of both data privacy and cybersecurity for internal operating systems. In 2017, the EU passed GDPR legislation that allows them to fine companies up to 4 percent of their annual income for data breaches or unauthorized use and distribution of *personally identifiable information* (PII). Additionally, ransomware attacks have become commonplace whereby hackers (many with support from their governments) break into company systems, steal sensitive data, and hold them for ransom until large sums of cash or digital currency is deposited in their accounts. Insurance rates for these types of business interruptions have also skyrocketed, forcing companies to accept more risk to operating income than ever before by increasing their insurance deductibles. Often times, these attacks involve not only company internal operations, but flow down to customers and/or the supply base, who are also victimized. Stopping these data leaks or intrusions by bad actors require companies to invest in greater cybersecurity hardware and software, as well as the writing and enforcement of policies that slow down the cycle times of business operations. They can also add significant cost to the IT, procurement, and legal functions tasked with identifying system weaknesses and negotiating more protective liability clauses and data integrity audits of its supply base. The most frustrating part is that the size of the customer or supplier needing this additional scrutiny does not fit any risk matrix — even small accounts with whom you do business can be points of intrusion or weakness and require the same level of scrutiny as large accounts.

Nascent procurement functions will need to establish a five-year plan that seeks merely to establish a deeper appreciation of the types of supplier relationships that exist based on risk. This may involve them in completing annual surveys on vendors as part of the operational risk assessments and have them weigh in through crowdsourcing activities. As one financial services executive noted:

"I'm not looking to build a big supplier management organization. I believe there is a lot of value in simply having the business aligned, and to provide some consistency and standardization and understanding on how we classify suppliers. I'd like our businesspeople to provide an impact, and to achieve that I need them to be part of the program. As such, I ensure that they participate in our risk assessments, and provide policies on what it means to be an approved supplier. As we eventually develop an approved supplier list across the business units, the business needs to know what we expect of them."

Segmenting Suppliers by Importance to the Business (Oil and Gas)

Oil and gas organizations are characterized by sourcing activity that is often dispersed across multiple projects in different parts of the globe. In order to drive category management across different technical and project activities, a three-tiered approach is typically adopted. Opportunities for strategic sourcing are identified through a centralized planning organization that establishes new projects and approaches and designates a sourcing team to engage the organization in this process, which is relatively well-defined in most organizations. The final cornerstone of category management is SRM that occurs once the contract has been established and is sustainable.

In this context, SRM involves typically four levels of segmentation based on the companies we interviewed in our research. At the lowest tier, "blanket" or "transactional" relationships include low-volume low-risk suppliers, that may span 90 percent of the supply base but less than 10 percent of the spend volume. This tier typically has no performance measures associated with their contract, as they are easily replaceable, and due diligence is restricted to whether a robust contract exists for these suppliers, or even whether POs are just being used. At the next level, "core" suppliers include those are that may be in one sector or local to a specific global region, who still have relatively low risk, who may have metrics that are monitored on a case-by-case business, but who are managed primarily at the category management or business partner level. Next, "managed" suppliers have detailed performance metrics, as they represent a high level of spend, but number perhaps fewer than 200 suppliers worldwide. These suppliers are engaged in detailed operational reviews in coordination with our category teams to monitor their performance on safety, on-time execution, and other purely performance-based metrics established through a scorecard. Also in this category are those suppliers that are critical from a supply perspective, but not particularly strategic and may not be engaged in long-term planning. (A good example would be niche software providers.)

Finally, strategic suppliers represent the most critical suppliers that span the business, and this is where the focus moves away from simple measurement to closer relationship management. These relationships typically include periodic meetings with management sponsors, and open and frank dialogues on subjects such as safety and value creation opportunities. As one executive noted, "unless you continue to work to improve a relationship, the opportunities to create additional value diminishes unless you do something more creative. So we have to get more innovative to ensure we are leaving no stone unturned."

A Procurement function's ability to execute category management (CM) and SRM is counter-cultural to the way most companies are organized and budgeted; therefore, significant leadership and change management are required to make it work. Functions and business units operate on their own budgets, whereas Procurement as a shared service function needs to consolidate requirements across these functions, business units, and geographies to work effectively. The coordination and communication with multiple stakeholders across these boundaries oftentimes requires that someone in the business compromise their needs for the greater good, yet their incentives for doing so within their P&L may be exactly the opposite. Only through the careful application of "stakeholder mapping" and understanding who the supporters and blockers may be in the process, who has influence and who does not, and painting the picture for the stakeholders that answers the question of WIIFM (What's In It For Me) can you overcome the organizational barriers that exist to operate in this manner. Somebody will always feel as if they are losing in some manner, whether it be budget or ceding control of decisions or ability to engage in supplier negotiations or communications at critical times. These need to be addressed up front, head on, and with complete and total honesty in order to move the needle. Once again, "Good luck with that!"

Oil and gas companies are also beginning to explore opportunities to build category teams around global projects. Historically, oil and gas companies have managed major projects on a project-by-project basis, sourcing each one independently. Recently, strategic suppliers such as the large *engineering procurement contracting* (EPC) companies are being managed more strategically. Although the scope of work changes across projects, the value-proven practices in the contract can be fixed through a master agreement. This enables them to move faster as new projects come along. As capital spending at one time was a big part of exploration expansion projects (less so today), the need to be able to build quality control, instrumentation, and other categories that cross projects presents an opportunity to improve operational improvements across categories.

It is important to note that designation of a supplier as strategic implies a real commitment, and as such, must be weighed against the level of internal investment and resources required to manage these relationships. One of the companies we met with recognized that they had "too many" strategic suppliers (in this case 45), and it sought to reduce this to a smaller number of under 20, which culminated in deep relationships with only a handful.

> *"We looked at the value opportunity versus the effort, and we decided to segment our strategic suppliers to the top seven who typically get the bulk of our attention. We recognized that they have been working with us for almost 30 years, but we didn't know if we were important to them or if they see us as an important customer. We recognized that they had a direct impact on our bottom line, and we made the decision to bring their senior executives in once a year to meet with our senior executives. These dialogues were purely strategic in nature, relative to what the future looks like, opportunities on the horizon, where they can come in to help us, not just on cost, but on speed to market, and entry into new regions where projects are beginning."[6]*

Another company also notes that they work with key suppliers in downstream refining to establish how to operate and transfer best practices on supply chain and business issues to improve end to end business processes. Projects are now being established on how to drive some of the "bottom up" lessons learned on safety, improvement, and turnaround projects to provide not just defined practices, but supply chain excellence.

Companies are also moving to designate executives with SRM accountability to manage the top 20 suppliers in a business or across businesses. In effect, SRM is becoming an enterprise-wide artifact and requires that all parties understand and work with suppliers in a consistent fashion. Secondly, supplier performance measurement (SPM) managers in procurement or in the technical community are also designated to manage the day-to-day report creation process, feeding data and analytics to the SRM senior executive on a regular basis. For example, they will develop the "prep sheet" when there is an explicit agenda to address. To be most effective, however, some companies have found that the senior SRM individual *not* be from Procurement, but be a senior executive who is a direct customer to the supplier (with no more than 10 to 20 SRM executives for the entire organization). This leads to a greater sense of the gravity of this role when a discussion takes place — the supplier recognizes that it is the voice of the business he is listening to, not just the noise made by a procurement team who he or she does not directly serve.

---

6 Interview conducted by Rob Handfield with industrial manufacturer CPO.

Does your organization have formal supplier relationship managers tasked with managing strategic suppliers across the organization, or is it just a part of a category/sourcing manager's responsibility?

Dedicated supplier relationship manager roles exist	21%
Part of category/sourcing manager's responsibility	71%
No formal supplier relationship manager	8%

0% 10% 20% 30% 40% 50% 60% 70% 80%

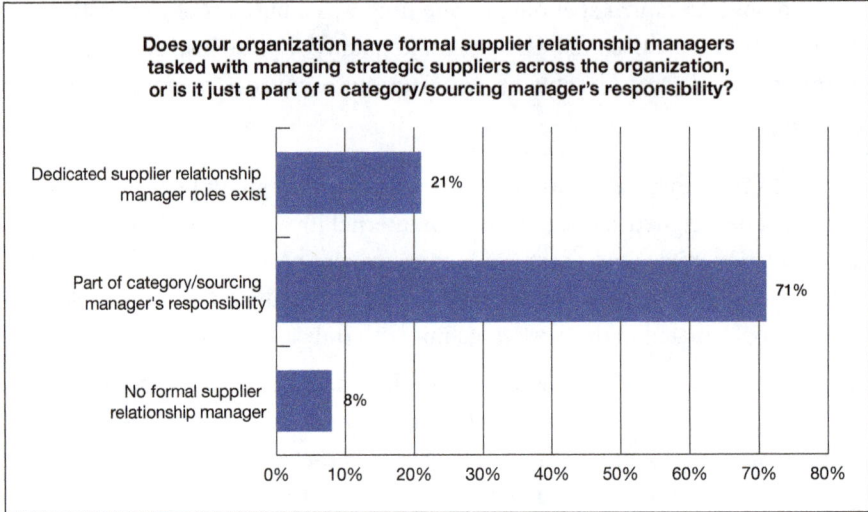

As shown in our study, most companies have not yet made SRM a full-time role, but designate it as a sub-element of the category or sourcing manager's role. The thinking on having someone responsible for managing a relationship is well established in many sales organizations but has not yet reached the point of being well understood or deployed in the supply community.

Talent Imperative: Finding individuals who have the energy to build subject matter expertise around supplier risk, who is well-regarded by the business unit, who understands business issues, and can use analytics to drive the right discussions is a primary challenge for organizations we met with.

Just as important as finding the right people who can add value to this assignment is figuring out the age-old question of "who benefits, who pays" for this individual? Often it is Procurement who pays, though the financial and operational benefits are realized by the stakeholder. As Procurement goes through its annual defense of its operating budget, there is a Procurement desire to get the beneficiaries to chip in some of their funds to pay for this. Yet this goes to the heart of Procurement's ultimate goal in most organizations, which is to become a "trusted advisor to the business," garner the respect that it deserves, and prove it is not just a "Negotiations R Us" or "Contracts R Us" function, but one that adds value to all commercial activities. As said in Chapter 7, "People are not your greatest asset … people are your ONLY asset!"

Segmenting Suppliers by Customer Importance

Companies (especially in financial services) are also considering the potential for revenue from suppliers and whether they can become future customers when sourcing segmentation decisions are made. The landscape can be viewed in the matrix shown in Figure 2. As shown, the upper right quadrant involves customers with whom your organization has both a high spend from a supply side and high revenue from the organization on the customer-facing side, this represents a win-win opportunity to grow the business. However, if a hugely important client is only a small supplier, there is a need to use caution and seek to create opportunity to expand

Figure 2: Financial Services Quadrant

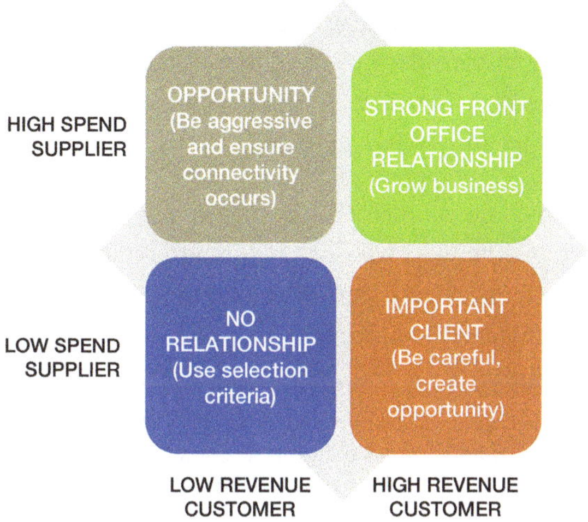
HIGH SPEND
SUPPLIER
OPPORTUNITY
(Be aggressive
and ensure
connectivity
occurs)
STRONG FRONT
OFFICE
RELATIONSHIP
(Grow business)
LOW SPEND
SUPPLIER
NO
RELATIONSHIP
(Use selection
criteria)
IMPORTANT
CLIENT
(Be careful,
create
opportunity)
LOW REVENUE
CUSTOMER
HIGH REVENUE
CUSTOMER

supply opportunities, in an effort to nurture the relationship. For example, Supply Management wouldn't want to put their business out to bid and destroy goodwill that could translate into lost customer revenue. One executive noted:

> *"Conversely, if we are spending hundreds of millions of dollars with them and they aren't even looking at us for institutional investing or transaction banking, we have to be careful to avoid reciprocity, but we can certainly take steps to be more aggressive and ensure that connectivity with our sales organization occurs so that they are aware of the situation. Normal selection criteria should always be used, and we can't ever cross the line when it comes to compliance, but these relationships do matter. Purchasing can become a big influence when a senior managing director sees banks as a commodity, and they can change the perception and create a new dimension to these discussions."*[7]

In effect, organizations must continue to apply independent supplier selection processes that are methodical in nature and independent from the notion of the client relationship. But in the process of negotiating, tendering, and evaluating suppliers around a requirement, there are separate and distinct sales operations occurring with the same organization. This represents a real opportunity for Procurement to operate in a way to create top line revenue with banking relationships, to work in a way that benefits both organizations, or at a minimum to ensure that there isn't a clash that occurs because of an oversight of this fact. This is an opportunity for Procurement to become the "air traffic controller" of these relationships for the company, adding significant value to its stakeholders.

Some organizations have assigned managers to consider the idea of a client relationship as a component and decision factor with the right level of weight as part of the supplier selection decision. Compliance officers need to be involved as well, and as the tendering process runs

7 Interview conducted by Rob Handfield with financial services CPO, December 2013.

its course, this officer can review it to, at a minimum, ensure that bad news isn't delivered to the supplier on a day that Sales is pitching them on a proposal, or that there is good news on a day when the information can be exploited. This is only the initial phases of this approach, but organizations are beginning to consider how best to manage these segmentation situations in the future and structure the decision in a comprehensive manner while maintaining the necessary firewall between buying and selling activities.

In general, our survey found that the majority of companies have some form of segmentation with critical suppliers, albeit at different levels of refinement, either through critical supplier identification (28 percent), various criteria for segmentation identified (36 percent), or some level of partial segmentation achieved (34 percent).

The issue of keeping the firewall between customers who are also suppliers is even more complex in the world of software and subscription services, as companies also collaborate and compete with one another simultaneously. Software, platforms, desktops, and infrastructure as a service (SaaS, PaaS, DaaS, and IaaS) are constantly evolving, and many companies are in "coopetition" with one another — they are not only buying and selling to each other, but they also collaborate by combining product and service offerings and leveraging off of each other's strengths to make and market unique combinations of services. At the same time, they are competing with one another in these strategic alliances. The immense competition that exists for smartphones between Samsung and Apple is legendary, as they constantly sue one another for patent infringements. At the same time, Samsung is selling $2 billion in parts to Apple.

This begs the question of whether a company needs an "air traffic controller" to manage how this works. Can the procurement category manager (PCM) take on this role? Yes, but only if the PCM has the knowledge base of its own company's product and services — and if firewalls between the buying and selling relationships are enforced.

Woe betide that PCM who makes a decision to switch from a supplier who is also a major customer of their business, just because the supplier won't budge on the price. The supplier's salespeople, especially commissioned ones, need to meet their sales quota, and if they are coming up short and their customer threatens to switch away from them (trashing their bonus and compensation), they may look to leverage the relationship by instructing their procurement function to look at bidding out its requirements for consideration of their customers' products. It can become a game of "chicken" to see who blinks first.

Some companies may try to deal with these situations by setting up strategic alliances or a global account manager (GAM) structure to play "air traffic controller" in these relationships; however, if each of the GAMs are incentivized to make their account the most successful, how does that help the company prioritize which relationship is the most important? Human nature and the desire to succeed will always be the biggest factor in all of these situations.

I (Howard) have seen this work the other way as well. In one instance, Procurement decided to terminate a relationship with a travel management/corporate card customer that was a big buyer of its technology services. Their sales team was furious when they found out about it, because their account (and commissions) were endangered by this decision. Six months later, the sales team came back to Procurement to thank them, as the new supplier relationship also incentivized the new supplier to look at their company's technology solutions and resulted in a new account that was 3 times larger than the account that left them! When it came to WIIFM, the sales team walked away with significantly increased commission. But how about the procurement team that took these risks, professionally and personally, in order to improve company cost and services? What did they get? I think we know the answer to that — zippo — along with a pat on the back (figuratively) and the good feeling of doing their job well (plus bragging rights about being a true value-added function!).

Supplier Segmentation

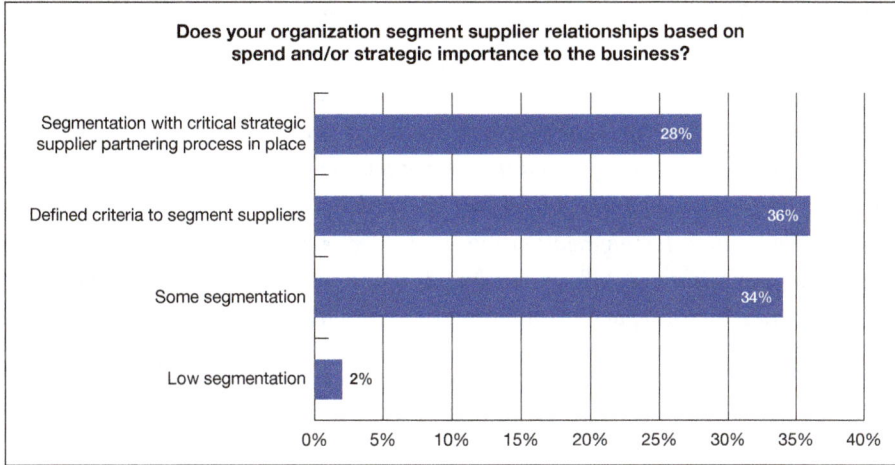

Does your organization segment supplier relationships based on spend and/or strategic importance to the business?

Category	Percentage
Segmentation with critical strategic supplier partnering process in place	28%
Defined criteria to segment suppliers	36%
Some segmentation	34%
Low segmentation	2%

Segmenting Tier 2 Supplier Relationships

Several companies also tier their supply base based on impact on tier 2 suppliers or commodities. As companies continue to outsource, one major segment is the management of leased equipment, which entails management of the aftermarket parts. One company we interviewed works with suppliers that are much larger than they are who are furnishing component replacement parts. This involves properly understanding the scale of relationships that exist up and down the supply chain, and building a deep understanding of the product component parts market that drives quick response time for part delivery. The company competes directly with the manufacturers of the equipment, but often has a quicker and more flexible response to customer requirements, which becomes a factor in a time-critical environment.

Another organization interviewed manages tier 2 raw materials for their automotive parts supply base on a global basis, with a global purchase team that looks at major categories such as steel, material, paint, adhesives, lubrication, and fuel. Each of these global teams have commodity strategies at a central location, as well as a developer who works directly with major tier 1 suppliers on cost strategies. The team is able to conduct global lowest total cost analyses to manage raw material supply to suppliers all over the globe, and conducts a complex analysis considering price analysis, logistics hubs, and supply routes that creates the optimized mix by location. Most of the contracts with tier 1 suppliers are local sources near assembly facilities, to promote the "buy where you sell, sell where you buy" culture that exists. To further promote collaboration with tier 2 steel suppliers, the supply organization has established multiyear agreements with steel producers to enable hedging on raw materials such as coke and iron ore, and they combine this with bank hedging agreements that also benefit steel suppliers. A three-month rolling price adjustment is established to enable long-term risk management on steel, a core component of tier 1 and 2 supply.

There is also an increasing recognition that supply base reduction poses a risk of pushing the contracting and relationship piece back onto tier 1 suppliers that are less capable of supply management than the buying organization. An executive at a major oil and gas company noted that:

"As we have reduced the number of tier 1 suppliers, we are forcing our suppliers to do more subcontracting, and we are seeing issues as we have forced them to become general contractors. They end up subcontracting the same people that we used to work with directly! But they are not good at managing them. So this raises a number of questions: Who is the best supply manager for managing second-tier suppliers? Should we be directing them to work with tier 2 suppliers? Do we have any business forcing relationships that didn't exist before? We are recognizing that supplier management is not a skill set that one develops overnight; it is a skill that needs to be built over time, and by reducing our supply base, we are creating something that the supplier is not ready to do!"[8]

As such, supply base reduction strategies should always examine the impact on tier 2 suppliers as well.

Establishing Supplier Performance Management Systems by Segment

The importance of performance measurement as the foundation for relationship building is a theme that dominated many of the discussions with senior executives on SRM. Performance measurement is what "drives" suppliers into different levels of the tiering pyramid, by getting people to think about "fitness for purpose" when they select suppliers. Business stakeholders may often pick suppliers they like based on the "beauty queen" syndrome, with the result that time and energy is wasted seeking to build strategic relationships with the wrong type of supplier. Suppliers should be required to move "up the tier," with new suppliers moving through a two- to three-year cycle where they start as managed or core suppliers, prove themselves through consistent performance metrics, and this establishes the basis for trust and exploring moving the relationship to the strategic level. As one executive notes: "We can get new suppliers to a strategic relationship in 18 to 24 months using a process that normally takes seven years. Because we aren't able to generate all of the performance measures internally, we rely on suppliers and collect the data either internally, externally, or a mix."

An important component of the supplier tiering process involves sending the right message to the supply base and then using tier structures as a means for driving the right types of relationships with the right set of suppliers. This presupposes that organizations have a good idea of what they want, which means establishing the right internal consensus on what constitutes an "ideal" supplier. This will also vary by tier.

When suppliers are first confronted with a buying company's attempt to measure their performance and build a relationship, the first impulse is typically one of distrust. This is particularly true in cases when the procurement function has a history of "beating suppliers over the head with a club" for price savings. On the other hand, when an organization has an

---

8 Rob Handfield interview with CPO oil and gas company.

established SPM system in place that values other factors (delivery, quality, service, technology, etc.), there may already be a solid foundation for building strong relationships. In cases when Procurement is only just initiating an SPM system, suppliers may need to move up through a performance management system for two or three years, especially when there is no trust based on prior relationships. A SPM system is an effective means of communicating requirements and rewarding behavior in a consistent fashion, which becomes the foundation for advancing the relationship to a higher level.

> The use of "balanced scorecards" for procurement performance reviews tries to encourage PCMs and sourcing managers to implement robust SRM processes, but the reality is that savings will always carry the most weight in these scorecards. The pressure to prioritize price reduction (as opposed to total cost of ownership, quality, service, and innovation improvements) is always there. So when times get tough or the situation gets dicey, Procurement's first reaction is oftentimes to reach for the hammer (because the problem starts to look like a nail). It's like the story of the scorpion and the frog. The scorpion asks the frog, "Will you swim me across the river on your back?" The frog says, "No, you will sting me and kill me." The scorpion says, "Why would I do that? If I sting you, we will both drown." The frog agrees to do it. Halfway across the river, the frog feels this terrible sting and screams at the scorpion, "Why did you do that? We'll both drown now," to which the scorpion replies, "I couldn't help myself … it's in my nature." Procurement has to be able to gravitate away from what it is in their nature to do, which is to go after savings above all else. But when procurement metrics are almost solely focused on "savings," however defined, can you blame the Procurement person for using a hammer to beat up the supplier? These behaviors are often reinforced at review time when it comes to doling out merit bonuses and salary adjustments after the leaders "totem pole" their PCMs based on savings performance. What gets measured, gets rewarded.

There exist a number of approaches for rolling out PMSs. Note that all supplier measurement systems have some element of subjectivity that supersedes simple transactional data generated by an information system. What data to analyze, what metrics to use, what performance categories to include, how to weight different categories, how often to generate performance reports, and how to use the performance data are all subjective to some degree. Moreover, there are no hard rules regarding the specific categories to include in supplier measurement systems; the selection of measures depends on what is strategically important to the buyer.

> The issue that nobody likes to talk about is whether this SRM/SPM system will be "flavor of the month" and change as the Procurement people (and leadership) change categories, change jobs, or leave the company. In many cases, companies still appoint CPOs from other functions to give them two to three years of "commercial experience," then move them to another (higher) role in the organization. The CPO position is not considered to be a terminal position but a steppingstone for developing leaders within the company. Without the continuity of leadership assured, neither is the continuity of such supplier relationship processes. We see this on the supplier side as well, especially in the software industry. As soon as the salesperson lands the new, big account and you start the process of SRM/SPM, that salesperson is taken off of the account (on purpose) so that they can be assigned to pursue the next big kill. Again, we are fighting not only human nature in these battles, but corporate nature.

The most common form of supplier performance system is a "scorecard" that utilizes a weighted point system. This approach overcomes some of the subjectivity in a categorical system. A weighted-point system weighs and quantifies relative scores across different performance categories, including measures that are generated by information systems, measures generated by individual assessments, e-mails, phone calls, etc., and measures generated by transactional data (such as delivery records).

At a major hospital, the CPO developed a simple scorecard based on quality, cost, delivery, and service. The CPO said, "Implementing scorecards involved leading change and seeking to influence individuals who were unfamiliar with the sourcing process." As this executive noted:

"We began by explaining to people that it is no different that the ratings you use for employee evaluation that are done once or twice a year. You have no problem doing these ratings. You also have no problem with the other types of ratings and evaluations we use, including patient satisfaction surveys, employee surveys, and so on. So why shouldn't we also rate our suppliers, who are effectively an extension of our organization? Even when we put it into this context, supplier performance measurement was still very much foreign territory for a lot of people to wrap their heads around…. We brought data to the problem that documented exactly what was happening in our facility. We organized that data in the form of a scorecard, which truthfully, has never been done before at this facility. The supplier had also never seen anything like it before, and they told us as much!"

As shown in Figure 3, understanding stakeholder requirements and building them into dimensions that are directly measurable is the most important first step. When the basic elements of a scorecard are constructed, a pilot rollout occurs, implementing it supplier by supplier. Many companies decide to begin with the worst-performing suppliers first, to fix a problem that is already an imperative.

Figure 3: Example of a Scorecard

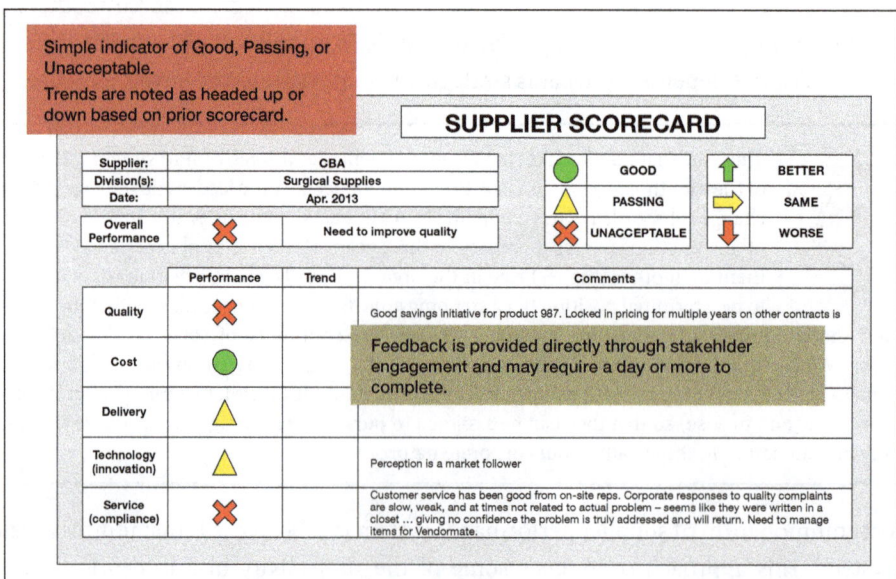

In building scorecards, the key is to begin by identifying stakeholder issues that are critical, without worrying about where the data will come from. Once the issues are identified, then the sources of data that can either directly or indirectly measure the issue can be developed. Note that the measures do not all have to be objective data pulled from a system, although this is always preferable. Some measures, because they are more about customer service, will require reaching out to measure customer perceptions based on recent experiences with that supplier.

A combination of methods may be required to establish relevant sources of data for a scorecard. Some data, such as on-time delivery, may require communication with receiving docks or electronic warehouse management systems. Quality data may also be buried in other systems across the hospital.

Central to the success of supplier performance assessment systems is the decision about what to measure and how to weigh various performance categories. An organization must decide which performance criteria are objective (quantitative) and which are subjective (qualitative), as the metrics used will be different between the two. Most of the objective, quantitative variables lie within the following three categories:

- *Delivery performance:* Purchase orders or material releases sent to a supplier have a quantity and a delivery due date. Therefore, a buyer can readily assess how well a supplier satisfies its quantity and due-date commitments. Quantity, lead-time requirements, and due-date compliance are all part of a supplier's overall delivery performance.

- *Quality performance:* Virtually all supplier measurement systems include quality performance as a critical component. A buyer can evaluate a supplier's quality performance against previously specified objectives, track trends and improvement rates, and compare similar suppliers. A well-designed measurement system also helps define a buyer's quality requirements and more effectively communicate them to its suppliers.

- *Cost reduction:* Buyers frequently rely on suppliers for cost-reduction assistance, which can be measured in a number of ways. One common method is to track a supplier's real cost after adjusting for inflation. Other accepted techniques involve comparing a supplier's cost against other suppliers within the same industry or against a baseline or target price. Some leading companies use the last price paid in the current year as the baseline price for comparisons during the next year.

- *Service and responsiveness:* Buyers may require some subjective measures of service, or responsiveness to requirements, particularly when a supplier is serving multiple business units. A common goal is to ensure that all business units are getting the same level of service, although suppliers may favor certain divisions more than others based on business volume. By establishing a common standard for performance across the business, the expectation is communicated that *"we expect equal treatment and performance across all of our business divisions!"*

In addition, a supplier measurement system must be compared against pre-established standards or goals so that actual supplier performance can be evaluated. These standards or goals must be attainable, readily measurable, appropriate to the supplier being measured, communicated to the supplier, and actionable.[9] For a goal to be considered actionable, it must be able to be acted upon; e.g., corrective action can be taken.

If somebody says, "It's not about the money," you can be sure of one thing: It's about the money! Larry Bossidy, former GE executive and CEO of Allied Signal and Honeywell, and later a director on the Board of Merck, first introduced the idea of building in six percent year-on-year supplier price reduction commitments into longer term contracts through productivity improvements, waste elimination, Lean Six Sigma, and other means. Very few companies actually try to negotiate this into contracts, but having a strongly supported SRM program with accurate scorecarding is essential to making this work. You often only get one chance to do this — during the initial bidding process while you still have leverage. Once you enter into contract for the goods and/or services from a leveraged position, you may quickly move into a critical or strategic quadrant (Kraljic) because the size of the commitment gets built into your infrastructure and the costs to change suppliers after implementation becomes huge.

So what's the real value of scorecarding suppliers that now have you over the barrel when you know that your organization doesn't have the wherewithal to make a supplier change for many years to come? The answer is that every supplier wants to grow their business with you, especially if it means expanding into their other lines of business and product offerings. And why would a supplier agree to pre-determined commitments to reduce prices every year? The argument best used is that by helping them become more efficient and reduce their cost structure, they will be able to extend that across their entire book of business/customer base with improved gross and operating margins. If they can find a way to reduce their costs through application of Lean Six Sigma and waste elimination with your company because you incentivized them to do so through such contractual commitments, everyone wins.

Routine reporting of supplier performance relative to a buying company's needs should also be considered. Performance reviews with critical suppliers should occur monthly or quarterly. Buyers should also meet with other tiers of suppliers on at least an annual basis to review actual performance results and identify improvement opportunities. However, a buyer should never delay reporting a supplier's poor performance, particularly when it adversely affects day-to-day operations. Poor performance must be addressed as soon as it is recognized to avoid financial or operational repercussions.

Some organizations also rely on non-internal sources to populate performance reporting. For example, third-party data collected on on-site representative badging data can be integrated into a service metric. Another example includes using suppliers themselves to self-report on performance, with periodic audits to ensure reliability. Finally, internal surveys can be used to collect data on suppliers using perceptual indicators from key stakeholders that interface directly with suppliers across the business. Such measures can also be applied at major project milestones, or other periodic points in time. Other types of objective data may be created using a third party responsible for data collection and reporting.

Talent Imperative: Organizations need to establish relationship managers who are able to effectively communicate with internal stakeholders and business units, listen to their requirements,

---

9 Monczka, Robert, Handfield, Robert, Giunipero, Larry, and James Patterson, *Purchasing and Supply Chain Management*, Cincinnati, OH: Southwestern Publishing, College Division, 5th edition, 2011.

establish relative performance measures that can be classified and quantified into supplier performance measures, and build these measures into contract negotiations. These individuals must also be able to effectively communicate to suppliers the requirements for doing business, clearly explain contractual performance expectations, and relate these to future business and relationship growth opportunities. Finally, individuals in SRM roles must be able to effectively assess suppliers and assign them to different relationship tiers, based on performance, deep understanding of supplier capabilities, and technological and performance roadmaps.

The Investment in SRM/SPM Resources and Systems, and Governance of Outsourced Relationships

Watch out — one of the biggest mistakes organizations make is underinvestment in the governance structures for the supply base. This has especially been true in outsourcing relationships because the act of outsourcing an internal function to an external third-party provider is almost always driven by cost reduction criteria, especially if moved to a low-cost country. Spending money to have robust governance of the outsourced relationship acts as a counter to why you outsourced in the first place, and Finance can be reticent toward funding such positions. This allows for extreme savings and productivity leakage to occur over time.

The same can happen to SRM programs. As Procurement's metrics for its cost as a G&A function get challenged over time, there will be pressure to "right-size" the organization, and this will be looked at as an overhead cost within the function as opposed to what it should be, which is a valuable arm of the function. There has to be performance measures for SRM that validate its value generation and are recognized/quantified by Finance as such, or else (over time) it will be setting itself up as a target for decentralization and cutbacks.

Summary

Developing consensus on the criteria for segmenting the supply base is an important part of building any external supplier relationship and is a foundational element in establishing the requirements for current and future business negotiations and contracts. One of the most important outcomes is to establish internal alignment, so that everyone in the organization understands the criteria for becoming a "strategic" supplier, and that the variety of existing relationships between internal business functions with key suppliers across all parts of the enterprise are clearly mapped out and understood. One executive we met with noted that "technology never solves business relationship issues, but technology platforms have the capability to help us better understand our supplier relationships." This executive noted that, in the future, there may evolve the need for a scale application, similar to Salesforce.com, which establishes a crowd-sourcing mechanism for tracking all of the contracts, reporting relationships, communications, and social interactions that take place between key suppliers and individuals within the organization. Today, that communication is largely unknown, much to the detriment of both organizational parties! Such a system would provide a systematic way of managing suppliers, and SRM could potentially become a revenue-generating function, where purchasing is enabling the front office sales team to have maximum contact with the supply side that can provide new technologies, new capabilities, and market intelligence that drives improved forecasting, planning, and order fulfillment functionality. Such an approach could also provide incentives for suppliers to offer suggestions and documented ideas on how to drive out cost, improve service levels, specifications, and TCO savings opportunities that benefit customers. This would also help drive improved performance management and create awareness around supplier relationship touch points within the organization.

Chapter 10:
Organizing the Procurement Function for the New Global Reality

In several instances throughout this book, we have harped on the fact that the chief procurement officer (CPO) role is often not a terminal position but rather a commercial or operational executive training position with a three- to four-year time horizon in major corporations that rarely reports to the CEO. The objective of the new CPO is often to make a big hit (savings), prove your toughness, and move on to higher roles in the company. With each changing of the guard comes a new "strategic initiative" to reduce costs, though it rarely results in repeatable, sustainable cost reduction and containment. Execution of long-term commitments, such as rigorous SRM programs, become a challenge in this culture. The professionals working in the procurement and supply chain functions know this, and their attitude toward implementing best practices can get squashed as they opt for being able to demonstrate short-term results. After all, what gets rewarded and measured gets done.

It is not like this everywhere, though, and there are companies willing to invest the time and resources to allow people to build careers and become professionals and executives in the procurement and supply chain functions. More often, this is in firms where margins tend to be lower due to competitive pressures, direct materials are the major expense item, and purchase price variance (PPV) to budget has a major impact on P&Ls. The expertise applied to these commodities has a direct impact on the bottom line, and it is more valued by the C-Suite executive leadership team.

But all of this still begs the question: Who should Procurement, Supply Chain, and the CPO position report to? And does this look like it will change going forward?

The Importance of CPO Reporting Relationships

The most common CPO reporting relationships are to one of the following positions:

- the chief financial officer (CFO);
- the chief accounting officer or corporate controller;
- the chief operating officer (COO);
- the head of manufacturing (usually an SVP or EVP rank who sometimes reports to the COO); or
- the chief administrative officer (CAO).

We also see companies initiating global or regional *shared services* initiatives, which usually involve Strategic Sourcing, Procurement Operations, Accounts Payable, Accounts Receivable, and possibly Accounting/Controllership, and the reporting relationship tends to be the C-Suite positions mentioned above, except Manufacturing. Depending on the business and where they are in the cycle of the pendulum swinging back and forth between centralization and decentralization, the CPO reporting relationship decision can make or break the mission of the procurement and supply chain functions. The supplier sales organizations need to know this in order to develop the right approach for selling into the business.

Why does this matter so much? Like we said in Chapter 8, "Culture eats strategy for lunch." The complete belief system of the procurement and supply chain organizations is driven by this reporting relationship.

We have observed that the CPO reporting relationship tends to vary by industry. Some examples:

- *Healthcare* — Procurement tends to report to the CFO with relationships to the chief medical officer.

- *Telecom* — Procurement reports to the COO or CFO. In general, COOs worked out much better, as Finance is generally focused on inventory and cost savings.

- *Industrials* — CPOs tend to report to a group president of corporate services (IT, Procurement, HR, etc.), which might be the COO or CAO. Some business divisions have their own procurement division, which reports to a centralized global VP of procurement. Supply Chain, however, reports to the COO and includes operations, engineering, and logistics, including shipping, finished goods, and movement of material.

- *Chemical* — Procurement reports to the CFO, who is often more aligned on numbers, or the president of manufacturing. But the COO has a broader view and is more emotionally tied to the outcomes.

- *Energy* — Major global businesses all have organizational heads. Each head has a manufacturing head who reports to the CFO or COO. The organization's CPO will usually have the same reporting relationship.

- *Retail* — Procurement tends to reports to the CFO.

- *Software* — Procurement often reports through to the CFO, with most spend being indirect services.

- *Electronics* — The CPO usually reports to the COO. An experiment was to have Procurement also manage logistics, but they realized this didn't always work out, so logistics became a separate functional lead.

When reporting through Finance and the CFO's organization, the bad news is that it pits the CPO against other finance executives in capital funding requests for procurement initiatives and technology investments. Finance usually runs the capital allocation and approval process, and the CFO's first priority will usually be to get the investments that the finance function needs, not its procurement function. This type of competition for funds is accentuated by the fact that both organizations are part of the G&A budget, and requests for capital at most large corporations are three times what they are willing to spend in any fiscal year. Procurement will usually be relegated to the back of the pack in this environment. This is not all bad news though, as the CFO can also drive compliance for the procurement function, and they can get budget holders in line with procurement strategic sourcing initiatives and automation of the buying processes that have the potential to lower the cost structure. Some CFOs see an empowered procurement function as a huge weapon that they can wield to keep the company in line and prevent budgetary expansion. They also can be the ones that insist savings (or a portion thereof) be incorporated in the functional budgets, thereby strong-arming functional managers to work with Procurement to assure mutual success.

When Procurement reports through the controller's office, the emphasis usually changes to a budget focus and one of adherence to processes and controls such as Sarbanes-Oxley (SOX), the travel and expense program, the requisitioning and order placement process, and accounting rules on purchases that impact depreciation and the accounting of capital and operating leases. Procurement activity will tend to lean toward acting as a police person (or worse, the IRS agent), making sure that stakeholder functional spending budgets are adhered to or that gift cards that are purchased and assigned to employees as "rewards" for projects get properly taxed. Initiatives to drive cross-functional category strategies and teams will usually take a back seat in this environment. This is not always the case though, as one of my most rewarding procurement leadership assignments was driven by a controller who was a visionary and also had responsibility for creating a *global shared services* function that promoted centralization, standardization across geographies, and investments in procurement tools. I would never have taken the assignment to build a strategic sourcing organization from scratch under this type of reporting relationship had I not seen her visionary approach and commitment to building a long-term global, centralized shared services function. This is a reminder that it's always about people and their WIIFM, and you work for a boss, not a company!

The CPO reporting to the COO may be the best of the reporting relationships (aside from directly reporting to the CEO, which is the best arrangement but rarely the case). The COO is responsible for the daily operation of the company and is often the #2 position in the company, reporting to the CEO or president. It is not uncommon to see a chief revenue officer (the senior sales executive), the chief marketing officer (CMO), or the head of manufacturing reporting to the COO. While Procurement also will have to compete for capital with the other functional heads that report to the COO, there is strategic alignment of the Procurement organization to the COO's goal of making the company's operating margins competitive and in driving efficiency throughout the company. Having Procurement aligned with the strategy of the company is the key to relevance and respect in any corporate culture.

A caveat to a COO reporting relationship is whether that pendulum in the company culture is swinging in the direction of centralization or decentralization, as well as specific business unit P&Ls that act as a deterrent to cross-functional team activities that are core to Procurement's strategic sourcing and operational success. The COO's view on this will determine the direction in which that pendulum is swinging and the momentum of that force (it all comes down to physics, I guess).

When the CPO reports to the head of manufacturing, you can usually guess the priorities — supply chain integrity, *just-in-time* (JIT) strategies for inventory management, availability and quality of material supply, material cost control of PPV to budget, and having a distribution/logistics/3PL strategy that optimizes the flow of parts to subassembly to final assembly to warehousing to the consumer or end customer, who could also be a broker or middleman. Then there are warehousing, customs, tariffs, tax schemes, and other concerns for those companies with international profiles. An enterprise requirements planning (ERP) system that drives visibility to all these aspects as well as sales projections that drive the manufacturing schedule and priorities is a *must-have* investment to make this work efficiently. If the company has a high percentage of its spending on direct materials, warehousing, and costs of distribution, then this CPO reporting relationship makes a lot of sense, as these factors can make or break the ability of the company to successfully meet its commitments to customers, shareholders, and suppliers.

The issue here is that indirect goods and services, other than distribution, logistics, and contract manufacturing, can take a back seat in all of this. The head of manufacturing may take a view that shadow procurement organizations within the functions are aptly suited to handle their needs, be it HR, Legal, Real Estate & Facilities, Marketing, Sales, R&D, Insurance/Risk, and especially IT. We can assure you from our years of collective wisdom that having shadow procurement in these functions leads to suboptimal sourcing arrangements, and a huge amount of money is left on the table when these functions apply their own sourcing practices to meet their company's needs.

As outlined in Chapter 8, Merck Procurement reported to the president of Merck Manufacturing Division (MMD), who saw things differently. He knew that 70 percent of Merck spend was on indirect goods and services, and he used Procurement to attack many of the third-rail categories of spend that had been untouched by Procurement in the past. These included *contract research organizations* (CROs) that conducted the clinical trials for drugs in Discovery & Development, and even HR Medical Benefits, which was a shocker! Why was that a shocker? Because before serving as president of manufacturing, Richard Clark was the president of Medco, a *pharmacy benefit management* (PBM) company that was owned by Merck but later spun off. Medco continued to be the supplier of Merck employees' HR prescription drug benefits.

Two days after Mr. Clark was promoted from president of MMD to CEO of the company, I (Howard) just so happened to be sitting next to him at a luncheon for the Efficiency organization. I broached the subject with him, asking if we could put Medco's business out for review and possibly bid. I wasn't sure if that was a stupid CLM on my part (*career limiting move*), but his reaction was precious. He told me a story about GE putting out its PBM business for bid when Medco was the incumbent, and they gathered the three bidders on the same floor in separate rooms of the same building and began a week-long exercise in parallel negotiations, jumping from one room to the next to negotiate with all three bidders. When GE came into his room on Friday morning, he had had enough and told them he was through, they weren't getting a single additional drop of blood from Medco, that they had made every possible concession they could make,

continues on next page

Procurement Confidential *continued*

and they were going home. Then the GE negotiator said to him, "Richard, don't worry, we sent home your competitors two days ago," and they closed the deal. He then gave me the green light for Procurement to do whatever it took to pursue a great HR prescription drug benefit plan, and it was one of the most successful sourcing activities that we carried out in the procurement transformation process. Once again, this was less about sourcing and more about culture, using procurement as the tip of the spear to drive cultural change in a company that was facing the jaws of death from stagnating sales and rising costs. He was as enlightened a leader as you could ever ask for.

The role of chief administrative officer is a powerful C-Suite position. In UK-based companies, the CAOs of public companies must be chartered secretaries (Institute of Chartered Secretaries and Administrators), lawyers, certified/chartered accountants, or others with equivalent experience (thanks again, Wiki!). The general counsel (GC) or chief legal officer may be reporting to or contained in the CAO role, as will the Accounting/Controllership function. For a CPO reporting to a CAO, there may be latitude to run a tight ship and focus on control and adherence to procurement policy and procedure by the company, which helps exert influence on a large number of categories. There may also be a focus on legal and legislative activities, such as strict SOX compliance, and attention to T&C boilerplate and minimized redlining of contracts. However, the caveat is the balance of power between direct reports, each of whom wants a measure of independence on how they run their function (which may include shadow procurement people) and the CAO's attitude toward enforcing them to comply and cooperate with Procurement on cross-functional and regional/international/global sourcing activities. Once again, Procurement and its remit will be greatly shaped by the culture of the CAO's organization and the CAO's own predilection toward autonomy for the functions reporting into the role.

Even worse — what happens when Procurement and Supply Chain report to different stakeholders? This causes the worst possible situation — where the two parties can become misaligned on priorities. A recent study found that supply chain executives were more focused on delivery issues, while procurement continued to focus on cost — which could produce some very different outcomes![1]

So what are the lessons in all of this? How can Procurement organize to effectively develop and execute leveraged transnational category sourcing strategies when the company's executives and P&L are organized along geographies, business units, and product lines while funding decisions are on a project-by-project basis, not a category of spend basis? The organizational structure and the reward systems for managers of these functions often (unintentionally) discourage collaboration across boundaries because they are not measured and rewarded at review time. I don't mean to be discouraging to professionals in the procurement and supply chain functions, as these are big hills to climb, but they can and must be climbed!

---

1 "Misalignment in Supply Chain, Procurement, and the Enterprise," GEP.com, https://www.gep.com/webcasts/misalignment-in-supply-chain-procurement-and-the-enterprise.

Getting Procurement Operations Right is the First Step

First and foremost, CPOs must fight for centralization of procurement operations for tactical buying through use of light, inexpensive plug & play digital technology investments that are user friendly and tied into a Procure-to-Pay (P2P) solution. The revolution in generative *artificial intelligence* (AI) makes this easier than ever, and users expect a buying experience as easy as any offered in their personal lives. Regardless of the reporting relationship, getting procurement operations wrong will shoot down anything that you are trying to accomplish in the strategic categories of your spend profile. Everyone says they want to be "strategic" or "global" and have those words in their job title, but you don't get invited to a seat at the table if you screw up the basics and make your user base miserable on the simple buys.

In procurement operations, controls to prevent abuse of the system and for compliance with company policy can sometimes be overwhelming, but controls must be tempered for reasonableness. If you clearly state what is allowed and what is not (and the likely punishment for abuse), and you monitor usage through spot audits and automated data analysis that clearly shows outliers to behavior, you can accomplish what needs to be done. Users will thank you for it, and the Pareto rule of 80 to 90 percent of transactions that impact 10 to 20 percent of the company's total spend can be relegated to the degree of importance that it needs to be. Even more simply, you can outsource management of this "tail spend" through companies such as Candex, which consolidates all of it into one supplier relationship. Many companies go down the route of outsourcing the activity to *low-cost countries* (LCCs), but without applying the right policies, processes, rules, and tools to the equation, it will just shift your mess from one place to another.

Outsourcing sounds simple, but there is always the concern that you are not managing the tail spend as best you should, or that it allows leakage of spend from category strategies that could use it to help create more leverage in the contracting process. However, that doesn't mean you can't manage and competitively bid punchout catalogue SKUs and give users a choice in which SKUs they order, or even conduct reverse auctions. SciQuest was offering catalogue choice solutions for laboratory supplies at least 20 years ago, and Amazon Business Services is not the only game in town. Competitive price is important, but there are a host of web-based solutions out there that will allow you to minimize your investment in manpower on the tactical buying, conduct regular sourcing or auction events, and focus instead on strategic sourcing solutions for much higher spend categories (and value opportunities). LCC solutions are only part of the answer.

Procurement operations still has to deal with other complexities, such as three-way matches of having receivers issued for all goods and services received before invoices can be matched to purchase orders and payments authorized. While you want to remain within a SOX-compliant system, users don't want to be bothered with having to issue receivers or with filling out a million little surveys on each transaction asking them to respond with a happy face or a frown. With proper spot-checking and AI-generated analysis, every item should not require a receiver issued to pay the invoice. But you still have to deal with the usual user disputes, such as actual quantity received (many places in the remote working world do not have receiving departments), quality of the goods, whether the price quoted to you was the actual price charged or was properly calculated using the company discount, whether the purchase was made in the correct currency and whether the currency hits your budget at the actual traded rate or the budget rate, getting returned goods authorizations and assessments of restocking charges, and every other conceivable problem that can creep up when ordering goods and services. The bottom line is that procurement operations has more complexity than most will see on the surface, but it's not worth the effort to find perfect solutions ... you will get bogged down in the minutiae, and whatever you do, you will not satisfy everyone's need or make everyone happy.

Complicating these matters are the existence of large, connected, multimodule upstream to downstream procurement solutions that add complexity every step of the way. More often than not, you work for the tool/system instead of the system/tool working for you. Breaking away from these P2P solutions is a difficult but necessary process if you want an organization based on speed, flexibility, innovation, and integration (the goal of the boundaryless organization), instead of hierarchical, rigid structures. The technology leap is making these systems obsolete (more on this in Chapter 11).

Positioning Strategic Sourcing and Category Management for Success

Selling (there's that word again, as part of the procurement organization and the CPO's job) the C-Suite reporting relationship on the role that Procurement can (and should) play has many facets to it. First, the CPO has to be able to read the room on where the culture of the function will lead them, and whether that is an acceptable end result.

- Will they accept and encourage cross-functional sourcing activity?
- Will they properly fund the function's need for investments in people, process, and technology?
- Is there a "stepped" approach that can be laid out that will migrate the function from one of control to one of influence over time as confidence builds in the procurement function's abilities?
- What will it take for the procurement function to see itself as something other than "Savings R Us," "Negotiations R Us," and "Contracts R Us" and to establish a reward system that focuses on long-term alignment with the company strategic plan, continuous value generation and improvement, and on solving business problems, not procurement problems?

Once the procurement function starts to see itself and its vision and mission differently, will the C-suite assist with the change management in philosophy and culture that will be required to make this work?

What it takes to execute a successful global transformation of a procurement function

I (Howard) have been part of leading six global transformations of procurement functions in multinational companies, and I have come up with a list of what seems necessary for this to succeed, regardless of the reporting relationship of the CPO:

- Timing — the business needed it to stay competitive and saw cost control as a strategic imperative;
- The CPO was recruited from outside the company with a mandate for change;
- A strong senior C-Suite/executive sponsor of the CPO who was willing to influence their C-suite peers;
- Increased budget allocation to bring in the necessary talent and invest in procurement people, process, and systems/technology;
- Moving to a centralized procurement reporting structure from a decentralized one, and the willingness to move site and functional shadow procurement people into the procurement organization;
- Introduction of a multistage *sourcing management process* (SMP) that is implemented globally in which all Procurement people are sufficiently trained, accredited, and reinforced in everyday use; and
- Establishment of a cross-functional support team, established by the CPO and sponsored by the C-suite, that includes representatives of the finance, business systems/IT, legal, HR, corporate communications, and change management organizations to help guide and support the procurement transformation.

Mind you, none of this is a guarantee for success, but it is a prerequisite. The internally appointed CPO who is rotated into the job for their three- to four-year assignment will NEVER be granted anything above the normal budget allocation to run a global transformation. It is the reality of corporate politics and the struggle for power and resources. Centralization and establishing a new way of working using multistage SMP is the only way to get the procurement function to speak the same language wherever you go, and for getting stakeholders to hear the same language throughout the company. The power of the consistency of that message, reinforced by a C-Suite sponsor and the support functions that can help facilitate and drive this cultural change, are necessary components of making this work.

Use of Outsourced Procurement Consultants

One of the clues as to whether the C-Suite reporting relationship is one that is dedicated to the success of the procurement function is their willingness to fund the use of consultants — outsourced procurement support — with category management expertise that have the experience to attack new categories of spend. It is rare to find a procurement strategic sourcing function with the expertise to do it all, especially if they are at the beginning of the transformation process and on the lower end of the procurement maturity curve. Bringing in this expertise fulfills several objectives:

- Flexibility to attack untouched categories of spend in a series of planned "Waves";

- Expertise in implementing multistage SMPs and defining that as the new way of working by the procurement function;

- Creating "quick wins" that build the confidence of the C-Suite sponsor in their investment in the procurement function;

- Giving less experienced procurement employees a learning opportunity to work with experts and duplicate their methods for driving results on other subcategories; and

- Creating credibility for the procurement function with stakeholders in the business.

When using outsourced consultants, there are legitimate concerns as to whether the benefits generated will be sustainable and whether the consultants can connect to internal stakeholders' real needs. The CPO has to guide this approach to be used by the consultants and message the stakeholders as to how this will all work, because without their cooperation in helping define the SOWs and their business requirements, the consultants will make the same rookie mistakes of negotiating for all the wrong things. The consultants also need to be reminded that when it comes to the stakeholders and working with them, "People don't care how much you know until they know how much you care."

The outsourced consultants need to have another deliverable in order to make sure they don't only pursue the short-term quick-win results — they need to help the global category managers (GCMs) and sourcing managers (SMs) establish a *source plan* document that creates a roadmap for how the category can drive value over time. The source plan in many ways is the procurement equivalent of the global account manager's (GAM) blue sheet, and it assesses the competitive landscape for the category, the processes and technologies that can be utilized, and the roadmap you need to follow to implement best-in-class solutions over time. This is a document that should also be shared with the primary stakeholders whose operations or budget might be impacted and aligned with their strategic objectives.

Just because you bring in outside consultants does not mean that you will have all of the market intelligence you need to be successful in achieving breakthrough results in new categories of spend. Making the investment — whether it be from less costly offshore resources like Beroe, generative AI tools, or more traditional sources such as Gartner (especially for large IT expenditures) — can provide the benchmarks that you need to know where to set your targets. An investment by the procurement function in establishing a permanent *center of excellence* (COE) will also signal to the stakeholder community that the CPO is going all out for sustainable, long-term solutions for the company in both process and market intelligence.

Communications and Cross-Functional Support

As noted earlier, successful transformations incorporate a change management strategy that includes the establishment of a cross-functional support team, established by the CPO and sponsored by the C-suite that includes representatives of the finance, business systems/IT, legal, HR, corporate communications, and change management organizations. By doing so, it sends a message to the business that the procurement transformation is a serious *business* initiative and priority, not a procurement initiative or priority. So when there is progress, such as a quick-win and savings impact, it is just as important to publicize it to the stakeholder community and give credit to the stakeholders that helped drive the process with Procurement. If the CPO insists on trumpeting the successes as procurement successes as opposed to business successes, you can also bet that they are the three- to four-year variety who care little about the sustainable impact of what is being done. But as said before, as a procurement professional, you can be successful and find rewards and advancement in such a culture, but be prepared for the change of direction that will come when the new CPO makes their way into that seat.

Co-locating Procurement with the Stakeholders

One of the biggest decisions that a CPO must make is whether or not to co-locate the procurement GCM or SM within the function that they support, such as marketing, R&D, IT, or engineering. The reason for doing so usually has to do with building bridges with the function to gain Procurement acceptance of its role. Assigning a subject matter expert (SME) who can speak their language and already understands the function's business shows a commitment to the function's sourcing needs (as opposed to assigning a "best athlete" that would have to ramp up a steep learning curve). As stated earlier, the major worry is that they focus on pleasing the functional stakeholder, forgetting that their role is to apply rigorous, agreed SMP to the category and that they are still expected to challenge and question basic assumptions as they go about their work.

A lot of effort goes into creating a centralized function. The goal is getting all procurement people — GCMs, SMs, and those in operations and COE support roles — to address the company's challenges in a formally consistent manner, using a common culture and language in doing so, thereby letting stakeholders around the world know that Procurement has its act together and is not "shooting from the hip." It can work as long as the co-located resources act like procurement people but are focused on solving business problems, not procurement problems. Their category strategies have to reflect that, and there has to be an added level of reinforcement of such through peer reviews of the work.

"It's the market, stupid" — the 80/20 Rule

One of the great frustrations, though, with procurement transformations is the fact that it takes so much investment in time and resources to work with stakeholders and define their real business needs. It is often undocumented, and development of specifications and SOWs take a lot of time. This is where having a source plan can be so valuable, especially one that is signed off by major stakeholders and is recognized as the long-term agreed strategy for the category. Without it, you are relegated, year after year, to repeating the process with your stakeholders. Yet with people constantly moving up and down in the company and in and out of the functions, there may be no way of avoiding it. Add to that the annual negotiation that has to go on with stakeholders and Finance regarding what savings gets built into the budget and what does not, and you end up with the following:

- Procurement spends 80 percent of its time on internal selling and negotiating with stakeholders and budget holders, and 20 percent of its time on analyzing the market, supply base, and market dynamics. It's the market, stupid! It should be the other way around: Procurement spending 80 percent of its time analyzing the market, supply base, and market dynamics, and 20 percent of its time negotiating business requirements with stakeholders! And it could be, but stakeholders must trust that you know their business requirements and will adequately address them in your sourcing activities.

> I have always had the experience and philosophy that procurement negotiations with internal stakeholders on savings for budgets, how the sourcing process should play out, how SRM should be done, and which KPIs and SLAs need to be incorporated in the SOW are much more difficult than negotiating with suppliers. Why, you ask? It always comes down to the WIIFM and the agenda ... you never know if you and your stakeholder have the same agenda. Your agenda may be savings and budget reduction, while their agenda may be control, maintaining the status quo, and dictating the supplier relationships. It's so difficult to get on the same agenda with internal stakeholders. But suppliers are easy — their agenda is to sell you something, and your agenda is to buy something, plain and simple. All the rest is commentary.

Achieving Win-Win — do you really want a long-term solution?

One of the great tests in a procurement transformation is being able to fight the war on two fronts:

- The battle for immediate, quick-win savings by moving more categories into the leverage quadrant through the creation of a competitive landscape; and

- Once achieving that leverage, deciding when and how to move to more strategic relationships with a small, select number of suppliers that can help the business truly align in a way that leverages the strengths of both organizations to create real value, and be able to measure and track that value generation.

The challenge is that this is usually a stepped approach that requires an agreed, long-term source plan signed off by the stakeholders and acknowledged to be part of the business strategy. Both sides have to have equity — "skin in the game" — for this to work. The GAM/SAM has to see a reliable revenue stream for the sales funnel and an opportunity to expand the commercial relationship with other functions in the company and along other lines of business products and/or services. The Procurement GCM needs to see a continuous improvement commitment that the supplier will reliably reduce cost, and that the supplier will reduce prices over time by eliminating waste and investing in technology that will add productivity to the goods or services being bought. Finally, the stakeholder needs to see that the function will continue to be enhanced in its ability to deliver against its metrics set by the company as measures of success and that their budget will be protected as this process unfolds. Therefore, Finance and Controllership must also buy into the long-term strategy (which means addressing their WIIFM as well). Nobody said this is easy, but the bottom line is this: **The culture set by the C-Suite executive and the CPO who reports into the C-Suite will let you know not only if this is achievable, but actually desirable.** If you see that the focus is only a continuous quarterly pressure to "show me the money," then my word of advice to all involved is this: "forgetaboutit." You are just going through the motions and wasting precious time.

Running Cross-Functional Sourcing Teams

The success of any procurement transformation will have at its center the launch of "waves" of procurement team initiatives on categories of spend, led by the GCMs and/or outside consultant SMEs, and the development of long-term source plans as the category strategy starts to unfold. This is where the rubber meets the road, and you find out whether team members from the stakeholder functions will adopt a WIIFM that includes a willingness to "lean into discomfort, and get comfortable in this uncomfortable place." Breakthrough solutions as opposed to incremental gains require this, which means taking on added risk for the members of the team. As I (Howard) have told such team members on many occasions, "If you don't have butterflies in your stomach from what you are about to do, then you are in the wrong place." Most of these teams will happily gravitate toward "lowest common denominator" solutions that make everyone on the team happy and comfortable that they will be able to carry out the team decisions without any friction from within their own functions. That is the wrong place to be. No true innovation happens that way, and barriers to success will never get broken.

The wave team needs an executive sponsor from the business who will push and encourage the team to pursue breakthrough solutions, and the CGM running the team has the awesome responsibility for facilitating the discussion and helping them set targets that will take them into that zone of discomfort. Stakeholders will see a personal risk of failure and an increased workload that they will have to shoulder as deterrents for doing so. Yet the GCM is expected to move them along and to shepherd them through the four stages of team dynamics — *forming, storming, norming,* and *performing.*

Getting through the storming phase is the tough part, and one way to do it is to create an environment where the members share and build with one another and challenge one another in a collegial manner, noting that "we are storming now, and we will get through this together." The team dynamic will help break down their functional siloed barriers, and they will become more dedicated to seeking out a team result.

The biggest issue, though, will be the soft skills of the GCM in leading this team through this process and a willingness to exert Stephen Covey's fifth habit: "Seek first to understand, then to be understood." If the GCM is seen as being "Savings R Us" and "Negotiations R Us," the team will be doomed to pursuing its lowest common denominator solutions and walking away, declaring victory. The CPO must, if committed to these category waves and pursuing break-through, long-term solutions, provide training and outside consulting assistance to the GCMs to help them maneuver the landscape and grow in the job.

What does all of this mean for you if you are a member of the procurement or supply chain organization?

If you are a member of the procurement or supply chain function and want to develop pro-fessionally, you also have to read the room to learn about the CPO and their vision for where they are taking the organization. Not everybody is cut out to lean into discomfort and drive toward breakthrough solutions in cross-functional team environments and then lead robust SRM processes. The soft skills required to be a team facilitator and influencing stakeholders who are often two to four levels higher in the organization is difficult, especially if it means moving to a different supplier and/or implementing a new process and technological solution in the company.

To GCMs and SMs in the procurement organization:

You have to be honest with yourself — is this the direction you want to go in, and can you develop the skill set required to be successful? Also, if this is an internally appointed CPO, will this just be a "flavor of the month" push for savings claims, and can you play this game successfully until the next regime comes on board? Is this really a "burning platform" situation, or can you get away with believing that "this too shall pass"? Does the CPO have an influential C-suite sponsor, or is this just a transitory situation?

Regardless of what eventually happens, you can be successful in this environment if you know what culture and which activities will be rewarded (such as taking risks, or not taking risks!), and if you feel comfortable and can acclimate to it. Falling on your sword is usually not rewarded, CLMs are to be avoided, and always remember, there's a difference between being right and being dead right. In the end, if you insist on being dead right, you are still dead.

What does this mean for you if you are a GAM/SAM or sales executive trying to sell into this business?

Watch out! In this environment, making an enemy of Procurement or trying to cut a deal around Procurement is one of the biggest mistakes you can make. Procurement will become a blocker to whatever you do, and you can be assured that in the end, it will screw up whatever commitments you made to your sales funnel, especially from a timing standpoint, and miss your quota target and bonus associated with that target.

My advice to Sales in these situations is to listen, and to look for ways that provide a solution that will make your Procurement interface look like they added value and savings, however they define it. Find out how they define it! Find out what the procurement person sees as a successful outcome, and work toward an end game that meets that outcome.

The good news is that if it is a true global transformation that is sponsored strongly by a C-Suite sponsor, there are ways to use this opportunity to build a long-term customer supply solution that will create an annuity for your sales funnel. Can Procurement help the business truly align with suppliers in a way that leverages the strengths of both organizations to create real value and measure that value generation? Do both sides have equity skin in the game? If you put together an approach that solves a business problem, or that creates a better end-to-end process solution that adds efficiency and competitive advantage for both you and the customer, your procurement interface can end up becoming a champion of your approach to the business. I have become that champion on a number of occasions when a dedicated sales team shows that they can simplify life for the business, add to their productivity, and reduce the *total cost of ownership* over the life cycle of the contract.

One risk in this is a decision on whether to deviate from what is asked for in the RFP process. The best way to address this is to add the new approach as an alternative proposal, but also address the direct request that is made on the RFP (unless you see it as a waste of your time and company resources). Attempts to go around Procurement to other functional executives as part of this process will always be met with contempt, so prepare for the blowback if you feel this is the only hope for you winning or retaining the business. You may win it in the end by going this route, but you will have to deal with the consequences later, as Procurement can make your life a living hell if it chooses to do so.

What does this mean for you if you are a stakeholder to the procurement and/or supply chain functions and need to buy or manage your goods and services with/through them?

Knowing the procurement process and its rules for engaging suppliers during a period of transformation can be a tricky balancing act. You need to gauge the influence of the CPO and the mandate that has been given to Procurement, especially if you have developed a preferred supplier relationship that you would like to extend, or if you have a new requirement and have a favored supplier in mind for meeting that need. It's important to understand how the procurement organization will react to a proposal that may have been solicited by you from the supplier, even if an informal one. A lot will depend on how busy the procurement function is, how much spend is at stake, and how much of a value opportunity may be available.

Most procurement functions set a limit on what they will get involved in from a strategic sourcing standpoint. It often mirrors whatever signature authorization rules are in place for the function — it could be $50k, $100k, $250k, or $500k depending on the size of your company and its total spend. Either way, they usually will appreciate if you involve them early in the process and may grant you more latitude and involvement for doing so, depending on their priorities and their bandwidth to handle the requirement. They will expect you to write the specification or SOW in a functional way that does not give favor to any specific supplier and to clearly define your business requirements, designating *must-have* criteria from *like-to-have* criteria. From this, they will craft the RFP process and an eventual negotiation plan. Under no circumstances are you to discuss your budget with the supplier, as that information represents a death knell for any value generation opportunity.

If the procurement function insists on no stakeholder communication with suppliers or potential suppliers on a bid list, and that Procurement be the only point of contact, there are ways to push back on this while not invalidating the process. Current operational discussions need to continue for providing the service during the bid process, and you should demand that they be exempted from this dictate as long as no discussion about the bid is entertained. Also, insist that Procurement issue "talking points" that all stakeholders can use during the bid process that keeps everyone on the same page and addresses what can be said and what cannot. This is a very powerful tool if used correctly because the supplier sales reps, as they make various inquiries throughout the organization looking for intelligence, will see that everyone in the company is on the same page and that circumventing the process will not be successful.

Some procurement organizations will push for bonus/penalty clauses in a contract tied to meeting or exceeding KPIs or SLAs, and they see this as a way to show their stakeholders/budget holders that they are tying the contract to successful performance. But I can tell you, delivering on those earned bonus payments can be difficult, especially if you, the budget holder, has forgotten that they are in the contract and has not budgeted for it. The real question for you becomes one of, "Did the supplier do anything to create additional tangible success that gave my function and my company a competitive advantage and higher revenue stream than normally anticipated?" If the supplier's actions create more revenue for the function or help avoid payments usually made by the function, at least you know the money will be there in the budget for them to share in your success. As a procurement person, I always felt that they were not only a nuisance, but also did not always promote the right supplier behaviors, as it gave a way for the supplier to buy their way out of their commitments by paying the penalty as opposed to correcting the problem. Also, Procurement knows that such penalty payments will rarely be allowed by Finance to count toward their savings metric, due to the tradeoff of quality and service.

Summary

We have entered a new world whereby people in an organization expect to be able to buy things for their company and their function in a frictionless manner like they do in their private lives. However, companies have to meet commitments to more stakeholders than just the function and have rules that have to be followed that assure integrity in all that is being done. Shareholders and investors as well as other stakeholder needs must also be addressed, whether its finance, controllership, legal, or the office of the CEO. The CEO has to sign off annually on SOX controls in U.S. companies and can come under personal liability for lack of proper controls.

Regardless of the need for controls, CPOs have the power to reorganize their functions from slow, hierarchical, unempowered organizational structures to ones that are built on speed, flexibility, innovation, and integration (the goals of "the boundaryless organization"). CPOs inherit the culture of their C-Suite direct reporting relationships, but have the power within the procurement and supply chain functions to drive a different culture if they choose to do so while still meeting the expectations of their bosses. The energy that can be generated by such cultural change can be transformational and can turn the functions into perpetual motion machines of value-added activity. This is the true definition of customer service, one that asks the 5 WHYs, and it differentiates the successful teams that are willing to "lean into discomfort, and get comfortable in that uncomfortable place" from the unsuccessful ones. They see their way, by sharing and building with one another, through the storming phase into norming and (high) performing, and by implementing breakthrough solutions that improve competitive advantage.

The reporting relationship of the CPO to the C-Suite will usually drive the priorities of the function, but it does not have to dictate the culture. There will always be short-term result pressures, but will there be a rigorous effort to also address long-term issues? ESG criteria, whether you support them or not, require a long-term approach and commitment to be successful. The same goes for moving into truly strategic relationships with suppliers. Understanding the culture, and then knowing its priorities and how they fit into the strategy of the company, is essential in knowing whether to pursue long-term strategies or just focus on quick wins (which are a necessity under any scenario). **Procurement, supply chain, and sales professionals can all be successful regardless, as long as they know the culture, landscape, and environment in which they are playing, and how they are truly being measured. You just need to ask yourself, "Is this what I signed up for, and am I excited about waking up every morning and pursuing this line of work?"** If you fit the culture, the strategy (or non-strategy) will take care of itself; but if you do not fit, make a plan to move on with your career or decide if it's worth the wait to see if this is the "flavor of the month" or a permanent state of affairs.

Chapter 11:
The Ongoing Transformation of Global Procurement and How We Work
(The digitization of the function)

In writing this chapter, which was started in March 2023, it was already obsolete by June. So we wrote it again in August, and it was obsolete by December. The rate, pace, and enormity of change in the ability to process data will make this chapter obsolete again by the time it is published, but publish it we must. You have to put a stake in the ground somewhere, sometime, and it's better to do so than not.

"People are not your greatest asset … people are your ONLY asset!" We've said this a million times (Chapter 7), and the reason we say this is because we truly believe it. We've never seen a high-performing team with great processes and technology run by mediocre people, but we have seen many times that great people can overcome the obstacles in their way of poor processes and technology, even poor culture. Throughout our years, we've seen so many hours of the talent and energy of great procurement people wasted, fixing problems created by the procurement systems that lead to more problems and frustration for internal stakeholders, internal functions like accounts payables, and especially suppliers. We end up working for the system and its tools, and developing rigid processes to feed the system, as opposed to the system working for us. It absorbs precious budgetary resources that could be devoted to global category management and supplier relationship management (SRM) that have the potential to add breakthrough value and results. But this is about to change, should the chief procurement officer (CPO) be willing to make the deep dive and jump into the new digital world.

Procurement functions, talent, and systems have come down a long road from its origins as bookkeepers and cost control mavericks as we seek to become part of the strategy of a company, top line and bottom line. We see our work as helping not only improve margins, but also giving our firms a competitive advantage in the marketplace, securing sources of supply in a high-risk global environment in an ethical manner, and introducing systems that create a great user experience at lower cost. **By focusing on true value-added activities and investing in "born-in-the-cloud" app and generative AI solutions, Procurement can lead the way in supplier collaboration and generating market intelligence that helps employees drive innovation and performance in their firms.**

If there was ever a need for Procurement to transform itself in this world of hybrid cloud technology, it could not be more expertly expressed than was done in the 2021 book, *Trade Wars, Pandemic, and Chaos: How Digital Procurement Enables Business Success in a Disordered World*, by Dr. Elouise Epstein, a partner at Kearney and one of the world's preeminent experts on digital procurement and how it affects supply chains. It is a must-read book for anyone in the procurement and systems world, and what is happening is nothing short of a revolution, as evolution never happens this quickly.

Systems to support global procurement functions have been going through a series of transformations over the years, and the recent challenges of maintaining and building reliable supply chains for delivery of goods and services during times of trade wars and pandemics has brought this topic to the forefront of the daily lives of people throughout the world. People expect that the ordering of goods and services in their company should be no more complicated than it is in their personal lives — Alexa- or Siri-enabled commands combined with great search engines and online subscriptions and e-catalogues to find what they need quickly with the push of a button. Of course, all of this has been enabled by the advent of public and hybrid cloud technology, big data, and the onward push of Moore's Law.

Moore's Law, which was first expressed in 1965 and named after Intel co-founder Gordon E. Moore, postulates that the number of transistors that can be packed into a given unit of space would double approximately every two years. The growth rates of the public and hybrid cloud providers that enable the server space to do this — Amazon Web Services (AWS), Microsoft Azure, Google Cloud, Oracle, and IBM Softlayer — along with the use of platforms like Linux, Apple iOS, and Android has been staggering, all driven by the law of big numbers as you double memory and computing space every two years. It has been the enabler of this new mobile world, as well as the race to the bottom of communications and connectivity costs.

As I (Howard) like to say, "Timing isn't everything, it's the ONLY thing." While writing this chapter (on March 22, 2023), the WSJ CIO Journal published an article on generative AI advances. Microsoft had announced a new chatbot embedded in its search engine Bing powered by ChatGPT-4, and Google's decided to expand access to its conversational computer program Bard. Bard is designed to respond to written prompts using information sourced from websites such as Wikipedia and can handle follow-up questions in a conversational manner. China's search giant Baidu Inc. also introduced a new chatbot named Ernie, and several other rivals including DuckDuckGo (which I use daily instead of Google because I don't want to give away my data for free) and Neeva, Inc. have also incorporated AI tools that can summarize information from the Internet.

Two days later on March 24, 2023, the WSJ reported that Databricks announced the launch of AI language module Dolly. Databricks stores and prepares data for AI applications, and Dolly will allow developers to build their own ChatGPT-like apps. Dolly can be used to generate natural language prompts. Further to that, they reported that the generative AI market was expected to reach $42.6 billion by the end of 2023, growing at a compound annual rate of 32 percent to an estimated $98.1 billion by 2026 according to market analytics firm Pitchfork Data, Inc. On the same day, at the age of 94, Gordon E. Moore passed away (but his "law" lives on).

By December 6, 2023, *Wired* magazine reported that Google had launched Gemini, and described Gemini as "multimodal" because it can process information in the form of text, audio, images, and video. An initial version of Gemini was made available through Google's chatbot Bard, and the company stated that the most powerful version of the model, Gemini Ultra, will be released in 2024; it will outperform GPT-4, the model behind ChatGPT, on several common benchmarks. Videos released by Google showed Gemini solving tasks that involve complex reasoning and examples of the model combining information from text images, audio, and video.

Google's Demis Hassabis, the AI executive leading the project, was quoted by *Wired* magazine as saying, "Until now, most models have sort of approximated multimodality by training separate modules and then stitching them together" in what appeared to be a veiled reference to OpenAI's technology. "That's OK for some tasks, but you can't have this sort of deep complex reasoning in multimodal space."

Wired magazine also reported that OpenAI launched an upgrade to ChatGPT in September that gave the chatbot the ability to take images and audio as input in addition to text. OpenAI has not disclosed technical details about how GPT-4 does this or the technical basis of its multimodal capabilities.

On February 9, 2024, Joanna Stern of the *Wall Street Journal* reported that Google announced that Bard — the company's generative-AI chatbot — has been rebranded as Gemini. She stated that "Gemini is going to be integrated into the company's voice assistant, still called Google Assistant. And there will be an advanced, paid subscription version of this new chatbot called Gemini Advanced (Google has long been the champion of a free, ad-powered search engine), matching Microsoft and OpenAI, which recently beefed up their own subscription offerings."

She reported that all of these are $20 per month subscription services: OpenAI, ChatGPT Plus, Microsoft CoPilot Pro (and if you are also a Microsoft 365 subscriber, the extra $20 a month gets you CoPilot integrated into Microsoft Word, PowerPoint, and other Office apps), and Google Gemini Advanced (that buys you 2TB of storage across Google, gets you access to Gemini Advanced, and the company's latest AI model, Ultra 1.0, which gets you Gemini in Gmail, Docs, Slides, Sheets, and more).

Like we said, from when we first started to write this chapter twelve months ago, most of what we wrote is now virtually obsolete!

It's helpful to look at the journey that got us to where we are now to give us perspective. In Dr. Epstein's book, *Trade Wars*, she documented how procurement systems have moved through three eras: 1) the *Application* era, 1994–2006; 2) the *All-In-One Suites* era, 2006–2016; and 3) the *Ecosystem* era, 2016–today. We believe that we are now on the verge of another new era. But first, let's build on Dr. Epstein's work as we examine the following progression of system applications to procurement and supply chains:

1. Dr. Epstein's *Application* era of 1994–2006 saw the founding of companies like Freemarkets in 1995, which provided for live, reverse auction capability on a host of commodities; and Ariba (1996) and Emptoris (1999) to establish comprehensive procurement on-premises server-based *enterprise requirements planning* (ERP) systems to link production with demand requirements. Ariba and Emptoris evolved to provide strategic supply and contract management software including applications for spend analysis, sourcing, contract management, supplier life cycle management, services procurement, compliance management, and telecom management.

    It is our experience, though, that one of the biggest flaws with ERP systems is human intervention in sales forecasting (often driven by hockey stick marketing projections, sales quotas, and revenue targets). This intervention changes production scheduling to meet forecast, which changes the timing and delivery schedules for ordering of goods and services to meet production requirements. In a world where nobody wants to be the one to shut down production on a just-in-time (JIT) system or be the source of a shortage that restricts revenue generation, people tend to "sandbag" their forecasts, causing inventory buildup and added cost in the supply base — the very problem that ERP and JIT were supposed to solve! ERP systems are supposed to be "the one source of truth," but rarely did they deliver the operational and strategic advantage they were designed to create. **They just didn't take into account the one thing that really matters — human nature — and the desire to under-promise and over-deliver against objectives in order to reap the rewards bestowed on those who do so.**

2. Dr. Epstein's *All-in-One Suites* era of 2006–2016 was driven by some major acquisitions and the introduction and launch of some new born-in-the-cloud competitors. IBM acquired Sterling Commerce for $1.4 billion from AT&T for its B2B and supply chain management solutions (2010) and then bought Emptoris (2012); SAP acquired Ariba for $4.3 billion (2012); and Coupa was founded in 2006 (and IPO'd in 2016), which looked to tie together modules for the complete procurement cycle — Procure-to-Pay (P2P) requisitioning, contracts, strategic sourcing, bidding, SRM, and payables. There were other born-in-the-cloud competitors emerging as well, such as GEP, and a host of specific functionality apps that addressed certain system gaps (see below). **Our issue with the original, larger "closed loop" on-premises software systems was their rigidity in process flows that did not mimic the way Procurement really approaches its work, the inability to integrate best-in-class applications into the suites, and the sheer number of people required to operate, manage, and update changes to the customized systems. This became a chain around Procurement's neck (in our humble opinion). They were bulky, not user friendly, and often delivered only a fraction of the functionality intended, making the procurement function more costly to operate and less efficient in driving value.**

    Why does this happen? Again, in our humble opinion, there are two reasons why the roadmap for transitioning from on-premises software suite solutions to digital subscription, born-in-the-cloud solutions encounters many obstacles:

First, these multi-suite solutions are designed to reinforce the use of multistage sourcing management processes. But oftentimes, the GCM doesn't start at Stage 1, especially if the category has been worked before and there are existing suppliers with whom you are conducting SRM. You may already know your stakeholder business requirements and have done the due diligence on the market and the supply base (and Porter's Five Forces), so you might start at Stage 2 or 3 in this case, or even jump straight to a Stage 4 contract renegotiation strategy instead of going out for bid.

Second, it's the finance capital funding model. Like in the wild of the savannah, you have to eat when you make your kill, or else it will be stolen away from you. There are no refrigerators. When you get funded, you have to spend it, and if you get one shot at upgrading your procurement function in a capital approval, you tend to buy everything that you need at once, which is a multi-suite solution. The alternative is to put together a roadmap for a series of born-in-the-cloud apps over several years to add functionality as you go and build up your capability with best-in-class digital tools, but there is no guarantee that you can make this happen year after year, getting the allocation of capital that you need to roll out this strategy.

3. Dr. Epstein's *Ecosystem* era 2016–today is marked by born-in-the-cloud easy-to-use apps, which works by layering different levels of capability on top of one another. Using a central hub software framework to ping a centralized database (a data lake, if you will), you can enable seamless integration to the latest app solutions and provide a great user experience (think "Amazon-like") using the P2P system as a foundation. Since the business selects the apps that give them the greatest value, it adds a sense of personalization that can allow Procurement to move from a "spend management" focus to a "value creation" focus, as many of the apps include a self-service element on traditionally low value-added transactional activity. You are not locked into the rigors of multistage SMP, as each of these apps can be accessed as needed at the most appropriate time in the process that you design.

However, once you invest in the earlier on-premises infrastructure, as many major corporations did, you have a lot of people in IT and Procurement whose jobs depend on supporting the system, especially as you attempt to functionally customize whatever parts you can to make them unique to your company's needs. Getting funding to invest in the new digital ecosystem technologies and platforms and moving extensive data residing in private servers into public and hybrid clouds can be difficult. It requires IT people with different skill sets, and a willingness to change procurement processes to adapt (such as signature authorization levels or SOX controls).

Dr. Epstein lists the many and varied apps that now exist for a variety of specific functional uses, such as *contract life cycle management* (CLM); smart contracts and analytics; sourcing analytics and supplier discovery/marketplace; identity verification; supplier performance tracking; automated tail spend rationalization (to manage the 10 to 20 percent of spend that is placed with 80 to 90 percent of the supply base); direct material optimization; supplier collaboration; strategy execution; complex/advanced sourcing/expressive bidding (and should-cost analysis); process intelligence; commodity indirects; bot and e-sourcing; spend analytics; purchasing automation; software reselling; catalogue management; ERP, P2P, and accounts payables; commodity indexes; risk (event, cyber, macro, financial, reputational, geographic, and supply); sustainability (supplier diversity, conflict minerals, forced labor); supplier golden record (single source of truth for spend by supplier that is cleansed, harmonized/parented, classified, and enriched); and services end-to-end management.

According to Dr. Epstein, this era has seen over 1,000 startups and over $2 billion in venture capital funding, focused on a microservices architecture approach and use of application programming interfaces (APIs) that allow for the easy integration of "best in breed," plug & play apps that easily tie into the hub. Licensing for use of these apps allows for "pay by consumption," or is subscription-based, and the ability to pull in and out of the ecosystem as one sees fit based on benefits received.

Some examples of companies that provide these functionalities include (but are not limited to):

- Fairmarkit — a Malden, Massachusetts-based SaaS platform that provides enterprise procurement and supply chain solutions such as automating the tail spend process with no-touch "3 bids and a buy" with preferred suppliers for requisitions under a certain value threshold and not on a contract.

- Candex — "Tail of the tail" solution — consolidates large numbers of tail spend suppliers for customers, providing efficiency in order placement and payment to address the 10 to 20 percent of spend that is ordered from the 80 to 90 percent of the suppliers in the supply base.

- Globality — a leader in autonomous procurement using an AI platform that creates precisely scoped requirements, identifies the most qualified suppliers, provides negotiation insights, and enables data-driven decisions. They provide a source-to-statement of work (SOW) platform for service categories using machine learning (ML) to help users create a scope, match it to prequalified suppliers and a marketplace of other suppliers (including small businesses and diverse-owned businesses), facilitate a tender process with side-by-side comparisons, then gather supplier ratings feedback on proposals from stakeholders, and push awards into a system of record — CLM/P2P/SRM. This satisfies stakeholder input on decisions and minimizes Procurement involvement while absorbing learnings from other system transactions in the marketplace.

- Workday (formerly Scout RFP) for bidding — an easy to set up functionality for issuing, evaluating, and awarding bids. Scout was bought by Workday in 2019 for $540 million and has been integrated into their suite of offerings to customers.

- Levelpath — a new procurement SaaS platform founded by CEO Alex Yakubovich and President Stan Garber (the previous founders of Scout RFP) to manage enterprise procurement services with a mobile-first interface, offering tools customized for each company's approval workflows. According to Kyle Wiggers, a TechCrunch writer, in an article published on September 18, 2023, algorithms built into the platform are designed to provide actionable insights, to reduce instances of vendor redundancy, and will include an AI model that understands the purchasing and workflow habits of employees, and adjusts the procurement experience based on this to make procurement "delightful."

- Sievo — based in Helsinki, Finland, and Chicago, Illinois, is a cloud-based procurement and spend analytics platform designed to help businesses manage spend analysis, contract management, procurement benchmarking, and spend forecasting using AI-enabled software to extract and classify data from across the entire company.

- Tealbook — a Canadian woman-owned supplier management company founded by Stephany Lapierre that seeks to deliver a "trusted source of supplier data" to an ever-growing e-procurement space. Tealbook takes "big data" and provides a self-enriching, self-maintaining mechanism that connects to all procurement software critical to the success of a digital procurement transformation to the supplier database with updated information to help manage risk, classify diverse suppliers (minority-owned, woman-owned, veteran-owned, disability-owned, LGBTQ-owned), and stay informed of critical changes in status.

- DocuSign — signature routing — IPO'd in 2018 and automates the signature process for documents and approvals. It e-mails a secure link to each recipient for document review and approval, with legally binding e-signatures.

- Icertis — ranked by Forrester as #1 in the CLM space, using AI to: 1) import and add appropriate metadata tags to legacy and third-party contracts; 2) provide chatbots for engagement with users; 3) guide users to assemble the right contract draft for their business purposes; 4) help assess risks in draft and existing contracts; 5) find contracts impacted by a new development where no preexisting metadata tags exist (e.g., a pandemic); and 6) help identify unknown or unidentified risks and anomalies within the overall contract portfolio.

There are also free online procurement communities based on open-source principles, such as Procurement Foundry, allowing members to share templates, supplier lists, SRM, and act as a repository for open software source code — the GitHub of Procurement — using Slack for its members to connect. Vendors and consultants are constrained to segmented sandboxes, and they promote the formation of group-buying exchanges, external collaboration, and procurement employee development.

Out of all of this innovation has risen DPW Amsterdam (Digital Procurement World), an annual procurement tech event that brings together the best and the brightest in the industry. This year's sponsors included some of the technology companies mentioned above as well as Accenture, akirolabs (a Germany-based SaaS platform for collaborative strategic procurement), Amazon Business, apexanalytix (supplier management), Archlet (intuitive sourcing analytics platform), Arkestro (embedding game theory in any process), Beeline (managing contingent workforce), Celonis (data intelligence), Certa (third-party risk platform), Cirtuo (category strategy creation), Coupa, Craft (supplier intelligence platform), Creatives (cleanse, enrich, and harmonize supplier data), Deloitte, EcoVadis (sustainability ratings), Emitwise (carbon management platform), Enable (rebate management platform), Everstream Analytics (risk & supply chain), Gatekeeper (CLM platform for regulated industries), GEP, HICX (supplier experience platform), IntegrityNext (supply chain sustainability), ISPNext (S2P spend management), Keelvar (sourcing/bidding), Kodiak Hub (SRM), LavenirAI (negotiation training & development), LevaData (direct materials supply chain), Lytica (spend analytics and risk),

ORO Labs (procurement workflows), Pactum AI (automated negotiation), Positive Purchasing (guided category strategy creation), Precoro (managing indirect spend), Promena (S2P and RFX), QAD (connected supply chains), Rosslyn (spend analytics), Sastrify (SaaS procurement), Scanmarket (source to contract & risk), Scoutbee (supplier discovery), SDI International (S2P & tail spend), Simfoni (spend analytics & tail spend), SpendHQ (spend analytics), Sphera (ESG & risk), Synertrade (S2P), The Smart Cube (BPO), Unite (sourcing & P2P), Valdera (direct materials sourcing), Vendr (SaaS buying), Veridion (AI supplier discovery), WNS Denali (BPO), and Zip (intake to procure solution).

While we do not endorse any of the companies specifically listed here, we wanted to show the enormity of the number of plug & play app AI and born-in-the-cloud SaaS solutions that are being developed and marketed for specific procurement and supply chain business challenges. This may be the most dynamic time for CPOs to reconstruct how procurement services are delivered and how procurement functions are organized, incentivized, and challenged to deliver business value that is actually valued by the functions that it supports.

This digital innovation has been going on for a while. As noted in a research report from The Hackett Group, "How Digital World-Class Procurement Organizations Outperform Peers" by Laura Gibbons, senior research director, and Christopher Sawchuck, principal and global procurement advisory practice leader, the change that Procurement needs to make to become digital is worth it.

According to Hackett, in 2021, a new bar was set by digital world-class procurement organizations, which spent 25 percent less than typical procurement organizations, and 6 percent less than even other world-class organizations. Digital world-class procurement organizations also employ 33 percent fewer full-time equivalents (FTEs) than peers per billion dollars of revenue. The gap is even greater for operations and compliance management FTEs (57 percent), enabling these organizations to deliver those processes at 55 percent lower cost. They are also able to deliver greater business value in the form of higher-quality services — better stakeholder engagement, SRM, and product innovation. Compared to peers, they have 2.5 times higher procurement ROI and 25 percent more spend influenced or managed by Procurement.

Hackett states that technology, of course, plays a key role in their efficiency and effectiveness. Digital world-class procurement organizations spend 20 percent more than peers on technology as a percentage of spend. They invest in emerging technologies such as smart automation, advanced analytics, and collaboration tools to reduce labor costs. They also automate more activity than peers — in some cases, reaching maximum automation levels. They have fully automated dissemination of purchase orders to suppliers, process 100 percent of requisitions electronically, and are quick to embrace new data and analytics techniques, such as predictive modeling.

Key to this is their ability to evolve their operating model to create a more fluid network of resources that can be deployed quickly to support the highest-value activities. They have 1) dedicated global process owners who can spot bottlenecks and make changes more easily;

2) 70 percent more staff in product design and development roles than peers; 3) 15 percent more in supplier partnering; and 4) provide 2.4 times more training hours for their workforce than peers do. The challenge, of course, is to continually demonstrate that the ROI of having this increased overhead cost for running the procurement function makes sense. It is a constant battle with Finance, especially if the pendulum is moving from centralization toward decentralization.

Deloitte, in a 2021 publication, "Turning the Corner on Digital Transformation with Global Business Services (GBS)," identified in its survey of organizations two key trends and findings: digital transformation, and the shift to global models. Based on a survey, the respondents state that GBS organizations should prioritize technology investments for several reasons: they boost collaboration, fuel innovation, and help generate tangible value. A majority of organizations, for example, are prioritizing single-instance ERP and cloud solutions and cited them among their most important capabilities. Other enablers include varying AI platforms for self-service, virtual assistance, and more, as well as case management solutions like ServiceNow and predictive and customer analytics. Any digital transformation journey, though, is only as successful as the people involved, meaning GBS organizations looking to level up their operations must prioritize talent (again, people are our ONLY asset).

However, there are several key obstacles to achieving digital outcomes, such as siloed processes or unorganized approaches to AI. Another key issue is technical complexity. Those who can navigate these challenges through open communication and collaboration organization-wide will be able to capitalize on the top three trends impacting GBS plans in the near term — which all happen to be digitally focused: expanded work-from-home capabilities (87 percent), digital agenda acceleration (61 percent), and additional virtual practices (59 percent). Still, there is no one-size-fits-all approach given the vast possibilities with digital.

One of the biggest challenges in the new procurement era is delivering company environmental, social, and governance (ESG) objectives through its supply base. Shareholders throughout the investment community are now demanding more from their board of directors and C-Suite in delivering not only profits, but those based on sustainable, diverse, and environmentally friendly approaches. The challenge for Procurement is not only in how the company sees the procurement mission and vision, but also in how Procurement sees itself and incentivizes, measures, and rewards its employees' contributions for not only savings, but the ESG and risk management missions of their company. If Procurement sees itself purely as "Savings R Us," "Negotiations R Us," or "Contracts R Us," then it will never be part of the company strategy or gain the "trusted advisor" moniker that it so actively seeks from its stakeholders.

The Role of Generative AI in Procurement

The ChatGPT platform came out in a flurry of activity and led to rushed faculty meetings at universities across the country, on the implications on how to use this technology in the classroom and the potential for students to cheat when submitting essays, homework, and take-home tests. These so-called *language learning models* (LLMs) are able to pull from billions of sources to create well-crafted narratives in response to user prompts. After the initial panic subsided, people came to understand that using ChatGPT has disadvantages as well as advantages. First, it does not cite the material it relies on. It pulls from billions of references to generate a narrative, but does not understand the reliability or applicability of these references. Second, the technology is heavily reliant on the ability of the human user to define and specify the questions that drive the engine of the system. If the question is not specific enough, the system will generate a nonsensical or irrelevant narrative. This has led to the field of *prompt engineering*, which is defined as the art of asking the right question to get the best output from an LLM. It enables direct interaction with the LLM using only plain language prompts. Google offers several important caveats to consider when conducting prompts to LLMs[1]:

1. *Clearly communicate* what content or information is most important.

2. *Structure the prompt:* Start by defining its role, give context/input data, then provide the instruction.

3. *Use specific, varied examples* to help the model narrow its focus and generate more accurate results.

4. *Use constraints to limit the scope of the model's output.* This can help avoid meandering away from the instructions into factual inaccuracies.

5. *Break down complex tasks* into a sequence of simpler prompts.

6. *Instruct the model to evaluate or check its own responses before producing them.* ("Make sure to limit your response to 3 sentences." "Rate your work on a scale of 1-10 for conciseness." "Do you think this is correct?")

7. *Be creative!* The more creative and open-minded you are, the better your results will be. LLMs and prompt engineering are still in their infancy and evolving every day.

The use of LLMs in procurement and acquisition is an evolving field, but there are a number of excellent models already developing. A great website that contains a number of procurement templates was developed by Dr. Daniel Finkenstadt, PhD, a colleague who worked for 18 years as a USAF acquisition officer. He has been experimenting with GPT and has developed a number of templates that can support different types of strategic procurement activities, including:

- Biobuilding GPT — Bioinspired design aide for survivable innovations
- Contract Performance Scribe — Craft and assess contractor performance narratives
- WhatIf_What Now GPT — Develop supply chain and event contingency plans
- Time to Lead — Navigate your leadership path
- Negotiation Coach — Negotiation improvement, preparation, and mediation tool
- Enterprise Sourcing Sage — Guide for sourcing strategies
- Contingency Contracting Advisor — Detailed guide for contingency contracting

---

1 "Prompt Engineering for Generative AI," Google.com, https://developers.google.com/machine-learning/resources/prompt-eng.

- Case Study Generator — Specialized in crafting business and operations case studies that can be used for scenario planning and other preparations
- Supply Chain Immunity Developer — Guide for measuring supply chain immunity (see Handfield and Finkenstadt, 2023)
- Performance Narrative Scribe — Generates narrative statements for employees and employers

These types of prototype GPT applications can be used to guide and support structured planning for major negotiations, cost management, strategic sourcing, and procurement leadership. See for example https://www.gartner.com/en/articles/what-s-new-in-the-2023-gartner-hype-cycle-for-emerging-technologies. The launch of the GPT store in 2024 brought a lot of pomp and fanfare but has proven to be a bit of a wild west. For instance, some of the GPTs developed by Dr. Finkenstadt were immediately copied by other GPT builders. The model performance differed as they were configured differently but other builders stole the name and likeness of his GPTs almost immediately after the store launched. This is just one more example of the tension between intellectual property/security and open-source development that has proliferated the Generative AI discourse lately.

To be effective in this new world of born-in-the-cloud digital apps, Procurement has to face the challenge from an organizational restructuring standpoint. But mostly, it's a change management challenge in creating the new mission and vision and culture of Procurement. Command and control, hierarchical organizations that follow strict processes and do not allow for deviation from the process will go the way of the dinosaur. Delegation of authority to act, and act quickly, has to be pushed down to the lowest level, to people working at the "coal face," to take advantage of the speed and flexibility that these new tools provide. This, combined with increased self-service, should significantly reduce the cost of the procurement function, but the processes and rules have to change to take advantage of the technology.

The culture must also change to tolerate more mistakes being made in this environment, as well, from quicker decision-making. The priority should not be in getting three-way matches of POs, invoices, and receivers issued by users to make payments when spot audits to assure compliance can do. Instead, the priority has to be the enablement of people to act in the best interests of the company in the most efficient way possible while also maximizing the leverage of its global spend footprint and encouraging its supply base to be part of the solution. Culture change is never easy, and this doesn't work well for the CPO who just moves in for three to four years as a weigh station to a bigger job. This causes a lot of headaches, and the changes will not be perceived well by some users who are now moving to a more self-service environment. But for the career CPO who has made procurement and supply chain their profession, it's an opportunity to reinvent the function!

In a lecture by three-time Pulitzer Prize–winning journalist Thomas Friedman, author of such books as *From Beirut to Jerusalem*, *The Lexus and the Olive Tree*, and *The World Is Flat*, he discussed Moore's Law and the law of big numbers and how we are moving to the second side of the chessboard. There is a story that the inventor of chess, when selling the game to the king, was asked how much he wanted to be paid for it. He said, "Give me one grain of rice for the first square, and double it for each succeeding square on the board." The king quickly agreed, not realizing the law of big numbers — he now owed the inventor 4 quadrillion grains of rice!

If we build off of Moore's Law (1965), we are only reaching the 30th space on the 64-space chessboard since that time, and the amount of data available in the world to learn and access pretty much follows Moore's Law, as it doubles every two years. There is no way that the human brain can keep up with all of these data being produced, as the law of big numbers continues to overwhelm our capability to process it all. AI and its march toward incredibly intelligent processing capabilities at incredible speeds will probably keep Moore's Law intact for a while longer. For people who do repetitive work, your job will soon be eliminated by the algorithms and the software. Only by being creative and having special knowledge and skills that are difficult to duplicate can you be assured that the machines will not make you obsolete. **Friedman's point was that what you need to learn most is how to learn,** because whatever facts and data you rely on for a specialty is quickly becoming a commodity. He then went on to read us a sports story of a college baseball game played between two DC area teams, then informed us that it was written by a computer that was fed data on every pitch of the game. This was 10 years ago, and journalism was also starting to become obsolete!

Who knows what the next *Ecosystem* era will bring, but there are two things you can count on: 1) There is nothing more constant than change; and 2) Learning how to learn, and how to quickly access and process data, will be at the heart of everything that you do. Culture eats strategy for lunch, and having a sales, procurement, and supply chain culture that focuses on how to change and adapt quickly and how to learn will differentiate the winners from the losers in all of this madness. Rigid, hierarchical, slow-moving processes based on command-and-control structures are being eaten alive by the competition, and if you've ever watched any videos of wild animals in the savannah, being hunted and eaten alive is not a very good way to go.

Index

Page numbers in *italics* refer to figures.